Solving Discipline Problems

Solving Discipline Problems:

Strategies for Classroom Teachers

Charles H. Wolfgang
The Ohio State University, Columbus

Carl D. Glickman
The University of Georgia, Athens

Allyn and Bacon, Inc.
Boston London Sydney Toronto

Dedicated to:

Louise, Helen, Mary, and Ellen Louise
C.W.

Harold, Ruth, Stuart, and Joanna
C.G.

Cover photo by Vaughn Sills

Series Editor: Hiram G. Howard

Designer/Production Editor: Gary L. Schmitt

Library of Congress Cataloging in Publication Data

Wolfgang, Charles H
Solving discipline problems.

Bibliography: p.
Includes index.
1. Classroom management. 2. School discipline.
I. Glickman, Carl D., joint author. II. Title.
LB3013.W62 371.5 79-22740
ISBN 0-205-06888-X

Printing number and year (last digits):
10 9 8 7 6 5 4 3 85 84 83 82 81 80

Printed in the United States of America

Contents

Preface

In this book we are trying to provide classroom teachers with a "rainbow" of discipline models, techniques, methods, and constructs to permit the teachers to move beyond a singular approach in handling classroom behavior problems. The teachers are encouraged to be professionals, to make the key decisions on what will be most helpful to them with their particular classroom and with their particular students. This unique model is titled *Solving Discipline Problems: Strategies for Classroom Teachers.*

Not long ago, we casually asked three of our friends, "What is the best route to take by car to a small town in a neighboring state?" The first friend quickly declared, "Go the scenic route," and he described a route through a series of beautiful mountains and valleys. The second friend disagreed, insisting, "Absolutely not. You will spend all day twisting and turning up narrow roads behind slow-moving trucks. That route is tortuous. Travel the interstate highway; you will save much time!" The third friend declared that they were both wrong. "The scenic route takes too long and the interstate has a dangerous twenty-mile section under construction. Take the secondary road. It has three lanes, and besides, it passes an outstanding restaurant that serves great lunches!

All three friends were true believers with total faith in their way. The classroom teacher faced with the problem of establishing discipline in his or her classroom also encounters true believers that range from Thomas Gordon in his *T.E.T. Teacher Effectiveness Training,* Eric Berne and Thomas Harris in *Transactional Analysis—TA,* and Louis Raths and Sidney Simon in *Values Clarification* to Rudolf Dreikurs in *Discipline Without Tears* and William Glasser in *Reality Therapy* to the proponents of Behavior Modification and corporal punishment. All these writers have total "faith" that they have discovered the "right way," much like our three friends who gave the road directions.

The classroom teacher faced with the daily realities of running a dynamic classroom with real students may be confused by these competing directions. The teacher wants practical actions that can be taken on Monday morning so that he or she can continue the job of teaching.

We are suggesting in this book that teachers do not need to be committed to one "faith" and instead can make their own choices. They can do as we did in traveling to the small town. We started on the interstate and later turned onto the secondary highway to bypass the dangerous construction. The secondary highway also permitted us to stop at the restaurant for a refreshing lunch, and then we ended the trip by transferring to the scenic route, where we enjoyed a view of the fall foliage.

It is our position that all models of discipline appear to be valid "routes to travel" with each model having its strengths and limitations. However, no one model contains the full "truth." Therefore, we have created constructs that permit the use of all teachers' actions from many models and provide ways to apply these techniques according to a teacher's beliefs and the stages of a student's social development.

Acknowledgments

We need to acknowledge the many people who have helped us in the development of this book. A special thanks is extended to the staff at Ohio State (Carolyn Wycuff, Charlotte Phillips, Amy Laurence, Karen Kitts, and Nancy Graham), our typist Mary Spencer, our proofreader "par excellence" Shirley Husted, production editor Gary Schmitt, and series editor Hiram Howard. Their help in refining our writing is much appreciated. We also would like to single out the contributions of Dr. C. Ray Williams, Dr. Roy Tamashiro, Dr. John Tewksbury, Dr. Steve Tipps, and Ms. Rose Ann Knowlton for their thoughtful feedback and contributions, and photographer Vaughn Sills for her fine work on the jacket photograph. There have been teachers and other school personnel, too numerous to mention by name, who have participated in workshops and courses with us in the field testing of our ideas. We thank them for keeping us "practical" and "rooted in reality." Finally, in a bit of immodesty, we would like to thank one another. The amount of energy and time spent in discussing and debating the development of this book have enriched us personally. We are proud of this book and hope that it will add to the professional growth of teachers and the well-being of students.

1

Introduction: Reaching the Breaking Point

Ms. Zunn is a quiet, composed woman who has been a fourth-grade teacher for six years. At the age of twenty-nine she has established herself in the eyes of her students' parents, fellow teachers, and school administrators as an above-average teacher. She is especially well regarded as a strong classroom manager. Her students have traditionally responded to her firm, calm manner with appropriately restrained behavior. They have always had true affection and respect for her.

This year, however, has not been one of Ms. Zunn's best. The community in which she teaches has begun to change from a basically middle-class to more of a lower-middle-class mix. The new trailer parks and housing projects have brought in populations of children who are new to Ms. Zunn's previous experience.

Although the great majority of her students are reasonably well behaved, there is one student in particular who constantly disrupts the entire class. His name is Joshua. Joshua, eleven years old, is new to the community and has already been in three different schools. His father is a warehouse manager, his mother a waitress, and he is the oldest of four children. He is an indifferent student, does not speak often, and is quick to physically lash out at others. He does not respond to Ms. Zunn's calm, stern manner the way that other students do. When she tells him to stop what he is doing (talking, dropping books, or bothering others), he ignores her and continues with his activities. When she finally has to resort to physical restraint, he loses all control and begins yelling, thrashing his arms, and flailing at her.

Ford Button, from *Phi Delta Kappan*

Ms. Zunn is near her rope's end. Yesterday, Joshua struck one of his classmates, and when she intervened, he swore at her. This morning, when he entered the classroom he immediately grabbed a fellow student's comic book and tore it to shreds. When Ms. Zunn ran over to him, saying, "Joshua, go sit in the corner," Joshua refused. When she started to pull him out of his seat, Joshua exploded, knocking his chair to the floor, striking out at her, and then, in pure rage, spitting at her. He finally broke away, ran out of the classroom, and disappeared down the corridor.

Ms. Zunn could no longer retain her composure. She told the class that she needed to step out of the room for a minute. Slipping into the hall, she leaned back against the wall and began softly crying to herself. Thinking of how helpless the situation with Joshua had become, she felt totally incapable of helping him. Not only were his needs unmet, but his excessive behavior was ruining the work she wished to do with the other children. She simply could not bear to think about facing an entire school year filled with problems related to Joshua and his problems.

Does this example seem exaggerated? Unfortunately, it is not. Rarely is there a classroom teacher who has not had the experience of a Joshua, or even worse, many Joshuas. We would venture to guess that the reader can readily identify one or more children in his or her own classroom who are providing a similar experience and creating similar concerns. What makes us venture this confident guess?

The National Education Association (NEA),[1] in its yearly survey of teachers, has documented that teachers are leaving the profession at an astounding rate. They report that only fourteen percent of teachers have been teaching twenty years or more. This is half the percentage of fifteen years before. Only a third of the teachers still in the profession believe they would make the same choice again. In other words, nearly two-thirds of our current teachers are discouraged enough to wish they had not chosen to be teachers. A major reason given for such feelings is "negative student attitudes and discipline."

Growing discontent with disruptive behavior in the classroom has been cited by the Gallup Poll as the public's number one school concern.[2] A leading educational journal has devoted an entire issue to this subject,[3] and a new term, "the battered teacher,"[4] has been coined. All of this documentation, however, does not bring the issue home as clearly as seeing a teacher like Ms. Zunn standing alone in a school hallway, crying quietly to herself.

Being teachers ourselves, we have had firsthand experiences with depression stemming from feelings of inadequacy in coping with a particular child. We know the reality of having this child constantly in one's thoughts day and night, of losing sleep in dread of facing the inevitable next school morning, and hoping that a weekend or vacation could last forever. Again, it might be thought that we are overstating the problem, and perhaps to some individual readers we are; however, in our experiences as teachers of children and of teachers we are convinced that this is the most real and common issue faced by those who work with children. We are assuming throughout this book that the reader has had or can anticipate a similar plight and wishes to learn of various ways to not only cope with disruptive children but to become a *proactive* source in helping these children grow and attain more socialized behavior. In doing so, it is hoped the teacher will gain some personal satisfaction and a good night's sleep as well.

Why Is Disruptive Student Behavior Such a Problem Today?

In an earlier point of time (according to the cited NEA report) when teachers seemed to be more satisfied with their profession, a teacher might have been able to get along by using techniques learned from experiences with his or her public school teachers or from experiences gathered through an undergraduate teacher training program. Teachers by and large worked with staid, homogeneous populations of students who could be expected to behave as previous youngsters did. Children in any one particular school generally came from the same family backgrounds, the same socioeconomic class, the same race, and often the same culture and religion. Techniques that worked with one child could be expected to have similar effects with others.

As the saying goes, "The times have changed." Public schools now contain a heterogeneous mix of youngsters. With increased mobility of families, we have in almost every neighborhood, families that come from various geographical regions and various cultures. Court-ordered desegregation has furthered this change. Also, public laws have added to the heterogeneous school mix, putting children with special needs, who were once separated from the regular classroom, into the regular classroom in the form of "mainstreaming." It can be safely said that as classrooms have become more heterogeneous, teachers have become increasingly discontent with their lives. More behavioral conflicts have erupted, with teachers discovering that their once "sure methods" no longer are working.

Please do not misunderstand us. We believe that heterogeneity is a healthy trend, one that is compatible with a democratic society. We do not advocate solving the issue of conflict in the classroom by suggesting that we retreat to homogeneous classrooms. This would be a simplistic effort to try to turn back the clock as well as to nullify some of this nation's hard-won civil and social advances. Instead, the answer lies in accepting the fact that working with diverse children who have different needs and styles is desirable and that teachers need to be educated in ways of making their own behaviors more compatible with such diversity.

We can compare the interaction of a symphony conductor with the orchestra to a teacher working in today's heterogeneous classroom. If the conductor gives the same signs to each musician, regardless of the tone and timbre of instrument played, then the sound that emanates from all the players would be, at best, monotonous and flat or more totally discordant. Trained and competent conductors know how to give different signals to various musicians to elicit the full quality of each instrument and player. As a result, the listener hears a dynamic mix of intensity and diversity that merges into an exciting blend of harmonious sound. So it can be with the classroom teacher. The use of the same approach to every child will be stifling and inadequate. A vital, developing classroom of children is created by a teacher who varies strategies suitable for each youngster. The end result is an optimal environment of individual children working cooperatively with each other.

The Teacher's Never-Ending Task

Working with children is a never-ending process. Teachers truly care about their students and want to provide them with the best possible learning experiences. However, unlike some professionals, educators have difficulty gaining a sense of satisfaction with what they do. If one has a wall to build, then one can go about doing the necessary construction, and in time the wall is done. However, a child is never "finished." Teachers can never be satisfied that a child has reached his or her optimal level. The teacher must always strive to constantly improve each student's situation. No wonder teaching is such a demanding profession, and one where the teacher finds it extremely hard to close the classroom door at four in the afternoon and forget about school until the next morning! Children are never "done," and this endless process is the ultimate beauty and ultimate frustration of our profession.

When a teacher encounters an extremely disruptive child, whatever sense of class achievement that has been previously attained begins to erode. Not only is the particular child's school life unhappy, but his or her actions scream for the teacher's constant attention. Such attention pulls the teacher away from what he or she desires to do with the other children. The teacher is caught betwixt and between. Is it fair to give this one child so much attention that it works to the disadvantage of the others? Or should the disruptive child be simply ignored or perhaps isolated in another area? The reality of most schools requires that the disruptive child be attended to. The teacher must live with the guilt engendered by not spending as much time as he or she would want to with the others. This guilt continues to compound. After all, if the teacher has decided to focus energy and attention on one child at the sacrifice of the others, the expectation would be to attain positive results and be able to return in short course to the rest of the classroom. To focus one's energies on one child and then to see no improvement, or perhaps to even witness a deterioration of the situation, brings the teacher to the breaking point and to the previously mentioned stage of helplessness.

What Can Be Done?

Let us begin this answer with some honesty. A cavalry of soldiers and horses is not likely to come charging down the hill to the teacher's rescue. Unless the child suddenly moves out of town (perhaps with the teacher paying the moving expenses!), it is most likely that the child is in the teacher's classroom to stay. The guidance counselor, the school psychologist, the school nurse, and the principal might offer some help, but it is the teacher who bears the brunt of the responsibility for the child.

Obviously the teacher must call upon many internal resources and skills to deal with the situation. The teacher has been through an undergraduate teacher training program and perhaps a graduate program as well. He or she might think back to courses in child psychology or classroom management. In most cases, these courses dealt with the general dimensions of children's behavior and did not offer much in specific application. On the other hand, the teacher might have been in a program that did stress certain specific applications such as behavior modification, student-centered counseling, or value clarification. If the teacher has been trained in a specific approach, or in no approach, the same problem will still exist.

The teacher has a limited range of techniques for dealing with limitless ranges of diverse behaviors in children.

The more resourceful teacher who is aware of his or her limitations will try to extend his or her "bag of tricks" by keeping current on the latest expert advice. The teacher might browse through a book store for professionals, or talk with colleagues about the newest approach. More than likely (as evidenced by the huge number of books sold), a glossy paperback will be purchased—one that gives assurance on its cover of providing "the answer" to working with children. Whether that book is entitled *T.E.T.: Teacher Effectiveness Training, Discipline Without Tears, Schools Without Failure, Transactional Analysis, Behavior Modification,* or is some other popular book, the teacher will have in hand a concrete approach to use. Again, however, the teacher remains limited. The specific approach that is read about and then implemented may or may not work. *The reason the newly learned technique may not work is that such popular books espouse one approach to working with all children.* It is our conviction that children are different and what works for one child will not be the same as the approach that works for another.

For this reason, what we will attempt to do in this book is to provide teachers with a practical demonstration and illustration of each of the major approaches to working with disruptive children. We do this by providing an eclectic *Teacher Behavior Continuum* (TBC) that encompasses all of the various behaviors and shows how the continuum can be used in different ways for different youngsters. In other words, our purpose is to fully acquaint the teacher with what is now known about working with today's children. In so doing, we hope to replace existing feelings of helplessness and not knowing what to do with a particular troublesome child with a sense of confidence and professionalism which emerges when one knows of the spectrum of strategies available and is thus able to make a suitable decision for each child.

The Teacher as a Professional

As we have mentioned, ours is not a "how to" book in the sense of giving a teacher a step-by-step approach to be slavishly followed when dealing with disruptive children. Our definition of professionalism is crucial for understanding how this book is to be used. We define a professional as one who gathers information about a problem, has a knowledge-base of possible alternative strategies, is aware of the consequences of employing each strategy, and then chooses the strategy which is most logically appropriate. This process is done from an underlying belief structure or philosophy pertaining to long-range goals for children.

We realize that this definition might sound rather vague, so we will try to operationalize it by looking at how a "professional" teacher would attack the problem created by a disruptive child. First, he or she would compile information on the nature of the child and the specific behaviors exhibited by the child. Secondly, this information would be checked against a spectrum of alternative ways to approach the child. The teacher would then carefully match each approach with what the predicted outcomes and consequences would be. This would be followed by choosing the most congruent approach. Finally, the teacher would use that approach only as a temporary stage of action, and would plan further steps leading to his or her ideal of how children should eventually be treated in the classroom setting.

To further clarify our definition of professional, we will contrast it with the term "technician," and show how a book written for technicians would be quite different. A "technician" is an individual trained to employ one exact approach to solving a problem. A technician does not need to judge alternatives, results, or long-range goals. He or she simply needs to do what is prescribed. The technician need not speculate about consequences before acting; he or she simply needs to act. As an automobile moves down an assembly line, the "door hinge" technician needs to simply make the proper hinge placement and secure the door. The teacher-technician, when confronted by a disruptive child, simply gives the same command or implements with an action that he or she has always given or implemented.

We believe that in contrasting these two terms we have defined our meaning of a "professional" teacher. We further assume that if the reader were already a *complete* "professional" in dealing with disruptive children, he or she would have not selected this book. Obviously, it would be nice if we were all "complete," but the reasons to write this book do exist, as does the need for its application.

We as authors do not believe in training teachers as technicians; we believe in educating teachers as professionals. We assume, as stated earlier, that teachers need to be educated in multieclectic approaches for dealing with children in our new, diverse classroom environments. It is the teacher who knows his or her own goals better than any outside "expert" and is the one who is most competent to decide and select those strategies most suitable for specific children. We will offer guideposts and case studies, but the ultimate decision is and should be the teacher's own. When a teacher is instructed to use only one approach, it suggests a denigrated view of that individual's competence. Teachers possess the capacity to make decisions from alternatives. Often, all that is lacking is the information about alternatives. This lack is created by the reluctance of the "experts" to give teachers credit for the ability to decide for themselves. Most experts try to force-feed their approach as the "right" one, and in so doing, they degrade both teachers and others who espouse different approaches. Fritz Redl criticized the experts in this way:

> All sides have pitched "belief" versus "belief," leaving the classroom teacher alone on the job in the process. Well, then, why the heck don't we forget about our theoretical disputes or convictional competitions and get together on the job?[5]

Getting Together on the Job

What this book intends to do is treat teachers as professionals in exploring the very troublesome area of classroom discipline and student management. We will first discuss our *Teacher Behavior Continuum* (TBC) and show the teacher the context of his or her own general behavior with disruptive children. We will use our continuum then as a construct for viewing three major schools of thought of managing students. The most popular authors of each major school will be discussed and their peculiar strategies will be explained in capsulized form, and then it will be pointed out how all approaches may be used in an eclectic manner based on the teacher's values. Subsequently, the stages of a child's social development will be explained as assessment criteria in determining appropriate strategies for individual children, and then a school process of "staffing" will be suggested to demonstrate how a school team might "mainstream" the difficult students for full schoolwide impact. Finally, we will point out the strengths and limitations of each model and make proposals for educational change.

Note: What This Book Is About

This book is only to a limited sense concerned about general classroom management. Our focus is on the individual child. Many readers will find occasions when they can extend the application of a single child's treatment to an entire classroom. Many of the authors we cite include in their description of teacher behaviors insights into the overall educational process. These added dimensions of classroom organization and management will also be discussed. Although an exploration of these dimensions is not our primary emphasis, the reader might garner some extra knowledge to successfully utilize specific techniques with entire groups of students.

Notes

1. "Who is the Classroom Teacher," *Today's Education*, November–December 1977, p. 11.
2. George Gallup, "Ninth Annual Gallup Poll on the Public's Attitudes Toward the Public Schools," *Phi Delta Kappan*, September 1977, pp. 33–48.
3. "Special Issue: The Problems of Discipline and Violence in American Education," *Phi Delta Kappan*, January 1978.
4. Alfred Bloch, MD, "The Battered Teacher," *Today's Education*, March–April 1977, pp. 58–62.
5. Fritz Redl and David Wineman, *When We Deal With Children: Selected Writings* (New York: Free Press, 1972), p. 259.

2

Beyond Theory to Classroom Practice

To know fully what one does as a teacher, one needs to understand the framework and consequences of behavior. Different teacher behaviors are compatible or incompatible with certain psychological theories. A teacher who chooses a certain behavioral strategy with children should be aware of the underlying psychological consequences of that choice. All too often, we unwillingly practice behaviors that are contrary to our own beliefs. Unless we behave towards children in ways that are reasonably compatible with our own values and ideals, we find ourselves working at cross purposes with our inner selves. In other words, what we desire in student behavior will not materialize until we choose those strategies that are most consistent with our own beliefs in achieving those ends. We cannot possibly know what is most congruent in these contexts until we understand the psychological basis for each of our actions. Therefore, we have a vital need for psychological perspectives in knowing what approaches to use.

This may sound rather abstract, but let us personalize our view. One of us was a teacher of sixth-grade children in a small, rural potato farming community in New England. (To escape the ordeal of going through a first-person confession, we will refer to this individual in the third person.) All through teacher preparation he had learned to value student independence and problem-solving. When it came to behavior, he believed that children should learn self-discipline and should be free to choose their own courses of action. All of this sounds fine, but within weeks of starting his initial teaching job this nice, idealistic teacher was screaming his head off at students. He found himself exerting physical pressure to prevent children from constantly moving out of their seats. The teacher was becoming more frustrated and more punitive in his behavior, while the students were raging further and further out of control. The teacher felt guilty. Something was obviously wrong, but what was it?

Unfortunately, at this point in time the teacher did not have the psychological perspective to re-orient his behavior. One one hand, he intrinsically valued self-discipline for children, but on the other hand he was using techniques that made it impossible to achieve self-discipline. He was taking more and more control away from the students. One might think, "The fool, why did he not use other approaches?" The answer is twofold. First, he was not totally aware of the inconsistency in his actions; secondly, even if he had been, he did not know of other, more consistent approaches. So what was he left with? He was left with a defeatist's attitude and a conviction that his students simply weren't capable of controlling themselves. These feelings led to a justification for continuing to use those teacher behaviors that made such convictions and prophecies self-fulfilling. With such teacher behavior, his students would never learn to exercise choice and independence. The infamous vicious circle was again off and spinning.

How Does Psychological Theory *Help the Teacher?*

If the teacher is able to view the context of his or her own behaviors as indicative of a certain psychological position, it will help to clarify the need to change either these beliefs or actions. In knowing the various major psychological theories, the teacher additionally gains a greater working knowledge of alternative approaches that he or she may use at different times in working with individual children. We should point out that we do not expect teachers to always use those behaviors that are totally consistent with their own philosophy. To expect this rigid consistency is unrealistic. Rather, we would expect teachers to use approaches drawn from various theoretical bases but to eventually move in the direction of one's own beliefs, or to use approaches consistent with stages of student development.

We understand how the mere use of the term "theory" or "psychological foundation" turns many readers off. The memories of sitting through courses dealing in theory have often been experiences of perceived irrelevance and consequential boredom. Much of what was learned in college was regurgitated on the final exam and then forgotten. This kind of experience is lamentable, as a solid grounding in educational psychology is of immediate relevance to anyone who works with children. Theories about how children learn, how they behave, the curriculum materials to be used, and the instructional methods to be employed do not originate in a vacuum. Whether we are aware of it or not, they come out of various psychological orientations. Unfortunately, the determinations about the materials, methods, and so forth that we use are usually made by those outside of the classroom. Decisions about these matters are usually made by commercial companies, school boards, or central office personnel. The teacher is not expected to choose, but instead to simply practice whatever is dictated by others. This lack of teacher input in these decision-making processes is unfortunate. Often those persons outside of the student and teacher process are mandating the what and how of teaching, and are making decisions about materials and curriculum based on superficial criteria (such as cost, public appeal, popularity, and so on) without giving proper thought to the ultimate psychological outcome of their choices.

What we are proposing is that, at least in the realm of student management, we return the power of decision-making to those on the "firing lines," the classroom teachers. To make wise choices, the teacher needs knowledge of the rudimentary psychological underpinnings of the alternatives. With this in mind, we wish the reader to follow us through a simplification of psychological theories of child development.

Three Schools of Thought

We have taken various psychological interpretations of child development and categorized them into three basic beliefs:

1. The child develops from an inner unfolding of potential.
2. The child develops as a result of external conditions.
3. The child develops from the interaction of inner and outer forces.

The first explanation presupposes that the child has an inner drive that needs to find its expression in the real world. The second explanation disavows any such inner force and instead emphasizes what the outer environment (of people and objects) does to the human organism to cause it to develop in its peculiar way. The third explanation presupposes that internal and external forces are constantly interacting and focuses on what the individual does to modify the external environment as well as what the external environment in return does to shape the child.

Using these explanations of social learning we have labeled three schools of psychological thought. They are the *Non-Interventionists,* the *Interventionists,* and the *Interactionalists*. The classical student of psychology might be ruminating at this point, trying to remember where in his or her studies have such psychological schools of thought been encountered. The answer is simple. They probably haven't been. These terms and categories, although not entirely original, have been so identified by us to give clarity to the practical applications of teacher behaviors that will be described later. To reassure the bewildered psychology student, the more familiar schools of psychological thought will be found in our following explanations.

The Non-Interventionists

The Non-Interventionists encompass humanistic and psychoanalytical thought. They share a belief in the inner person. The humanists believe that within every child is an inner rationality which is constantly striving to improve.

As Carl Rogers, who is perhaps the most popular proponent of the humanist movement, has written:

> Human beings have a natural potential for learning . . . this potentiality and desire for learning, for discovery, for enlargement of knowledge and experience can be released under suitable conditions. It is a tendency which can be trusted, and the whole approach to education . . . builds upon and around the student's natural desire to learn.[1]

The psychoanalysts might find themselves feeling uncomfortable being grouped with the humanists, but their founder Sigmund Freud was a pioneer of the "inner person" concept. The psychoanalysts, however, do interpret these inner elements quite differently from the humanists. They believe that instinctual inner drives can be destructive and must be raised to a conscious level in order for the individual person to channel and control these forces in a constructive manner.

Briefly, we can conclude that the Non-Interventionists agree that the child's outward behavior should not be the primary focus for understanding his or her development. Instead they look to inner emotions and feelings. Behavior is only symptomatic of inner processes. Any increased growth is found in facilitating expression of those inner dynamics.

The Interventionists

The Interventionists encompass experimental behaviorist psychologies. They all hold to the premise that human development can be explained through an understanding of the quantity and quality of external stimulation. They believe observable behavior is the only key to understanding a person's social growth and that adjustment in human behavior comes about through the changes in outside conditions. (To them, there simply is no inner or emotional dimension to human growth.) As B.F. Skinner, the leader of behavioristic theory, wrote:

> An experimental analysis shifts the determination of behavior from autonomous man (free to decide for himself) to the environment—an environment responsible both for the evolution of species and for the repertoire acquired by each member. . . . It is the autonomous inner man who is abolished and that is a step forward.[2]

The Interactionalists

The Interactionalists include practitioners of Social, Gestalt, and Developmental psychologies. Although they may differ in their particular emphasis, they all concur that an explanation of development must take into account a multitude of factors. The whole child can only be understood by the interrelationship of all the parts. A child must be viewed as part of his or her total environment, in terms of what goes on both internally and externally. Growth is seen as a result of the constant interplay between child and society. Jerome Bruner, America's foremost cognitive developmentalist, wrote:

> One finds no internal push to growth without a corresponding external pull, for, given the nature of man as species, growth is as dependent upon a link with external amplifiers of man's powers as it is upon those powers themselves.[3]

Similarly, Alfred Adler, with his emphasis on living in a group, described the socialization process this way:

> . . . we always come upon the outstanding fact that throughout the whole period of development, the child possesses a feeling of inferiority in its relations both to parents and the world at large . . . this feeling of inferiority is the cause of his continual restlessness as a child, his craving for action, his playing of roles, and pitting of his strength against that of others. . .[4]

Both Bruner and Adler take note of the dynamics that occur between child and environment. Bruner refers to external amplifiers; Adler refers to the world of other people.

Guidelines for Classroom Practice: The Teacher's Role

Our terms *Non-Interventionists, Interactionalists,* and *Interventionists* should become clearer as we describe the popular applications of the various psychologies of social learning theory to the classroom. Writers who share the common assumptions within each of our three categories propose different roles for the teacher in relation to his or her troublesome child. Non-Interventionists emphasize the role of the teacher as being supportive to the child's own attempts at problem solving. The Interactionalists emphasize a parity relationship between teacher and student in arriving at joint solutions. The Interventionists stress the role of the teacher as planner and organizer of the environment for shaping the student's behavior.

Non-Interventionists

The Non-Interventionists have an abiding faith in the child as master of his or her own destiny. The function of the teacher is to provide a facilitating environment so that children can give vent and free expression to their feelings. The teacher empathizes with the child as he or she wrestles with inner emotions. This view is evident in the writings of Carl Rogers *(Freedom to Learn)*[5]; Virginia Axline *(Play Therapy)*[6]; Clark Moustakas *(The Authentic Teacher)*[7]; Thomas Gordon *(Teacher Effectiveness Training)*[8]; Thomas Harris *(I'm Ok—You're Ok)*[9]; Louis Raths, Merrill Harmin, and Sidney Simon *(Values and Teaching)*.[10]

Clark Moustakas expressed this application of Non-Interventionist beliefs when he wrote:

> Personal interaction between teacher and child means that differences in children are recognized and valued . . . Relations must be such that the child is free to recognize, express, actualize, and experience his own uniqueness. Teachers help to make this possible when they show they deeply care for the child, respect his individuality, and accept the child's being without qualification.[11]

The Non-Interventionists believe in a supportive, facilitating environment where the teacher is present to accept and emphathize with the student in his or her inner struggle.

Interactionalists

The child is not viewed as developing solely from either inward unfolding or from the conditioning of outside forces. Instead, it is felt that development occurs with the simultaneous pushes and pulls from within and without. Boundaries must be established and students must be made aware of behaviors from others that enhance or detract from their functioning in society.

The role of the teacher is to be one of constant interaction with the child. He or she allows freedom of behaviors up to a circumscribed point. A child who transgresses acceptable boundaries then comes into conflict with the teacher. The teacher takes command and jointly forces a mutually acceptable resolution. This theoretical view is broadly evident in the writings of Rudolf Dreikurs (*Discipline Without Tears,* 1972)[12] and William Glasser (*Schools Without Failure,* 1969).[13]

Dreikurs's work (1972) is indicative of the Interactionalists' position. He stated:

> Conflicts cannot be resolved without shared responsibility, without full participation in decision-making of all the participants in a conflict. Democracy does not mean that everybody can do as he pleases. It requires leadership to integrate and to win mutual consent.[14]

The Interactionalist theory of coping with child behavior is based on the teacher being able to assume the role of a clarifier, a boundary delineator, and finally as an enforcer. These theorists believe that children should take responsibility for their actions but need the active involvement of a kind but firm teacher. The child and/or teacher may decide on the remedy. Regardless of action, a solution acceptable to all must result.

Interventionists

The Interventionists share the assumption that a child develops according to the conditions of his or her environment. It is only with the implementation of a logical system of conditioning serving as reinforcement that socialized behavior can be assured.

The teacher is thus the controller of the environment. His or her task is to select the appropriate conditioners in direct commands and physical punishment to insure the proper learning behavior. Examples of Interventionist theory are evident in the writings of James Dobson *(Dare to Discipline)*[15]; Lloyd Homme *(How to Use Contingency Contracting in the Classroom)*[16]; Garth Blackham and Adolph Silberman *(Modification of Child and Adolescent Behavior)*[17]; Siegfried Engelmann *(Preventing Failure in the Primary School)*[18]; Saul Axelrod *(Behavior Modification for the Classroom Teacher)*[19]; and Charles Madsen and Clifford Madsen *(Teaching Discipline)*.[20]

Saul Axelrod (1977) echoes the Interventionists' point of view. He wrote:

> By accepting a position as a teacher, a person has not only a right but an "obligation" to modify student behavior. Children enter the schools without the necessary social and academic skills to function independently and productively in adult society . . . Teachers who do not bring about suitable changes in student behavior are failing to live up to the responsibilities of the profession.[21]

With the Interventionists there is no recognition of either the child's inner emotions or the child's capability of rational decision-making. The teacher takes command over the child's disruptive actions and makes immediate use of directive techniques to channel the child into constructive behavior. In order to keep a child learning efficiently, misbehavior is dealt with by selective reinforcement until the undesirable behavior is extinguished and the desired behavior is obtained.

Teacher Behavior: The Use of Power

After years of observing teacher behavior, we have found seven typical techniques that teachers utilize in dealing with misbehavior.[22] If you were to reflect on your own classroom experiences as a teacher, you might be able to identify your own immediate response to sudden misbehavior. Whether it is a book flying over your head, a scuffle, or abusive language, you probably would react in some of the following ways:

Visually Looking On: Some teachers 1) simply look over at the offender as if to say, "I see what you're doing but I know that you can take care of yourself,'' 2) observe the behavior and collect information on the entire situation be fore acting, or 3) gaze directly at the student with a penetrating frown.

Nondirective Statements: Some teachers immediately reflect the episode back to the student (''John, I saw you throw the book,'' or ''You must be angry to throw that book.'') or they reflect internally about what their next steps should be.

Questions: Other teachers react with such questions as, ''What do you think you're doing?'' or ''Jimmy, why are you doing that?''

Directive Statements: The habitual response of many teachers is to immediately correct the child with such statements as ''Stop that,'' ''Get back into your seat,'' or ''Don't do that again!''

Modeling: There are teachers who react to disruptive situations by moving over to the child, taking him or her by the arm, returning with the child to his or her seat and concretely showing the child what he or she should be doing. For example, the teacher opens the book to the correct page, puts the pencil in the student's hand, and begins to work on the next problem. Other teachers might elect to point out a well-behaved child as an example to be followed.

Reinforcement: Some teachers attempt to ignore the disruptive behavior and reward the child's next appropriate behavior with praise or privileges. Other teachers will punish the child by removing privileges, sending a note home, and so forth.

Physical Intervention and Isolation: Teachers who have experienced much frustration often will physically remove the child from the situation. This is done by isolating a child to a place in the room or out in the hall. Some teachers exert physical pressure by grabbing, shaking, or paddling the child.

We could categorize behaviors in other ways, but for purposes of this book we believe that these seven categories encompass most of the individual variations of teacher action. A few teachers use all seven, some use four or five, and many use only two or three.

The seven behaviors have been listed in a purposeful way. After delineating these seven behaviors, the authors noted that each behavior reflects a certain power relationship between teacher and student. Some teacher behaviors obviously provide the child with a great amount of time and opportunity for self-improvement. Other behaviors clearly give the teacher immediate control over the child. With these differences in mind, we conceptualized a power continuum. At one end of the continuum, strategies are used whereby the child has the most control of his or her behavior and the teacher has minimal control (this has been illustrated by the use of a capital *C* for child and a lowercase *t* for teacher); in the middle and at the other end of the continuum, the teacher subsumes the child's power (note the use of a lowercase *c* and a capital *T*). The seven teacher behaviors are inserted along this continuum as shown in Figure 2–1.

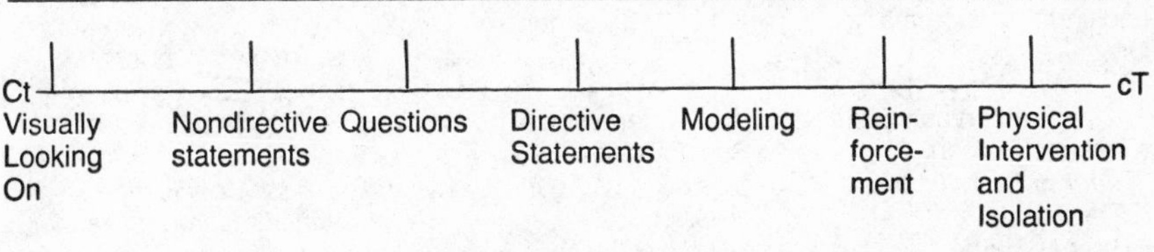

FIGURE 2–1. *Teacher Behavior Continuum (TBC)*

The reader can see how teacher behaviors such as visually looking and nondirective statements will encourage the child to find his or her own solutions, while behaviors such as questions, directive statements, and modeling tend to diminish the child's control and increase the teacher's power until finally modeling, reinforcement, and physical intervention move the source of power from the child and give it fully to the teacher. Therefore, what we have is a continuum of teacher behaviors that reflects a graduated scale of teacher control.

Now here comes the tricky part, so read carefully! As stated earlier, in describing major psychological theories of managing children, we have found and identified three distinct perspectives of the developing child. These are the *Non-Interventionists,* who believe that the child develops by having a supportive environment that encourages his or her own problem solving; the *Interactionalists,* who believe that a child develops through a constant give-and-take relationship with others; and the *Interventionists,* who believe that the child develops only by the conditioning of outside forces. Therefore, the application of these various theories emphasizes teacher behaviors that reflect the corresponding degrees of power possessed by child and teacher. The Non-Interventionists stress the use of teacher behaviors on the left of our continuum, the Interactionalists stress teacher behaviors that cluster in the middle, and on the right side the Interventionists see the teacher as having maximum power over the students' actions. This is illustrated with writers in Figure 2–2.

The techniques or methods imbedded in each major psychological school of thought can be understood accordingly. At the child-centered end of the continuum, the *Non-Interventionists* use minimal teacher power. The teacher uses an empathetic glance and reflective questions. The teacher utilizes only supportive and accepting behavior toward the child in order to maximize the chances of a child working through his or her own misbehavior.

The *Interactionalists* have the teacher move in more boldly by the act of drawing attention to the behavior through nondirective statements, questions, and directive statements. The Interactionalists strive for a solution, wherein the teacher and child attempt to find an integrative answer to the inappropriate behavior. The

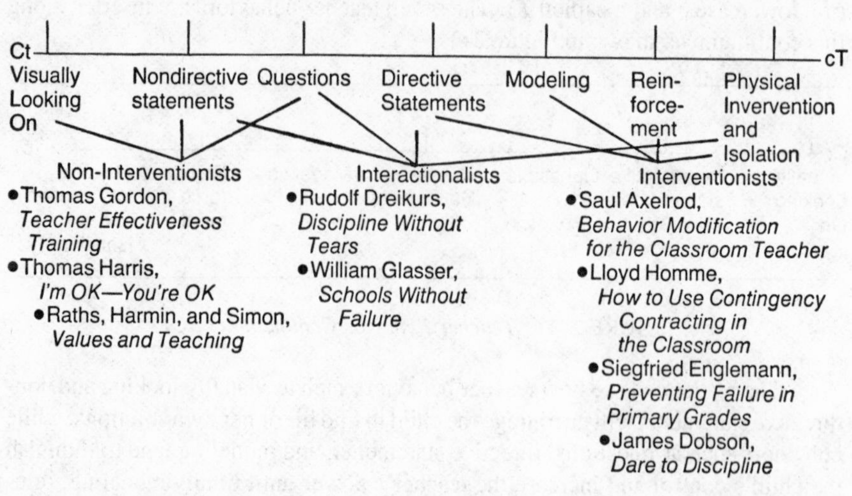

FIGURE 2–2. *Teacher Behavior Continuum (TBC)*

Interactionalists employ some of the techniques of the Non-Interventionists and Interventionists, but they are wary of any unilateral control of behavior by either student or teacher.

On the teacher-centered end of the continuum, the *Interventionists* have the teacher take control of the situation. The student corrects his or her behavior as the result of commands, explicit teacher modeling, rewards, and/or being physically restrained or isolated. In all, the Interventionists look for a tangible and immediate way to correct the misbehavior of the student.

Although these are somewhat simplistic explanations, the Teacher Behavior Continuum (TBC) will provide the reader with a ''handle'' for understanding the following sections where detailed explanations of some of the most popular student management approaches will be provided. The TBC also establishes a framework for a teacher to reflect on his or her own teacher behaviors and to compare the TBC with one's personal belief about children and their development.

Most of the popular approaches address in some way all seven behaviors on our continuum, and we will include an explanation of how each behavior is portrayed within those contexts. Some specific teacher behaviors from the TBC will prove to be more vital tools than others for a teacher implementing a specific approach. Often, those behaviors that are not central to a specific applicator are given very different interpretations by that individual. For example, the Non-Interventionists stress visually looking on, nondirective statements, and questions, yet they also speak of modeling, reinforcement, isolation, and physical intervention. However, they explain these latter behaviors quite differently from the interpretations heeded by the Interventionists and Interactionalists. For each popular application and its aligned proponents we will go through the seven teacher behaviors of the continuum and show specific strategies and interpretations, and thus permit the highlighting and comparison of each model.

Organization of the Following Chapters

What follows will be a delineation devoted to each school of thought in the next three chapters; i.e., Non-Interventionist, Interactionalist, and Interventionist. Within each of these chapters we will describe in some detail the actual techniques suggested by two (or more) of the more popular teacher-student interactive models representing that particular philosophy. The reader will be shown the central techniques suggested by each writer and how they are to be used in the classroom. We will at the same time compare and contrast each model with others.

Notes

1. Carl Rogers, *Freedom to Learn* (Columbus: Charles E. Merrill Publishing, 1969), pp. 157–58.
2. B. F. Skinner, *Beyond Freedom and Dignity* (New York: Knopf, 1971), pp. 214–15.
3. Jerome S. Bruner, et al., *Studies in Cognitive Growth* (New York: John Wiley and Sons, 1966), p. 6.
4. Alfred Adler, *The Practice and Theory of Individual Psychology* (Totowa, New Jersey: Littlefield Adams, 1972), p. 33.
5. Rogers, *Freedom to Learn*.
6. Virginia M. Axline, *Play Therapy* (New York: Ballantine Books, 1969).
7. Clark Moustakas, *The Authentic Teacher* (Cambridge, Massachusetts: Howard A. Doyle Publishing, 1972).
8. Thomas Gordon, *T.E.T.: Teacher Effectiveness Training* (New York: Peter H. Wyden Pub., 1974).
9. Thomas A. Harris, *I'm OK—You're OK: A Practical Guide to Transactional Analysis* (New York: Harper & Row, Publishers, 1969).
10. Louis E. Raths, Merrill Harmin, and Sidney B. Simon, *Values and Teaching: Working with Values in the Classroom* (Columbus: Charles E. Merrill Publishing, 1966).
11. Moustakas, *The Authentic Teacher*, p. 31.
12. Rudolf Dreikurs and Pearl Cassel, *Discipline Without Tears* (New York: Hawthorn Books, 1972).
13. William Glasser, *Schools Without Failure* (New York: Peter H. Wyden Pub., 1969).
14. Dreikurs and Cassel, *Discipline Without Tears*, p. 71.
15. James Dobson, *Dare to Discipline* (Wheaton, Illinois: Tyndale House Pub., 1970).
16. Lloyd Homme, *How to Use Contingency Contracting in the Classroom* (Champaign, Illinois: Research Press, 1970).
17. Garth J. Blackham and Adolph Silberman, *Modification of Child and Adolescent Behavior*, 2nd ed. (Belmont, California: Wadsworth Pub., 1975).

18. Siegfried Englemann, *Preventing Failure in the Primary Grades* (New York: Simon and Schuster, 1969).
19. Saul Axelrod, *Behavior Modification for the Classroom Teacher* (New York: McGraw-Hill, 1977).
20. Charles H. Madsen and Clifford K. Madsen, *Teaching Discipline: A Positive Approach for Educational Development*, 2nd ed. (Boston: Allyn and Bacon, 1974).
21. Axelrod, *Behavior Modification*, p. 158.
22. Charles F. Wolfgang, *Helping Aggressive and Passive Preschoolers Through Play.* (Columbus: Charles E. Merrill Publishing, 1977).

3

The Supportive Model: Gordon's Teacher Effectiveness Training

The scene is a fifth-grade classroom after school dismissal, and one child has remained behind. He approaches the teacher.

Student: "I hate this school!"

Teacher: "School is making you very unhappy."

Student: "Yes. I'm going to go back to my old school."

Teacher: "You're unhappy with this new school and you would like to go back to your old one."

Student: "Yeah, I never get to play. Every recess Tommy and Jeff pick the team, and they never pick me. No one likes me in this 'dumb' school."

Teacher: "You don't get picked for the teams and it makes you feel that no one likes you."

Student: "Bill and Mike don't get to play either. And we are going to get that ball first, and we won't let anyone else play! But, we tried that yesterday and Jeff knocked us down and took the ball—and, you know, the playground teacher wouldn't do anything about it! If I brought my ball from home they wouldn't do that!"

"Douglas, what I think I hear you saying. . . ."

John Anfin, from *Phi Delta Kappan*

Teacher:	"The other boys take the school ball away from you and they would not be allowed to do that if the ball was yours."
Student:	"Yes. Could I bring my ball from home to use?"
Teacher:	"Yes, if you think that would help."
Student:	"Then I can start my own team and not let Tom and Jeff play!"
Teacher:	"You could start your own team and not let Tom and Jeff play."
Student:	"Well, I would, if they let me pitch."

This dialogue is an example of one child's attempt to adjust and find his place in a new school, and it is typical of hundreds of similar problems that students bring to teachers. We see the teacher using the techniques suggested in Thomas Gordon's problem resolution model called *T.E.T.: Teacher Effectiveness Training*. The teacher did not advise, judge, or criticize this child on how to solve his problem, but instead simply listened carefully to the child's statements, appeared interested, and showed understanding of the student by mirroring the student's feelings and perceptions. Each time the student spoke, more of what was bothering him emerged and the parameters of his problem became clearer. Intellectually the child explored ways of solving his problem and finally was able to decide on a course of action. The *T.E.T.* techniques provide many helpful tools for the classroom teacher, and it will be our purpose to explore the theoretical roots and principles of such an approach and then show how these techniques relate directly to our own Teacher Behavior Continuum.

Gordon and Rogerian Theory

T.E.T.: Teacher Effectiveness Training,[1] created by Thomas Gordon, is based on a school of thought first conceptualized and popularized by Carl Rogers in his books entitled, *Client-Centered Therapy,*[2] *On Becoming a Person,*[3] and *Freedom to Learn.*[4] Rogers's therapeutic concepts were a departure from the highly deterministic Freudian psychology therapy of innate inner aggressive drives. Although the belief in the inner person remained, Rogers did not accept the position that the child is inherently ruled by destructive forces. Instead, he aligned with A.H. Maslow's belief that the child is born "prior to good and evil,"[5] a belief that would suggest that what a child grows to become will be a summation or embodiment of the child's experiences. The child does have an inherent capacity, but it is a capacity of being rational and capable. Rogers believes that given empathetic understanding, warmth, and openness one will choose what is best for oneself and will become a fully functioning person, constructive and trustworthy. The child is seen as "exquisitely rational," and it is believed that problems arise from the conflict that occurs when that inherent rationality is stifled. It is felt that this "stifling" happens in the classroom when we as teachers set about to order, direct, or make the student behave according to our will.

The underlying assumption of Rogerian theory is that each person is uniquely different and thus it is impossible for one person to make appropriate decisions for another. Any two people in a given situation will experience that situation in a way that is distinct from each other. This is because we experience and interpret stimuli based on our prior encounters, goals, expectations and attitudes. Each person will "screen" the event according to who he or she is as a person, and this screening, to a great extent, occurs at the unconscious level. Life, then, according to Rogerian theory, is a process of continually changing situations and continually changing problems in which we must make a multitude of decisions based on our individual experiences and perceptions. Many of these factors about making decisions ourselves are hidden from our consciousness. Therefore, the process or goal, within the Rogerian theoretical framework, for the individual experiencing problems is to consciously process his or her difficulties through the vehicle of language. By expressing one's feelings and concerns, an individual can make decisions that will result in the most appropriate rational solution.

Let's return to our beginning example of the student who "hates school." This first expression of "I hate this school!" was just the tip of the iceberg. Underneath there was a collection of fears and disappointments. "I hate school" might be more adequately interpreted as a message reading, "Dear Teacher, I'm very unhappy in this school because I have problems. Will you listen to me and help me?" The Rogerian teacher hears this wider message and does not fall into the trap of denying the child's underlying message by lecturing or advising the student; i.e., "Oh, come on, 'student,' this is one of the best schools in the state. You ought to appreciate what you have and how lucky you are!" or, "Well, young man, that attitude will never do. You must change your behavior if you want to get along here."

The teacher, as we saw, took an empathic, nonjudgmental position and simply mirrored the student's statements. This mirroring enabled the student to feel that the teacher followed what he was saying, that not only was he being permitted to talk but that he was being encouraged to continue and to expand on his feelings and ideas. The teacher believed that, given a supportive climate, the student would be able to express his problem(s) and feeling(s), and then suggest his own solutions. Whether the solutions are successful or not is not as important as the student being able to trust his own capacities to eventually master his problems.

This theory holds that a faith in one's own problem-solving capacity relates directly to the idea of "self-concept." Self-concept can be defined as a set of ideas that one holds about oneself as a person. You may see yourself as basically competent or incompetent in meeting life's continual challenges. It is only with the opportunity to wrestle with your own daily problems that you become master of your own destiny. The reader might see that in the "I hate school" example the child has been able to enhance his self-concept by realizing that he can define his own problems and make attempts to solve them. If the teacher had lectured or advised the student, the opposite effect might have occurred and the child's self-concept would have been weakened in the process.

Based on this theoretical position, the teacher's role is primarily one of being a supportive, non-critical facilitator with a total commitment to the rational ability of a child to identify and solve his or her own unique problems. With this understanding we may now turn to the techniques of Thomas Gordon and observe how he has operationalized Rogerian theory into specific teacher practices, as described in *T.E.T.: Teacher Effectiveness Training*. We will follow Gordon's procedures, using the Teacher Behavior Continuum (TBC) as our organizer in comparing the central elements or behaviors. Again, please keep in mind that these behaviors are: (1) visually looking on, (2) nondirective statements, (3) questions, (4) directive statements, (5) reinforcement, (6) modeling, and (7) physical intervention and isolation. As previously stated, the ranked order of these behaviors suggests an increasing use of power by the teacher and a decrease on the part of the student. It should be obvious that, given Gordon's theoretical framework, he will stress those behaviors (1, 2, and 3) that give most control to the child. With this in mind, let us begin.

T.E.T. and the Teacher Behavior Continuum

Visually Looking On

Central to the *T.E.T.* model is the expression of open and authentic communication between teacher and student. By definition, the word "communication'' suggests an exchange of ideas between people. Obviously, there is a difference between talking and hearing versus communicating. Communicating is a process whereby each party understands what the other has to say and formulates responsive messages in a way to create further understanding. Of course, all teachers will ''hear'' what a child says. The child who screams an obscenity is clearly heard, but, according to Gordon, the child is often not understood in terms of the meaning of the ''real'' message and the impact of strong feelings being expressed. Stress is placed on the teacher to use the least control possible in the process of understanding a student. That minimal control is described as *visually looking on* as the teacher *critically listens* to what a student is trying to say.

The first step on the Teacher Behavior Continuum is for the teacher to simply look at a misbehaving child. The look should be one of saying, ''I see what you are doing. I have trust in your ability to correct yourself. If you need my help, I am here.'' The student who cannot achieve his or her own immediate solution to the problem should then be encouraged to verbalize the issue. The teacher gives the student much time and encouragement to express what is troubling him or her, with the teacher nodding or using various gestures to encourage the child to continue.

Student: ''Janie is a stuck-up snob. She wouldn't go to the game with us!''

Teacher: ''Uh-huh.'' (Teacher nods while looking at the child.)

Gordon, in *T.E.T.: Teacher Effectiveness Training*, states, ''Saying nothing actually communicates acceptance. Silence—critical listening—is a powerful nonverbal message that can make a student feel genuinely accepted and encourages him to share more and more with you. A student cannot talk to you about what is bothering him if you are doing the talking.''[6]

Questioning (Skipping Nondirective Statements Temporarily)

At times while students are talking to us, they seem to have trouble beginning, or, once started, they pause in the middle of what they are saying and cannot appear to get started again. In these instances, it might be necessary to use what Gordon called ''door openers or reopeners.'' Examples would be such questions as, ''I'm interested, would you like to talk more about that?'' or ''Would you like to go on?'' Such ''door openers'' (questions) are of a nonevaluative nature. They encourage the student to explore his or her feelings more fully.

Teacher: ''Hello, Tommy. I think I see a worried look on your face. Would you like to talk about it?'' (This is the use of *questioning* as a ''door opener.'')

Student: "Someone stole my pencil. This has happened three times this week!"

Teacher: *"Uh-huh."* (Nods with *visually looking on* as critical listening.)

Using these supportive questions as "door openers" is quite different from using those kinds of questions that Gordon calls "roadblocks to communication." The latter are questions that probe, cross-examine, or accuse and are of little help to a student trying to find his or her own solutions. For example: "How much time did you spend on this project?" or "Did you ask permission before you did that?" are all questions that impose the teacher's will and dominance. These are really camouflaged directive statements that say, "You are wrong. You need me to tell you want to do." Gordon is adamantly opposed to the use of questions or direct statements that diminish the student's capacity to rationally alter his or her own behavior. On the other hand, making nondirective statements is seen as a more active way of helping the student.

Nondirective Statements

The question now arises as to exactly how we can use language to communicate with students most effectively. The most important use of language by the teacher within the *T.E.T.* model is called "active listening." To employ silence, to acknowledge responses by visually looking on, or to use "door openers" as questions has a positive but limited use and, in general, reflects passive behavior on the teacher's part. Effective communication between teacher and student involves a much more *active* response by the teacher through "active listening" and the use of *nondirective statements*. The teacher can actively communicate to the student that he or she is being understood by summarizing or mirroring the student's feelings or problems as the teacher comprehends them.

It might be helpful to look more closely to see how true communication really works, or, in short, "Why people talk." Gordon says that people talk when they have an internal need, either physical or emotional, and that people encode that need in the form of spoken language so that they can be understood by others. Unfortunately, many needs, especially those related to feelings, are difficult to express in language. If we return to the initial example in this chapter, which began with, "I hate this school," we realize it was only after much active listening that we discovered the child's real feelings and problems. The student first attempted to "encode" his feelings by stating, "I hate this school," which was a "unique coding" and revealed only the surface of the deeper problems that he was facing. We must not take such "uniquely coded" statements at face value, but permit the child to continue expressing through language while we mirror with "active listening" *(nondirective statements)* our understanding of what the child is attempting to say. For example, a student who has just been expelled from gym class and returns to the homeroom teacher might be dealt with as follows:

Student: "I hate folk dancing . . . that sissy stuff is for girls."

Teacher: "You don't like folk dancing because you think it is sissy stuff." (*Nondirective statements* as "active listening.")

Student: "Yes. Mrs. Jones in music class makes us folk dance on Fridays."

Teacher: "Uh-huh." (Nods with *visually looking on* as "critical listening.")

Student: (Drops eyes and gives no further verbal response.)

Teacher: "Would you like to tell me more about that?" (*Questioning* as a "door opener.")

Student: "Yeah, Mrs. Jones is unfair!"

Teacher: "Mrs. Jones has done some things that you feel are unfair." (*Nondirective statements* as "active listening.")

Student: "Yeah, she made us dance boy-girl and boy-girl, and there weren't enough girl partners and she made me be a 'girl,' and all the boys laughed."

Teacher: "You felt angry with Mrs. Jones for making you take a girl's part, and then you felt silly when the boys laughed."

In the preceding dialogue, we see the teacher helping the student express feelings that were "uniquely encoded" and unclear at first ("I hate folk dancing . . ."), and through "critical and active listening" the teacher finally hears the student's central problem and the feelings that were deeply troublesome.

Now that the teacher has some understanding as to what the problems of his or her student are, what should he or she do? Should the teacher tell the student how he should respond to the music teacher? Gordon would say "no." He would describe such a response as another "roadblock," called, "advising, offering solutions or suggestions."[7] Should the teacher confront the music teacher? Should the teacher call in the principal or guidance counselor? *T.E.T.* provides a helpful construct for the teacher to use in answering these questions and for defining what the teacher's response should be.

The central key to these issues in *T.E.T.* is, "Who owns the problem, the teacher or the child?" As shown in Figure 3–1, all behaviors of the student can be placed on a "window" and divided into three areas: (1) those behaviors that indicate the student is having a problem (i.e., other students will not pick him as a team member); (2) a no-problem behavior (i.e., a child works quietly at his desk); (3) those behaviors by the student that have a direct and concrete effect on the teacher, causing the teacher to "own" the problem (i.e., student interrupts while another child is being helped).[8]

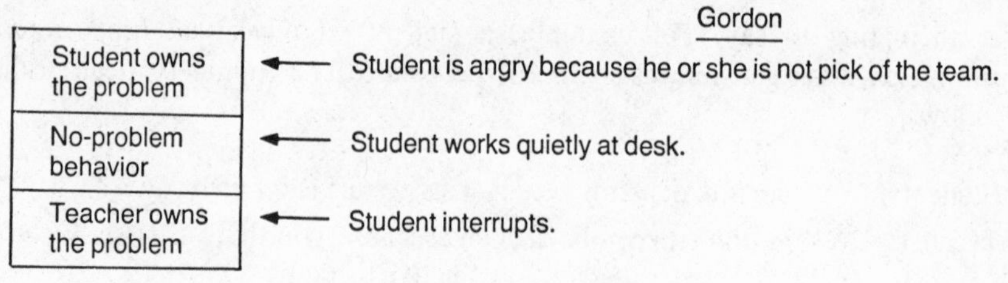

FIGURE 3–1. *Problem of Ownership*

When the problem belongs to the student ("I can't find my pencil" or "Mrs. Jones won't let me do so-and-so"), the role of the teacher is to use critical listening *(visually looking on)* and "door openers" *(questions)*, and to periodically mirror the child's concerns or messages with active listening *(nondirective statements)*. If the problem is owned by the teacher, in that it has a concrete effect on the teacher, then he or she may introduce an "I" message. This is a matter-of-fact *directive statement* containing the word "I" that expresses to the student the description of the student's behavior and how it is having a negative effect on the teacher. It also tells the student how the teacher feels about these actions; for example: "When gym equipment is left in the aisle, I might trip, and I'm afraid I might fall and be hurt." The "I" message must contain the sequence of "behavior, effect, feeling." Once an "I" message is expressed and the student has heard how his or her behavior is interfering with the teacher's needs, the teacher returns to critical listening *(visually looking on)*, active listening *(nondirective statements)*, and, if need be, to using "door openers" *(questions)*. The following dialogue provides examples of each of these behaviors.

Teacher: "Carol, when lunch papers are left on the table instead of being thrown away, I must pick them up before the next lunch group can be seated. I find this frustrating!" ("I" message)

Student: "I'm always getting picked on! Everyone *always* picks on me!"

Teacher: "You feel that everyone is making unfair demands on you." (active listening, *nondirective statement*)

Student: "Well, everyone picks on me."

Teacher: "Uh-huh." (critical listening, *nondirective listening*)

Student: (Silence)

Teacher: "Would you like to tell me more?" ("door openers," *questions*)

Student: "Well, Mrs. Jones makes me pass out the papers and erase the boards, and Miss Anderson makes me clean out the hamster cages three weeks in a row. And no one else gets jobs but me."

Teacher: "You feel that it is unfair for you to be given extra jobs by teachers, and therefore you do not need to clean up after yourself at lunchtime." (active listening, *nondirective statement*)

Student: "Well, it is unfair, but I guess I could throw my lunch papers away. Gee, I didn't know it was such a problem for you. But, I'm going to tell Mrs. Anderson, 'No more hamster cages for me!' "

The preceding dialogue reveals a problem clearly owned by the teacher. The student's *behavior* (leaving behind lunch papers) had a concrete effect on the teacher (the teacher had to pick them up and it interfered with her ability to seat other children), and in turn the teacher described her feelings (frustrated). We can also see that the teacher did not use any forms of teacher behavior or power-related behavior to manipulate the outcome. After delivering an "I" message, the teacher returns the problem to the student, and the teacher maintains a nonjudgmental stance.

There are other behaviors engaged in by students about which the teacher might hold very strong feelings. However, when these are investigated closely it is found that they do not have a concrete effect on the teacher and in turn the "I" message has little impact. How a student styles his or her hair, or the issue of wearing short dresses, or students holding hands in the halls, or poor posture, or the choosing of friends all might evoke strong feelings in the teacher, but these student behaviors involve clashes in values and cannot be said to affect the teacher directly. They are simply matters of personal taste. Gordon warns against trying to change the students to conform with a teacher's values by using "I" messages or "roadblocks." Gordon suggests the use of values clarification, one of our models described in Chapter 5, to deal with value-laden problems.

Directive Statements

We can imagine some of our readers shaking their heads in amazement and thinking, "Do you mean to say that this fellow Gordon says for us never to tell students what to do? He must be some kind of a crazy guy!" Never fear. Actually, Gordon does believe that there are times when teachers must use very strong directive statements with students, such as the giving of orders, directions, or commands. When *directive statements* are used correctly they are described by Gordon as strong "influencing attempts" by the teacher. If the child should be in some immediate danger, naturally it is appropriate for the teacher to command, "Turn down that flame, quickly, it's in danger of exploding!" or "Don't jump now, someone is climbing underneath!" or "Watch your head!" Such "influencing attempts" are generally acceptable to students, and they are willing to comply. We see no true conflict arising between teacher and student as a result. The difficulty occurs when teachers overuse commands or too strongly direct. Then, in reaction, students begin to resist and the teacher and student find themselves in conflict. When this occurs, such *directive statements* again become roadblocks, and the teacher will need to return to "active listening" to reestablish the relationship.

Gordon cites the following examples of directive statements that should be avoided by teachers:

1. *Ordering, commanding, directing*. Example: "You, stop playing with your pencil, and finish that test right now."
2. *Warning, threatening*. Example: "You had better straighten up, young man, if you want to pass this course."
3. *Moralizing, preaching, giving "shoulds" and "oughts."* Example: "You know what happens when you hang around with "that gang," you get into trouble. You ought to choose your friends more wisely."
4. *Advising, offering solutions or suggestions*. Example: "What you need to do is make a list and then put yourself on a time schedule to get these things done on time."
5. *Teaching, lecturing, giving logical arguments*. Example: "Let's look at what is going to happen. If you do not bring your gym clothing you will not be able to take PE and you will fail that class."

(Each of the preceding roadblocks presents a teacher's solution to a student's problem. The next five communicate judgments, evaluations, and, at times, put-downs.)

6. *Judging, criticizing, disagreeing, blaming*. Example: "You're just not the student that your sister was."
7. *Name-calling, stereotyping, labeling*. Example: "You're always acting like the class clown. When are you going to grow up?"
8. *Interpreting, analyzing, diagnosing*. Example: "You're always trying to find the easiest way to get around your homework."
9. *Praising, agreeing, giving positive evaluation*. Example: "You are my best student in this class. I'm sure you will want to be chairperson of this committee."
10. *Reassuring, sympathizing, consoling, supporting*. Example: "I also found that course difficult when I first tried it, but once you get into it you'll find it easier."[9]

The last two roadblocks (numbers 9 and 10) are examples of strong reinforcing techniques that are central to some of the models that will be summarized in following chapters. It is interesting to note that certain strategies held to be of utmost importance to some experts are scorned by others. Gordon's interpretation of reinforcement must be closely read to understand the later differences with other writers.

Reinforcement

The resolution of conflict within the *T.E.T.* models relates to Gordon's definition of two types of authority and how the teacher uses his or her power with students. *Type I authority* is desirable and is based on a person's expertise, knowledge, and experiences. An individual obtains the power inherent in Type I authority by being judged as one who is wise and expert enough to be listened to by students, and is an individual sought after for advice. *Type II authority* is undesirable. It is aligned with a power-based position that enables a teacher to (1) dispense certain benefits that students need or want (reward or positive reinforcement) or (2) inflict discomfort or painless punishment on students (negative reinforcement). Later we will discuss how the Interventionists use reinforcement and rewards as a central tool in their techniques to get students to change. The Non-Interventionist writers such as Gordon dramatically disagree with such an approach. Gordon sees the use of both positive and negative reinforcements as a manipulation and misuse of power by a teacher which will eventually produce defensive reaction mechanisms in students so they may deal with such authoritarian power. Gordon would suggest that if we see the following behavior in our students, we may need to investigate our use of power. These following behaviors indicate the use of Type II authority:

— rebelling, resisting, defying
— retaliating
— lying, sneaking, hiding feelings
— blaming others, tattling
— cheating, copying, plagiarizing
— bossing, bullying, pushing others around
— needing to win, hating to lose
— organizing, forming alliances
— submitting, complying, buckling under
— apple polishing
— conforming, taking no risks, trying nothing new
— withdrawing, dropping out, fantasizing, regressing[10]

Finally, even the teacher who has Type I authority and uses visually looking on, nondirective statements, door openers and ''I'' statements will still run into conflict with an individual child. The occasions will be less frequent but still inevitable. The *T.E.T.* model provides a resolution for such conflict. Gordon has defined conflict as a collision occurring between teacher and student where their *behaviors* interfere with each other's attainment of their own needs and thus *both parties own the problem*. For example:

Teacher: (Returns to the classroom to discover a student taking a pencil from the teacher's desk.)
"When pencils are taken from my desk, I cannot find one to do my work and I must pay to purchase new ones. This has happened a number of times, and I find it annoying." ("I" message, *directive statements)*

Student: "Well, each time I return from Music Class I find someone has taken my pencil. This has happened three weeks in a row."

In this example both teacher and student own the problem and they find themselves in conflict. Gordon suggests that such problems are usually resolved by using two methods that result in either the teacher or the student winning. In Method I, the teacher wins by using authority and power, and the student loses.

Teacher: "Well, you're just going to have to learn that you cannot be permitted to steal from the teacher's desk. For the remainder of this week you will not be permitted to go for recess (or to the pep rally)." (Judging, criticizing, blaming, and punishing are creating an obstacle to the student's rational capacity to solve his or her problems.)

We can restate the dialogue to show Method II, where the student wins and the teacher loses.

Teacher: "Someone has taken your pencil."

Student: "Yes, and if you had not left class to go to the teacher's lounge to smoke a cigarette, you would have been here to prevent someone from taking my pencil. My father is really angry, and he said if I have one more thing stolen from my desk he is going to come to see the principal."

Teacher: "Well, uh, I don't ever want you to take things from my desk again."

This is an example of *Method II,* where the student "wins" when the teacher gives up or ignores the student's actions. These win-lose methods both center on a "power struggle" between teacher and student, and in each case the loser goes away feeling resentful and angry. Many teachers unknowingly use one of these methods. Some teachers use both, which is even more destructive as the teacher swings from an authoritarian position to one of being permissive. They appear highly erratic and unpredictable, and leave the student confused. Gordon proposes an alternative solution called *Method III* "no lose," where the conflict is resolved without the teacher or student using or losing power.

Teacher: "Someone has taken your pencil." ("active listening," *nondirective statement*)

Student: "Well, I probably shouldn't have taken yours, but I really need a pencil for the test next period—and someone keeps stealing mine."

Teacher: "Can you think of how we may solve this problem for now so we will both have our pencils and both feel OK."

Student: "Well, it only happens on Tuesday when I go to Music Class. I could take my pencil with me, but I don't use pencils in Music Class, and I really don't want to carry it around."

Teacher: "Taking your pencil to Music Class does not seem to be the solution. ("active listening," *nondirective statement*)

Student: "Yeah, I wonder if I could put my pencil somewhere else in the classroom on Tuesdays when I go to Music, somewhere where it will be safe. And, I'm going to bring this problem to our class meeting to see if we can get people to stop taking my pencil."

Teacher: "It sounds like you have begun to solve your problem." ("active listening," *nondirective statement*)

Student: "Could I put it in your desk?"

We can see that Method III "no lose" is a conflict-solving process in which the teacher does "active listening" and uses "I" messages until he or she fully hears what the child's problems and needs are, and then they "put their heads together" until a solution can be found that is acceptable to both. Method III creates a "no lose" result, and no power struggle is involved. The solution can be suggested by either the student or the teacher, but the final agreement must be acceptable to both members involved with the conflict. Method III, a final departure point for Gordon, is a central beginning point for the Interactionalists (Dreikurs and Glasser), who see all student misbehavior as affecting others. These Interactionalists would agree with the general steps described here, but not with the teacher's behaviors. Gordon also suggests that to create a "no lose" climate, the teacher can introduce the "scientific method," involving the following six steps developed by John Dewey as a format for Method III.

STEP 1. Defining the Problem

With the use of active listening and "I" messages, the teacher would help a student or an entire class focus on a problem that affects them. During this defining step, one should not attempt to provide a solution or make an evaluation, but, instead, simply attempt to get everyone involved to clarify their needs.

STEP 2. Generating Possible Solutions

During this second step, the goal is to "brainstorm" many different solutions for the problem, again without attempting to make an evaluation of the ideas presented. Early evaluation of solutions will limit creativity, and the teacher might need to use "I" messages to keep the discussion guided towards brainstorming.

STEPS 3 and 4. Evaluating and Deciding on Solution(s)

Having made a list of the possible solutions in Step 2, the teacher and student, or group, need to go over each solution to determine which ones can be agreed upon by all involved. If the teacher or student cannot live with the solution being considered, they can express this through "I" messages. It is important that all solutions be considered fully, and the teacher will have to use much active listening to achieve this end.

STEPS 5 and 6. Implementing and Evaluating Solution(s)

During the final steps, a clear agreement must be established as to who will do what and when they will begin. At this time, those involved should set a time to meet again to re-evaluate the results.[11]

In using the Method III "no lose" conflict-solving process, Gordon suggests that there are some problems outside the teacher's "area or spheres of freedom." He provides a chart that looks much like a target with a bull's-eye, and places the teacher in the center.[12] This center area represents activities such as classroom organization, rules, assignments, and so forth, that are within the teacher's "area of freedom." In turn, each circle moving out from the center is labeled "school principal," "district superintendent," "local laws," "state laws," and "federal laws." Each new circle represents a higher level of authority that can limit the teacher's freedom to make certain decisions. For example, the state law requires compulsory education for all students, so if by Method III the teacher and class were to decide that school attendance should be elective, there would be no way to implement their decision. This issue is simply outside their realm of decision making. In other words, there are certain social constraints within which both the student and teacher must live.

Although *T.E.T.* rejects the systematic use of *reinforcers,* which we will see described in the Interventionist models, Gordon does acknowledge the need to create a classroom that is supportive of various activities. He suggests the classroom environment can be modified (a word used heavily by the Interventionists) in a systematic and creative way to alleviate student disruption. It can be changed to enrich the learning space and activities. In modifying the environment, time is another variable that relates to certain student problems. The effective teacher knows that at certain times in the day it is better to introduce difficult concepts to students, while at other times students tend to be irritable, which can make such learning difficult. Time, within the *T.E.T.* model, is organized and viewed in three ways: (1) diffused time, (2) individual time, and (3) optimum time.[13]

When students are working closely with others in a busy classroom, they need to use a lot of energy for screening out stimuli in order to concentrate on such work as reading or working a math problem. *Diffused time* is the time period in which the student works in close social contact. The student can only function effectively for a limited time in such a stimulating environment before becoming fatigued. It is necessary, therefore, for students to have some *individual time* where they can be by themselves for a short period (for example, a "quiet corner" or an individual study carrel). The third classification, *optimum time,* is a period during the day when a student is able to meet individually with the teacher or a fellow student. If this time is not provided for, the child might attempt to fulfill his or her need for personal attention by being disruptive. This misbehavior forces the teacher to deal with the student and in turn gives the one-to-one contact that is desired. With these time classifications in mind, the teacher is encouraged to deliberately plan the day to create a balance of all three forms of time to maintain a teaching-learning environment that maximizes a "hassle-free" climate for child growth.

Modeling

Although the use of modeling is a technique more systematically used by the Interactionists, the *T.E.T.* model acknowledges its importance. For the teacher using *T.E.T.,* the rule of thumb is, "Do it, don't talk about it! Practice, don't preach!" In other words, the teacher, by his or her every action, is modeling to the students behaviors that reflect the teacher's values. Greater problems arise when the teacher attempts to "teach" students to behave in one way while he or she behaves in an opposite manner. The injunction to "Do as I say, not as I do" produces a double standard that is easily recognized by students. Gordon would suggest that we as teachers look closely at our school and class rules and ask, "Do the rules allow the adults to behave in one way while denying the same behavior to non-adults?" Can teachers hit students (corporal punishment) while acts of fighting among students are severely punished? Do teachers "cut" the lunch line, while students must wait their turn? Are teachers permitted to smoke in school while students are not? Such questions require us to introspect closely and ask ourselves what exactly are the values that we are modeling. A teacher's modeled behavior has a powerful effect on student behavior.

T.E.T. also addresses the modeling of behavior that a teacher uses while resolving a conflict with a student. Do we retreat to *Method I* power behaviors that enable only the teacher to employ his or her authority to win? Or, do we give in and use *Method II,* wherein we become permissive and lose to the student? The

Method III "no lose" technique of problem-solving models the type of authentic behavior that helps relationships between teacher and students. A youngster, having seen *Method III* "no lose" techniques modeled by the teacher, may then begin to use similar techniques with adults and peers.

Physical Intervention and Isolation

The use of such physical behaviors by the teacher as inhibiting a disruptive child by removing him or her from the classroom is not explicitly dealt with in *T.E.T.* We may infer, though, that such strong measures would not be acceptable within the *T.E.T.* framework, except in a case where a student physically endangered himself or others. A reasonable teacher would be justified in intervening to keep students safe. The use of isolation or physical force to coerce students would be an extreme form of a "roadblock" to communication and would be clearly rejected by *T.E.T.*

Summary

By using the Teacher Behavior Continuum (TBC) in Figure 3–2 we may now summarize and outline the "tools" that Gordon has provided to the teacher in his *T.E.T.: Teacher Effectiveness Training* model. Those tools are classified into overt and covert teacher behaviors in Figure 3–2. The overt behaviors are those outward actions taken by teachers that can be clearly observed and defined. These are (1) critical listening or (2) acknowledging responses and gestures, (3) door openers or re-openers, (4) active listening (mirroring feelings) and (5) "I" messages, and finally (6) strong "influencing."

The covert behaviors suggested by *T.E.T.* are actions that run through the teacher's mind in reflecting, planning, predicting, and preventing, and do not deal with direct action or conflict resolution between student and teacher. These covert actions can be listed as (a) planning Method III "no lose" conflict resolution, (b) modeling teacher behavior consistent with expected student behavior, (c) reorganizing classroom space, and (d) reorganizing classroom time (diffused, individual, and optimum times).

Notes

1. Thomas Gordon, *T.E.T.: Teacher Effectiveness Training* (New York: David McKay, 1974).
2. Carl R. Rogers, *Client-Centered Therapy: Its Current Practices, Implications, and Theory* (Boston: Houghton Mifflin, 1951).
3. Carl R. Rogers, *On Becoming a Person: A Therapist's View of Psychotherapy* (Boston: Houghton Mifflin, 1961).

Ct ——— cT

Visually Looking On	Nondirective Statements	Questions	Directive Statements	Modeling	Reinforcement	Physical Intervention and Isolation
(1) Critical Listening (silence) (2) Acknowledgement Responses (gesture)	(4) Active Listening (mirroring feelings) "You're worried about getting an exam soon." (5) "I" messages "When I find papers left on the floor . . ." (behavior, effect, feeling)	(3) Door Re-openers "Do you want to talk more about it?"	(6) influencing "watch your step"	(a) Method III "no lose" (b) Daily actions	(c) reorganizing space (d) reorganizing time (diffused, individual, optimum)	

Supportive Model

Author: Thomas Gordon

(numbers) overt behavior (letters) covert behavior

FIGURE 3–2. *Teacher Behavior Continuum (TBC)*

4. Carl R. Rogers, *Freedom to Learn* (Columbus: Charles E. Merrill Publishing, 1969).
5. Abraham H. Maslow, *Toward a Psychology of Being,* 2nd ed. (New York: D. Van Nostrand, 1968), p. 3.
6. Gordon, *T.E.T.: Teacher Effectiveness Training,* p. 61.
7. Gordon, *T.E.T.*, p. 48.
8. Gordon, *T.E.T.*, p. 40.
9. Gordon, *T.E.T.*, pp. 51–52.
10. Gordon, *T.E.T.*, p. 200.
11. Gordon, *T.E.T.*, pp. 227–234.
12. Gordon, *T.E.T.*, p. 275
13. Gordon, *T.E.T.*, pp. 169–175.

References

Related Readings

Clark, D. H., and Kadis, A. *Humanistic Teaching*. Columbus: Charles E. Merrill Publishing, 1971.

Holt, John. *Freedom and Beyond*. New York: E. P. Dutton, 1972.

Research on T.E.T.

Aspy, David. Unpublished report of T.E.T. Evaluation. Newport News School District. Gatewood Building, 1241 Gatewood Road, Newport News, Virginia, 23601.

For information about how school districts can offer the Teacher Effectiveness Training Course to their teachers, write to School Programs, Effectiveness Training, Inc., 531 Stevens Avenue, Solana Beach, California 92075.

Instructional Media

Films

Title:	Carl Rogers on Education (Part I)		
Time:	30 minutes	Color	
Rental Fee:	$25	Purchase Price:	$250
Company:	American Personnel and Guidance Association 1107 New Hampshire Avenue Washington, D.C. 20009		
Synopsis:	Describes how people acquire significant learning and indicates the directions in which the educational system must change to have a real impact on students. Covers such topics as: the role of the student		

in formulating his or her curriculum; the circumstances under which learning will be a lasting and meaningful process—the activities a teacher should engage in to be a facilitator of learning . . . and the qualities in the interpersonal relationship between facilitator and students which foster and encourage the learning process.

Title: Carl Rogers on Education (Part II)

Time: 30 minutes Color

Rental Fee: $25 Purchase Price: $250

Company: American Personnel and Guidance Association
1107 New Hampshire Avenue
Washington, D.C. 20009

Synopsis: Analysis of the educational system by focusing on the following topics: implementing "freedom to learn" within restraints and obligations imposed upon teachers in the usual educational setting, coping with the different expectations students have of what they want or need from a teacher; the role of the educational system in transmitting societal values and in helping young people resolve value questions; the characteristics in young people that are fostered by teachers who facilitate freedom to learn.

Title: Three Approaches to Psychotherapy, No. 1
Dr. Carl Rogers

Time: 48 minutes Color

Rental Fee: $75 Purchase Price: $375

Company: Psychological Films, Inc.
1215 East Chapman Avenue
Orange, California 92669

Synopsis: Describes client-centered therapy as practiced by Dr. Carl Rogers. Shows interview with patient, Gloria, and gives a summation of the effectiveness of the interview. Correlated with the textbook *Therapeutic Psychology* by L. Brammer and E. Shostrom.

Title: Three Approaches to Psychotherapy, No. 2
Dr. Frederick Perls

Time: 32 minutes Color

Rental Fee: $75 Purchase Price: $375

Company: Psychological Films, Inc.
1215 East Chapman Avenue
Orange, California 92669

Synopsis: Describes the Gestalt therapy as practiced by Dr. Frederick Perls. Shows his interview with patient, Gloria, and gives a summation of the effectiveness of the interview.

Title: Three Approaches to Psychotherapy, No. 3
Dr. Albert Ellis
Time: 42 minutes Color
Rental Fee: $75 Purchase Price: $375
Company: Psychological Films, Inc.
1215 East Chapman Avenue
Orange, California 92669
Synopsis: Describes rational-emotive psychotherapy as practiced by Dr. Albert Ellis. Shows his interview with patient, Gloria, and gives a summation of the effectiveness of the interview. Includes an evaluation of her therapy with Dr. Rogers, Dr. Perls, and Dr. Ellis.

Title: Actualization Therapy—An Integration of Rogers, Perls, and Ellis
Time: 27 minutes Color
Rental Fee: $20 Purchase Price: $250
Company: Psychological Films, Inc.
1215 East Chapman Avenue
Orange, California 92669
Synopsis: Presents sequences from the film series, "Three Approaches to Psychotherapy," illustrating the work of Dr. Rogers, Dr. Perls and Dr. Ellis. Includes an analysis of each of the styles by Dr. Everett Shostrom, contrasting them and describing each of their contributions. Describes how Actualization Therapy represents an attempt to integrate each of these approaches into a working unit.

Title: Teacher Effectiveness Training
Author: Thomas Gordon
Time: 29 minutes Color
Rental Fee: $45 Purchase Price: $395
Company: Media Five
3211 Cahuenga Boulevard, West
Los Angeles, California 90068
Synopsis: Outlines the methods used by teachers to build more effective classroom relationships. Illustrates and explains the concepts of active

listening, "I" messages, and the "no lose" method for resolving conflicts.

Title:	T.E.T. in High School		
Author:	Thomas Gordon		
Time:	29 minutes	Color	
Rental Fee:	$45	Purchase Price:	$395
Company:	Media Five 3211 Cahuenga Boulevard, West Los Angeles, California 90068		
Synopsis:	Demonstrates the "no lose" method of resolving conflicts, and improving human relations in the secondary level classroom.		

Title:	Be an Effective Teacher		
Author:	Thomas Gordon		
Time:	55 minutes (Two Reels)	Color	
Rental Fee:	$30 per day	Purchase Price:	$300
Company:	American Personnel and Guidance Association 1107 New Hampshire Avenue Washington, D.C. 20009		
Synopsis:	Teacher Effectiveness Training approach provides a sound basis for promoting a powerful learning environment in the classroom. Reel One: Presents role-play demonstrations of the T.E.T. approach in action, through the application of active listening when the child has a problem and "I" messages when the teacher has a problem. Reel Two: Conflict-resolution skills are presented. Discusses the origins and underlying philosophies of the central concepts, as well as the techniques of implementation.		

4

The Communication Model: Berne and Harris's Transactional Analysis

Mr. Tyler, the kindergarten teacher, turns to discover a large pool of paint at the feet of a five-year-old girl standing before the painting easel. Sally, a bold little girl, has spilled paint on the floor for the third time this week. She looks at the spreading paint, wraps the end of her smock around her hand and hugs it like a blanket. At the same time, she sucks her thumb and looks away from Mr. Tyler's gaze. Mr. Tyler's immediate inclination is to say words to this effect: ''Sally, why in the world do you always make such a mess? You never pay attention to what you're doing.'' Instead he pauses. He is a teacher trained in Transactional Analysis. He knows that Sally's behavior indicates she is being the *Child,* impulsive and irresponsible. Mr. Tyler realizes that if he goes ahead with his retort he would be perpetuating the *Child* in Sally by taking the role of admonishing *Parent*. Instead, he must speak as the rational *Adult,* and in so doing, hope to bring out Sally's *Adult* as well. With these thoughts, he says: ''Sally, paints are hard to control but you can clean them up. What do you need to clean up this mess?''

What were all of the verbal options open to Mr. Tyler? The following are a number of responses that the teacher might have made:

Questions

Who made this mess? *(Parent)*
What do you need to clean this up? *(Adult)*
Why is it that I always have to clean up your mess? *(Child)*

Directive Statements

See this mess you made because you never pay attention to what you're doing. *(Parent)*
Paints are hard to control but you can clean them up. *(Adult)*
I'm so mad, I'm not giving you any more paint! *(Child)*

Transactional Analysis

We have all heard teachers make these kinds of statements to children as well as to each other. Transactional Analysis (generally referred to as TA) provides the teacher with a helpful framework for viewing what is said to and by students and to ascertain whether their verbal interactions are conducive to dealing with misbehaving students. Transactional analysis was first presented in *Games People Play* by Eric Berne[1] and *I'm OK—You're OK* by Thomas A. Harris.[2] These books primarily dealt with communications between adults. Later, these same principles and concepts were used to help adults deal with children in such books as *Born to Win* by James and Jongeward,[3] *TA for Tots* by Alvyn M. Freed,[4] and *Games Students Play* by Ken Ernst.[5]

If we place ourselves in the shoes of the teacher encountering the kindergarten child, described in the beginning of this chapter, we might think about the many occasions when we would have liked to have retracted what was said and rephrased it in a more positive manner. However, according to TA, there are many different persons in ourselves. It is believed that our inner energy is often diverted into opposing factions. First delineated by the early works of Sigmund Freud, this idea of inner energy was tied to the existence of three constructs: (1) the *Id,* representing our instinctual selfish needs or drives, (2) the *Superego,* representing a restrictive force over these selfish drives, and (3) the *Ego,* which serves as a referee balancing the forces of hedonism and repression to attain enlightened self-interest. The teenager finds a sporty looking car parked at the corner with the keys in the ignition. The *Id* says, "Go on, take it for a ride. What a thrill!" The *Superego* shouts, "No, you will be arrested. You and your parents will be embarrassed and ashamed." In a healthy individual, the refereeing *Ego* resolves the dilemma with thoughts such as, "I will not take the car now, but if I want a car like this, then I will work overtime, save my money, and by the summer I will be able to purchase my own car." Life for every individual is a dynamic process of interplay of urges and checking forces. These concepts, although interesting and maybe helpful for the highly trained psychoanalyst, have been generally too abstract to be useful to the classroom teacher who must deal with everyday behavior. Such TA writers as Berne and Harris have attempted to operationalize these Freudian concepts into ways that adults can use readily. A TA model for teachers has been developed that describes direct actions and behaviors to be used in their work with students of all ages.

The Theory

Theorists in the process of documenting the basis for the principles of TA have leaned heavily on research done on memory processes and the experiments done by such neurosurgeons as Dr. Wilder Penfield.[7] Such experiments have involved stimulating the various parts of the brain with mild electrical waves. It was discovered that such shocks elicited from the subject a recall of historical events and feelings. Subjects reported feelings that "they were there," and they could relive past incidents. From these experiments it was hypothesized that day-to-day experiences serve as stimuli that evoke memories of past situations and cause the person to relive the events with vivid images and feelings. The brain can be thought of as a recorder of experiences. All events from birth onward are put on "tape" and are stored for instant retrieval. One might recall walking past a restaurant and smelling the aroma of fresh bread and roast turkey. The mind is quickly flooded with images and feelings about Thanksgiving dinner as a child. It is almost as if the person were a child again. Obviously other stimulations can trigger negative recordings. The smell of wood burning could conjure up recollections of a traumatic house fire or the smell of oils, a car accident.

Life is a process of dynamic urges and counter checks. We have a stored memory of our past experiences that can be quickly invoked with the accompaniment of vivid images and feelings.

The central principle of TA is called the social "transaction."

Eric Berne states:

> The unit of social intercourse is called a transaction. If two or more people encounter each other . . . sooner or later one of them will speak, or give some other indication of acknowledging the presence of the others. This is called the *transactional stimulus*. Another person will then say or do something which is in some way related to the stimulus, and that is called the *transactional response*.[8]

From a classroom perspective, the transaction just described would be either the teacher initiating action toward the student and the student acting back, or the student acting toward the teacher and the teacher responding. What teachers or students "do" or "do back" is to a great extent a reflex response whereby the student or teacher hears a "tape" of a similar past experience and simply "acts" it out in reality. For example, the classroom teacher needs to move her students to the auditorium, and this present situation triggers a memory-bank response: 'Boys, line up; girls, line up.'' This act of verbalization has never been thought out consciously by the teacher. It is simply what he or she has experienced in his or her own school experiences as a student. The teacher simply ''replays the tape'' and says to the students what was said to him or her as a student. What TA can do for the teacher is to provide another repertoire of words that will bring out positive and constructive responses from the students.

Berne closely observed people's outward behavior and actions as they replayed their internal ''tapes.'' He frequently saw a metamorphosis occur before his very eyes. At one moment a person's manner, appearance, words, and gestures were indicative of a confident ''adult'' who could respond to information in a business-like, rational manner. At the next moment the same person might change and employ the ''childish'' actions of being impulsive, demanding, and whining. Soon the person might change again to become a harsh ''parent'': judgmental, sounding off with advice, and evaluative. After extensive observations Berne concluded that in all people there exist three states of being. One state is that of a ''little person'' much like a three-year-old, which he called the *Child*. The second state is an imitation of all the stored-up experiences a person has had as a child of his or her own parents; this state is called the *Parent*. The third state is called the *Adult*. The *Adult* is quite different from the other two states and is rational, responsible, and objective. These three states, *Child, Parent,* and *Adult,* are more readily understood and applied than the previous Freudian terms of the *Id, Superego,* and *Ego*. Following are more detailed explanations of each of Berne's states.

Parent

The *Parent* state is based on all the ''tapes'' we have stored from those experiences we have had with our parents or parent substitutes which we recorded in total when we were very young. They are recorded as ''truths'' because, as helpless children, we were totally dependent on our parents for security and lacked the intellectual ability to evaluate our parents' actions. In these tapes are recorded, not only the external admonitions and rules as heard from parents when they were stern, but also the pleasures given to us by a happy and proud parent. The *Parent* contains a controlling side and a nurturing side. Much of a parent's rules were for the child's own safety; i.e., ''Don't run into the street.'' Difficulty arose, however, when a parent told us to do one thing while he or she did another. Our memories record both the verbal and behavioral experience. ''Don't tell lies!'' exhorts the parent, but the child often catches the adult telling lies; i.e., ''Tell the salesman at the door I'm not at home.'' Usually these unedited contrary tapes hidden in our *Parent* state contain imperatives and extremes about what the child should or should not do. The words and terms ''never,'' ''always,'' and ''never forget that'' come out of the *Parent* state.

Child

While we are recording the external rules as part of our *Parent* state, we are simultaneously recording the same internal feelings as part of our *Child* state. Since the child does not have the vocabulary or intellectual ability to question and evaluate his experience, the "seeing, hearing and feeling data" become our *Child*. Because a young child is far from behaving in socially decreed ways, the *Child* takes great joy in exploring, testing, and generally getting into the world with ceaseless energy and noise. In turn, when these explorations conflict with parental values, the child must give up much of his or her desires for unlimited exploration to win parental approval. Because of the frustration caused by the parent's demands for a civilized child, the young child begins to feel that, "I'm not OK." These "Not OK" feelings are permanently recorded in our *Child* state and can never be erased from memory. We can all remember (at least a few times, and in some cases, many times) when we have felt inadequate in controlling ourselves, even when we know that we are acting wrong. We might uncontrollably and irrationally explode at someone. The *Child* has taken over.

The *Child,* however, also has a positive side. On these tapes are the "OK" recordings of good feelings that go with exploring, touching, and feeling. "OK" feelings come from memories of being held warmly and closely, or the carefree times playing in the park, or the glorious feelings of licking a cold, smooth ice cream cone. All tapes of positive and negative feelings have been recorded before the age of five, and they will always be there to be replayed.

Adult

As the young child moves out of toddlerhood, he or she begins to store information for use in understanding future events. The child begins to think and the rational abilities of categorizing and generalizing begin to develop. As early as ten months old the child is able to do things that provide both awareness and thoughts about himself or herself. These beginning *Adult* data are quite different from the *taught* concept of life in the Parent stage and the *felt* concept of life in the Child stage. The *Adult* develops a thought concept of life based on information gathered and rationally processed. The *Adult* as a rational state in the early years of life is weak and can be easily displaced by the demands of the Parent or Child.[9]

It is the task of the *Adult* to test the rules and information of the *Parent*. Through experience, the *Adult* discovers it is true that one "should not run into the street" (Parent) and this information in the Parent can be trusted and is dependable. The "Not OK" feelings first associated with these early reprimands, although now seen as justified by the Adult, are still not erased, and such "Not OK" feelings can still swell up. An individual always needs the rational *Adult* to turn off these "Not OK" feelings. It is also the *Adult's* job to determine when the

Child's feelings can be expressed. As a mature person, the *Adult* knows that it is acceptable to cry at a wedding but not appropriate to scream at the school principal (even when the son- or daughter-of-a-gun deserves it!).

The general day-to-day job of the *Adult* is to "check out" old information found in the *Parent* and to update and validate it for future use; e.g., does drinking coffee really stunt growth? Hopefully, if the information in the *Parent* is found to be accurate by the *Adult,* the person is free to obey the messages—"Walk on the right side of the hall," "Don't go down one-way streets," "Fasten the seat belt"—and there is no further need to expend energy debating these issues. This saves the *Adult* from having to "reinvent the wheel" and make every decision from "scratch." If the information from the *Parent* is prejudicial ("Don't play with any children that have slanted eyes") and the information gained by the *Adult* is contradictory ("My teacher has slanted eyes and she treats me warmly and is always helpful"), the youngster must use a lot of energy to try to resolve the differences between *Parent* information and *Adult* information. When such *Parent* information wins out, we have the roots of prejudices and mistrust of others with a view that others are "Not OK."

The premise of TA is that all individuals need to feel adequate. Within them are three states or forces; if the *Adult* state is given ample opportunity to develop, then the youngster will become a rational and wise person who will be understanding of others and himself. He or she will be able to use the other states of *Parent* and *Child* in a constructive manner.

The *Adult* force tests the rules and information of the *Parent.* The *Adult* also determines when the feelings of the *Child* can be expressed. When there is little conflict between the *Parent, Child,* and *Adult,* the student has a lot of energy left to explore and to creatively use his world. Harris states that creativity is born from curiosity in the *Child* when it provides the "want to" and the *Adult* provides the "how to."

A student who constantly misbehaves does so because of an untenable tension among the three inner forces. If the *Child* holds the greater influence, the student has an attitude of "I'm not adequate but others are." If the *Parent* holds the greater influence, the youngster has an attitude of "I am all right, the rest of the world is to blame for every problem that occurs." If the student is severely caught by both *Parent* and *Child* working against each other with little adult intervention, we have the most severe attitude of "I am inadequate and so is everyone else. Everything is hopeless."

The teacher's job is to approach the misbehaving student in ways that affirm the attitude that the child is capable and that he or she can also trust the rest of the world. This is done by interacting with the child in two ways. The first way affirms the positive and valid dimension of the inner *Parent* and *Child.* The second way is to appeal to the child's *Adult* by approaching the student with the teacher's own *Adult.* These two ways are forms of "stroking."

Stroking is the expression of affection given to one individual by another with the use of physical or verbal behaviors. All of one's life might be viewed as an attempt to acquire such strokes.

Let's stop for a moment. We can sympathize with the reader having such words as "transaction," *Child, Parent, Adult,* and "stroking" reeling off these pages. What does this mean? How, as a teacher, can I use this information? We admit that such terms, although perhaps less obtuse than *Id, Ego,* and *Superego,* are nonetheless still difficult to explain and summarize in a few pages. You have persevered long enough; we will now plunge into applications. Hopefully, the reader will be better able to understand the TA terminology as we give examples and move through our Teacher Behavior Continuum. Remember, though, the basic aim of TA is to promote rational thought (the *Adult*), to affirm the positive aspects of restraint (the *Parent*), and to facilitate creativity (the *Child*).

TA and the Teacher Behavior Continuum

Visually Looking On

First of all, teachers need to find clues that will help them decide what internal state they are operating from and what internal state the particular student with whom they wish to deal possesses. Teachers need this vital information to ascertain the most appropriate approach to use in dealing with a disruptive student. Nonverbal clues can be found in facial expressions, vocal tones, and body gestures.

The following clues signal that the *Parent* is in control: "Furrowed brow, pursed lips, the pointing index finger, head-wagging, the 'horrified look,' foot-tapping, hands on hips, arms folded across chest, wringing hands, tongue-clucking, sighing, patting another on the head . . ."[10] There are also nonverbal actions that are unique to each teacher and to which students can easily see and interpret as, "Oh, Oh, here comes the Parent." Usually students will have great fun mimicking our idiosyncratic mannerisms when we are not in sight.

Following are nonverbal clues that indicate the *Child* is in charge: "Tears; the quivering lip; pouting; temper tantrums; the high-pitched, whining voice; rolling eyes; shrugging shoulders; downcast eyes; teasing; delight; laughter; hand-raising for permission to speak; nail-biting; nose-thumbing; squirming; and giggling."[11]

Finally, how will the *Adult* look nonverbally? The face will not be blank or dull, but the face, eyes, and body moving continually with short periods of non-movement as we or the student listen closely to what is being said.[12]

Just as there are many nonverbal clues that enable us to view the transaction of teacher and student, we find similar clues in key phrases or spoken words.

Parent clues are in the use of words like the following: "I am going to put a stop to this *once and for all;* I can't for the life of me. . . ; Now always remember . . . ; ('always' and 'never' are *almost always* Parent words . . .)." The evaluative words *may* identify the *Parent* such as: ". . . stupid, naughty, ridiculous, disgusting, shocking, asinine, lazy, nonsense, absurd, poor thing, poor dear, no! no! sonny, honey . . . , How dare you? cute, there there, Now what?, Not again!" The automatic or the unthinking use of "should" and "ought" are again near giveaways to the Parent state.[13]

The *Child* state's verbal clues can be seen in the following words: "I wish, I want, I dunno, I gonna, I don't care, I guess, when I grow up bigger, biggest, better, best (and many similar superlatives)."[14]

Finally, language can give us clues that the *Adult* state is in control: "How much, in what way, comparative, true, false, probable, possible, unknown, objective, I think, I see, it is my opinion. Basic vocabulary words such as why, what, where, when, who, and how."[15]

The teacher, after observing both his or her own behavior and the student's, is now ready to make an assessment of stages and plan an appropriate action. This assessment or analysis of stages has to be primarily reflective. As Mr. Tyler did with Sally, the teacher needs to ask, "Is the child's behavior indicative of the *Child,* the *Parent,* or the *Adult?* Is my behavior indicative of the *Child,* the *Parent,* or the *Adult?*" After an assessment of the answers to these questions, the teacher is prepared to change his or her behavior with nondirective statements, questions, and directive statements that are more in keeping with constructive purposes and will elicit the child's rationality.

Let's see how this assessment might work. A middle-school teacher might have just undergone the following experience. The scene is a junior high school classroom of low achievers.

Teacher: (Looks at watch, takes a deep breath, and lets it out slowly with a hissing sound, glances at student, and frowns.)

Student: (Glances at teacher, returns frown, pushes papers aside, and crosses arms across chest.)

Teacher: Do you have work to do? (In a tone of disgust.)

Student: Unfortunately I do.

Teacher: I cannot believe your work. You're so immature. Of all the eighth-grade classes that I have had in my ten years of teaching, your class is the worst!

Student: I can believe it! This class is terrible. I can't get any work done.

Teacher: I've told you over and over again that you have to do your work or you're not going to pass this course.

Student: (Nods) Yeah. Well, this is a waste of time.

Teacher: You and some others need to be taught a lesson in this class. You people never should have been promoted to the seventh grade. But you know the administration. Anything to please the parents.

Student: Yeah, anything.

The teacher might walk away from this interchange knowing that little has been accomplished. Certainly the student is not about to finish his work any quicker than before. By reflecting on the transactions, the teacher might be able to find out why nothing was accomplished, and later, in a similar situation, might be able to take a different tack. In analyzing this transaction and the exchange of "strokes" between these two people, we see the *Parent*. The teacher is scolding and judging while the student is agreeing with an "I could care less" attitude. The conversation is carried on without any attempt to get the facts or to test the reality of the participants' statements. They appear to enjoy their "misery" while exchanging "Aren't things awful for both of us" messages. This occurs because such blaming permits each participant to feel "OK" by blaming the present situation on others.

The teacher using TA to analyze the situation might later be able to approach the student through the use of the *Adult* state.

Teacher: (Looks attentively at student and smiles.)

Student: (Looks up at teacher, looks bewildered, and then frowns and crosses arms.)

Teacher: Is the work too difficult to do?

Student: No, there's too much of it.

Teacher: How much can you get done by the end of class?

Student: Only one page (out of eight).

Teacher: Oh come now, the most you can do is one page?

Student: Yeah.

Teacher: All right, if they're not too hard to do, when will you finish the rest of the pages?

Student: Tomorrow.

Teacher: Well, then, if you have to do these pages as extra homework I guess it's all right. However, if you don't have them done by tomorrow then we'll have to decide how we can make sure they get done.

The reader will notice that the teacher has avoided using the evaluative, belittling *Parent* and the stubborn, emotional *Child*. By responding as the *Adult*, the game of "ain't it awful" cannot be played. The student continued to try to be the *Parent* and place the blame elsewhere. The teacher remains the *Adult*, keeping the problem focused and realistic.

Before we proceed to nondirective statements, we must stress that the teacher act as an *Adult* and appeal to the child's *Adult*. This, however, does not mean that there aren't instances when a teacher and student cannot respond to each other as *Parent* to *Parent* or *Child* to *Child*. These are acceptable transactions (although limited in promoting rationality) in affirming (or stroking) each person as adequate. For example, the student finally finishes all his work and laughs with uncontrollable glee and says, "See, 'teach,' I told you I could do it!" The teacher responds with a spontaneous victory gesture. In this case we have a *Child*-to-*Child* transaction that sends positive vibrations back and forth. Here is another example: The student looks up in the middle of his work and says, "I know that I have to finish this work no matter how hard it is!" The teacher responds with "Yes, that's right. You have to finish that work." What we have is a *Parent*-to-*Parent* transaction that, again, is complementary and productive.

Although the adult state of rationality is prized, other complementary transactions are valuable. What is to be avoided are crossed transactions that create pain and difficulty between people. For example, the student asks, "What time is lunch?" and the teacher replies, "You're always thinking of eating. Why don't you finish your work and stop thinking about your stomach." This is a case of the student's *Adult* being violated by the teacher's *Parent*. Harris gives many examples of various interactions called complementary, crossed, and ulterior. An ulterior transaction is more subtle because it involves a surface message that is different from the real intent. In this chapter we will stick to 1) the use of *Adult* messages to promote rationality and 2) complementary messages that promote positive self-concepts.

Nondirective Statements

Although the use of nondirective statements by teachers is not as central a tool as seen in the previous chapter on *T.E.T.*, it is a viable *Adult* technique for a teacher to use in having a student explain his or her behaviors and thoughts.

Student: I hate those kids. They are driving me crazy!" *(Child)*
Teacher: The students are doing things that you do not like. *(Adult)*

The statement by the student is coming from his or her *Child,* while the teacher's nondirective statement can be thought of as a response coming from the *Adult*. In other words, the teacher is dealing with reality and his or her words reflect for the student the "facts" as the teacher interprets them. Generally, then, nondirective statements communicate from the *Adult* states and help students to verbalize and clarify the true meaning of their actions.

Questions

The use of questions can become more effective if teachers can analyze the messages they send as "OK" or "Not OK" with the help of the *Parent, Adult, Child* construct. To demonstrate, we return to the introductory example: The kindergarten teacher turns to discover a large pool of paint at the feet of a five-year-old standing before the painting easel. The teacher's question-responses could have come from these alternatives.

Questions

1. Who made this terrible mess?
(Parent to Child)

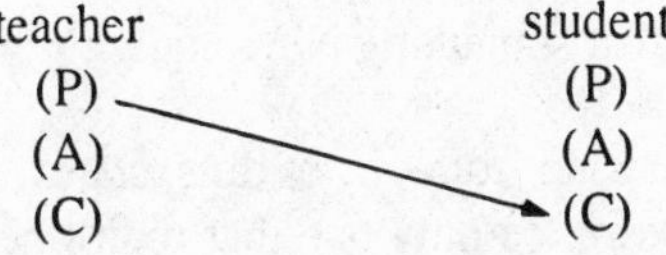

This question indicates that the teacher is making an evaluative *Parent* statement (terrible) and treating the student as a wayward *Child.*

2. What do you need to clean this up?
(Adult to Adult)

teacher — student
(P) — (P)
(A) → (A)
(C) — (C)

This question indicates that the teacher is acting in a constructive "Let's get about it!" manner. The teacher is responding to the student in a way that indicates that the student is capable of solving this temporary problem. It is one *Adult* speaking to another.

3. Why is it that I always have to clean up your mess?

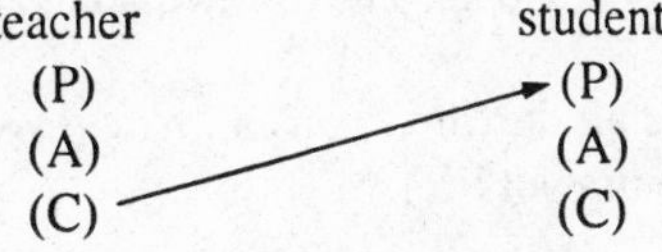

This question indicates that the teacher is acting from his or her own childish impulse to see every act as being personally related to self. The teacher is seeking an answer to the egocentric perception that "everything wrong always happens to me." He or she asks the question as if the student has an evaluative, authoritative *(Parent)* answer. The teacher, if thinking rationally, would know that the student is not capable of supplying such an answer.

Now let's reverse this situation. What are the alternative replies that a teacher can make to a student's question? Often, in a classroom, students bait their teacher with hostile questions. For example, Billy receives his test paper, looks at his grade, and yells out, "Why didn't you tell me beforehand that you were going to grade this test?!" The student's *question* was from a "you (teacher) are not OK" posture by sending a message from the student's *Parent* to the teacher's *Child.* (Alternative questions could have emanated from the student's *Adult,* such as, "What criteria did you use in order to give a grade?" or from the *Child,* "I'm never any good at taking your tests.") The "Why didn't you tell me?" question is judgmental and implies that something is wrong with the teacher's rational abilities.

The teacher can respond from one of three states. If he or she responds as a *Parent* with, "Well, you're the only one that didn't hear the directions. Maybe you had better start listening!" then the teacher has intensified the battle by inferring that it's not his or her fault that the student can't hear. With a statement such as this, the teacher can hardly expect the student to rationally discuss the issue.

If the teacher responds as a *Child* with, "I'm at my wit's end. I do not know what I'm doing!" then the teacher has affirmed the student's *Parent* question. The teacher has said in effect that the student is right and that the teacher is inadequate. Such a response encourages the student to continue with the attitude that he is "OK" and it's the teacher who is always wrong.

On the other hand, if the teacher responds as an *Adult* with, "I thought I did explain that this paper would be graded. Everyone else seemed to know it. Perhaps you weren't listening or were absent on the day I told the class. Let me check." then the teacher has presented the facts as known and has encouraged the student to look for the reasons for the apparent miscommunication. The teacher has turned the student's baiting question into a learning experience that is profitable for both.

Directive Statements

We have seen that there are questions and then there are questions! The same can be said for directive statements. The following are all directive statements.

1. You are so loud all the time, you can't keep your mouth shut! Shut your mouth for once in your life!
2. You make me so mad. All you want to do is drive me crazy. Please keep quiet!
3. I can't teach the class when you talk so loudly. If you have something to say, raise your hand and I'll listen to you.

Here are three direct statements with the same purpose in mind, to keep the student quiet, yet they are very different. The first statement tries to shut the student up by sending an evaluative *Parent* (I'm OK, you're not) message. The second one attempts to quiet the student by pleading with the student for mercy. It is a *Child* (I'm not OK, you are) message to a *Parent*. The third is a reasoned statement that looks at cause and effect and a possible solution. It is an *Adult* (I'm OK, You're OK) message to another *Adult*.

In commanding disruptive children, the teacher might analyze his or her own verbalizations to see what hidden messages they might contain. Are the commands reinforcing the *Child, Parent,* or the *Adult?*

It is misleading to think that a teacher should never use *Parent* or *Child* directive statements. These are healthy and natural when used in appropriate situations. For example, when informing children about "hard and fast" classroom rules, the teacher should be the authoritarian *Parent*.

—Do not go up the left side of the stairs!
—Be in your seat when the bell rings!

Where the *Parent* gets into trouble is when such statements become destructive and emotionally "loaded" between teacher and student ("You must have a vacuum between your ears. I've told you a thousand times, you're supposed to be in your seat when the bell rings!").

Child statements that are natural are those that reflect uncontrolled enthusiasm.

—"Jimmy, you make me feel terrific when you behave that way!"
—"Wow, what a super kid. I must be a super teacher!"

Such instances of *Child* states illustrate strong positive emotions between teacher and student. *Child* states become destructive when emotions of anger, vindictiveness, and apathy emerge and overwhelm rational restraint (i.e., "Go away! I can't stand the sight of you!").

Reinforcement

Reinforcement of desirable behavior through a reward system is not directly mentioned in the TA model. The idea of conditioning a student's behavior is foreign to the Non-Interventionists' position. Instead, the Transactionalists use the notion of "stroking." Every person needs to be accepted as "OK." Children who have a "Not OK" image and who are expending their inner energy in conflict need the greatest affirmation of self-worth. As Harris wrote, a parent (or teacher) working with a child with problems should "whenever in doubt, stroke." The greater the percentage of time that classroom teachers give and receive ''strokes'' through complementary messages, the greater the chances of students having a positive image and thus being able to go about the business of correcting their own behavior.

We have seen in the previous sections of this chapter how a teacher's verbalizations can affirm or denigrate a child's image. The teacher should be conscious of and verbalize complementary messages.

Modeling

Harris suggests that teachers should teach TA to their students. It is his opinion that if students and teachers had a common language for analyzing behavior, it would be easier for them to clarify and correct their own actions. As he wrote:

> Education is heralded as the greatest medication for the ills of the world. Those ills, however, are deeply embedded in behavior. Therefore *education about behavior* through an easy-to-understand system like P-A-C, [*Parent, Child, Adult*] could well be the most important thing we can do to solve the problems which beset us and threaten to destroy us.[16]

The teacher can therefore demonstrate transactional analysis through lectures, role-playing, and discussions. Alvyn Freed has written a book for teachers and parents that tells the TA story to children.[17] Teachers can read the story to their students. Such stories can help students recognize their own inner feelings and categorize their verbalizations.

Physical Intervention and Isolation

The use of physical intervention and isolation is the antithesis of what TA proposes. An approach that is based on revealing inner patterns through analyzing coded messages between people and on having the child ultimately be responsible for his or her own solutions would regard such use of the teacher's power as being detrimental to a child's development.

Games

The study of the games that misbehaving children use is a powerful tool for the teacher. By understanding such games, the teacher can put together all the gathered knowledge of TA into a comprehensive plan.

Many children continue to see themselves as ''Not OK.'' They will act in ways to receive attention from their teacher. They have generally not received warmth and positive attention, and rather than go unrecognized altogether, they resort to "acting out" in order to receive a negative reaction such as "cold pricklies," which further reinforce their "Not OK" scripts and serve as an excuse for not improving behavior. Children manifest this misbehavior in the form of individual "games." Ken Ernst has classified many of these games into such categories as "Uproar," "Chip on the Shoulder," "Stupid," "Clown," "Schlemiel," and "Make Me."[18]

"Uproar": These children engage in "knuckle-cracking, gum-popping, finger-tapping, pen-clicking, hair-combing, dress-straightening, pencil-sharpening, paper-rattling, clock-watching, turning around, wiggling, coming in late, acting stupid, and trying to sidetrack the lecture." When admonished by the teacher, such students say they are being picked on and shortly resume the game with another form of distraction.

"Chip on the Shoulder": The student that plays the game of "Chip on the Shoulder" will at times throw things, be verbally abusive, and generally cause a classroom disturbance that appears to be similar to the child playing "Uproar." The student in "Uproar" is constantly looking for ways to "bug" the teacher's *Parent,* while the student playing "Chip on the Shoulder" only causes a disturbance when he or she is called upon or some demand is made to perform. This behavior is simply a cover for "I'm Not OK" feelings, whereby the student fears being considered "dumb," and rather than running that risk, the student decides to be a "devil" by striking out.

"Stupid": The game of "Stupid" is played by children who are performing a host of acts that make them appear "dumb." They collect an audience and get others to make fun of them, while they show their delight with nervous smiles. These students might "accidentally" do the wrong assignment, injure themselves while using school equipment inappropriately, or participate in a host of similar acts that eventually get them called "Stupid" by peers.

"Clown": The "Clown" is generally well liked by teacher and students, and can be found mimicking the actions of teachers or others to the delight of his or her peers. Usually this is done when the teacher's back is turned.

"Schlemiel": This student repeatedly bumps into others, knocks things over, and disrupts others' belongings and activities. They quickly volunteer to help "clean up the mess," and succeed in making things worse. Generally they respond to criticism with, "Well, it was only an accident," or "I was only trying to help."

"Make Me": Students playing "Make Me"simply refuse to do assignments or to perform the requirements necessary. When questioned by the teacher

they will lay down the challenge of "Make Me." The "Make Me" student puts the teacher in the position of a persecutor or a rescuer.

Although there are various treatments for each diagnosis, generally the teacher can use the following strategies:

- First, *analyze the game that the student is playing*. What is the student looking for? (What kinds of strokes? From whom?) What state is the student operating from and to which of the teacher's states is the student directing messages? *(Child? Parent? Adult?)*
- Second, *don't play the game!* Come back as the *Adult*. Allow the child to see the game for what it is.
- Third, give "strokes" or attention *that affirms the child's worth*.
- Fourth, *allow the child to find his or her own solution*.

Taking the example of the "Stupid" game, let's apply the strategies.

Hector is bumbling, incoherent, and "dumb," or at least this is how he appears. Whenever called upon, he vacantly stares, says something unintelligible or nonsensical, and then sheepishly grins to himself as the other students roll their eyes and giggle. The teacher should:

1. Identify that Hector is acting stupid as part of his "I'm not OK" self-perception. The frustration and impatience that he causes the teacher is also evidence of a "Not OK" perception of the teacher. Hector is acting as the helpless, bad *Child* and is appealing to the domineering bad *Parent* to always correct and control.
2. Act as the *Adult* and not as the rescuing or scolding *Parent*. The teacher should meet with Hector in private and tell him that the "game is up." The teacher will not persecute or rescue Hector when he raises his hand. He will be called on, and if no intelligible answer is forthcoming, nothing will be said or done to him.
3. Meet with Hector after class, if he is embarrassed to answer correctly in front of the class. Then he can tell the teacher the answers that he "would" have given in the classroom. The teacher should give "strokes" by touching, smiling, or verbalizing.
4. Allow Hector to decide when to venture forth with correct answers in class.

Summary

We can now refer to the Teacher Behavior Continuum (Figure 4–1) and summarize Transactional Analysis. Covertly, the teacher needs to use the *Parent*,

Ct —————————————————————————————— cT

Visually Looking On	Nondirective Statements	Questions	Directive Statements	Modeling	Reinforcement	Physical Intervention and Isolation
(a) Diagnosis of teacher and student internal states	(1c)—Use as an *Adult* response to clarify student's explanation *Adult* to *Adult*.	(1a)—Ask student Adult questions *Adult* to *Adult*.	(1b)—Reply to student's actions with *Adult* statements *Adults* to Adult.	(3)—Teach and demonstrate the principle of T.A. to the student.	(2)—Affirm the student as "OK" with complementary transactions *Child* to *Child*, *Parent to Parent*, *Adult* to *Adult*.	
—The teacher is acting as *Child*, *Parent*, *Adult?*				—Lecture role playing, story telling.	Avoid cross transactions *Parent* to *Child*, *Child* to *Parent*, etc.	
—The student is acting as *Child*, *Parent*, *Adult?*						

Communication Model (TA)

Eric Berne, Thomas A. Harris, and others

(numbers)—overt behaviors, (letters) —covert behaviors

FIGURE 4–1. *Teacher Behavior Continuum (TBC)*

Child, Adult construct to analyze the teacher and student transaction (letter *a*). When dealing with disruptive behavior, the teacher then overtly sends messages from his or her *Adult* to the student's *Adult* by the use of Questions, Directive Statements, or Nondirective Statements (1a, 1b, 1c). The teacher must continue to "stroke" the student with complementary transactions that affirm the "I'm OK, You're OK" perception (2). The teacher helps the student to analyze his or her behavior by teaching TA (3). Finally, the teacher allows the student to make his or her own solutions.

Notes

1. Eric Berne, *Games People Play: The Psychology of Human Relations* (New York: Grove Press, 1964).
2. Thomas A. Harris, *I'm OK—You're OK: A Practical Guide to Transactional Analysis* (New York: Harper & Row, Publishers, 1969).
3. Muriel James and Dorothy Jongeward, *Born to Win: Transactional Analysis with Gestalt Experiments,* (Boston: Addison-Wesley, 1971).
4. Alvyn M. Freed, *TA for Tots, (and other Prinzes)* (Sacramento: Jalmar Press, 1973).
5. Alvyn M. Freed, *TA for Kids, (and Grown-Ups, Too),* Transactional Analysis for Everyone Series, (Sacramento: Jalmar Press, 1971).
6. Ken Ernst, *Games Students Play, and What to do About Them*. (Mellbrae, California: Celestial Arts, 1973).
7. William Penfield, "Memory Mechanisms," *A.M.A. Archives of Neurology and Psychiatry,* ed. L. S. Kubie et al., 67 (1952): 178–98.
8. Harris, *I'm OK—You're OK,* pp. 29–30.
9. Harris, *I'm OK—You're OK,* pp. 43-50.
10. Harris, *I'm OK—You're OK,* pp. 65–66.
11. Harris, *I'm OK—You're OK,* p. 67.
12. Harris, *I'm OK—You're OK,* p. 67.
13. Harris, *I'm OK—You're OK,* p. 66.
14. Harris, *I'm OK—You're OK,* p. 67.
15. Harris, *I'm OK—You're OK,* p. 67–68.
16. Harris, *I'm OK—You're OK,* p. 161.
17. Alvyn M. Freed, *TA Stories for Kids,* (Mellbrae, California: Celestial Arts, 1977).
18. Ernst, *Games Students Play, and What to Do About Them,* pp. 13–36.

References

Berne, Eric. *Games People Play: The Psychology of Human Relations*. New York: Grove Press, 1964.

Ernst, Ken. *Games Students Play, and What to Do About Them*. Mellbrae, California: Celestial Arts, 1973.

Freed, Alvyn M. *TA for Kids (and Grown-Ups, Too)* Sacramento: Jalmar Press, 1971.

Freed, Alvyn M. *TA for Tots (and Other Prinzes)*. Sacramento: Jalmar Press, 1973.
Harris, Thomas A. *I'm OK—You're OK: A Practical Guide to Transactional Analysis*. New York: Harper & Row, Publishers, 1969.
James, Muriel, and Jongeward, Dorothy. *Born to Win: Transactional Analysis with Gestalt Experiments*. Boston: Addison-Wesley, 1971.

For information on the International Transactional Analysis Association (ITAA), which holds study groups, seminars, and institutes and publishes the quarterly *Transactional Analysis Journal,* write to The International Transactional Analysis Association (ITAA), 1772 Vellejo Street, San Francisco, California 94123.

Instructional Media

Films

Title: Games We Play in High School
Author: Eric Berne
Time: 29 minutes Color
Rental Fee: $45 per week Purchase Price: $395
Company: Media Five
3211 Cahuenga Boulevard, West
Los Angeles, California 90068
Synopsis: Concepts of Transactional Analysis are introduced as a means of improving secondary discipline, human relations, and learning. Describes techniques and games students and teachers play in the classroom.

Title: The OK Classroom
Author: Thomas Harris
Time: 29 minutes Color
Rental Fee: $45 per week Purchase Price: $395
Company: Media Five
3211 Cahuenga Boulevard, West
Los Angeles, California 90068
Synopsis: Discusses Transactional Analysis concepts, explains special meanings of the terms: Parent, Adult, Child, Transaction, Strokes, Life Positions, and Games. Documentary examples of theory in action.

Title: Transactional Analysis
Time: 30 minutes Color
Rental Fee: $30 Purchase Price: $300

Company: University of California, Extension Media Center
2223 Fulton Street
Berkeley, California 94720

Synopsis: Introduces the use of TA in management, illustrates the reasons for people's actions in organizations, and shows how to promote productive employee behavior. Uses interviews, dramatic re-enactments, and animation to explain and demonstrate such principles of TA as game playing, the three types of transaction-stroking, trading stamps, and life scripts.

Title: Transactional Analysis

Author: Eric Berne

Time: 70 minutes Color

Company: Human Development Institute
20 Executive Park West, NE
Atlanta, Georgia 30329

Synopsis: Outlines Dr. Berne's thoughts on the importance of having a theoretical basis, the intake process, the significance of the fee, and the necessity of a therapeutic *Contract*. Describes his goal in therapy as being "Game Free Behavior." Shows the use of TA with a group of 6 people.

Title: Concepts in Transactional Analysis: Therapy in a Group Setting with Morris & Natalie Haimowitz: Charlotte

Time: 25 minutes Color

Rental Fee: $30 per day Purchase Price: $300

Company: American Personnel and Guidance Association
1107 New Hampshire Avenue
Washington, D.C. 20009

Synopsis: Presents the Transactional Analysis (TA) constructs of rubber bands (attaching to a current situation feelings from the past) and rackets (a person's existential position which finds its expression in "saving stamps" or collecting enduring nongenuine feelings, which can be traded for a guilt-free "blow up"). Also covers the four TA life positions.

5

The Valuing Model: Raths and Simon's Values Clarification

Miss Jansen stops her sixth-grade social studies lesson and tells the students to put their books away and take out paper and pencils. It is time to do an exercise on personal values. Miss Jansen spends twenty minutes, twice a week, on these types of lessons. Today's lesson will be role playing around a common dilemma that students might face. She walks to the front of her desk, leans against it, and begins:

"Class, I'm going to tell you a story, and after the story you are to write down what you would have done if you were Peter."

> This story is about Peter and his best friend Bob. Both boys have decided that they need a new baseball for the upcoming ball game. Together they have two dollars. They go into the local discount store that is advertising a sale on baseballs. The boys immediately head for the sports department. At the baseball table, they see a sign saying that some baseballs are for sale for only one dollar and fifty cents. Looking at the balls, Bob discovers that all the balls on sale are gone. The only ones left are the higher-priced ones costing three dollars. Peter says to Bob, "Heck, let's go; we don't have enough money." Bob says, "Wait, there's an empty box left over that is marked at the sale price. Let's take one of the three-dollar balls out of its box and put it into the lower-price box. No one will ever know." Peter is not sure, but before he can act, Bob has made the exchange and is walking to the check-out counter. Bob yells to Peter to hurry up with the money. Peter runs to the counter, Bob hands

> him the box, and the cashier asks for a dollar and fifty cents. Peter pays, gets his change, and walks out the door with his purchase. At that moment, a large man grabs Peter by the arm, turns him around, and says, "Son, let me see that box." Peter glances up at the man and sees a badge on his coat that reads *Store Detective*. Peter looks quickly for Bob, but his friend has disappeared. . . .

Miss Jansen looks up and tells her students to think very carefully about what they would tell the detective if they were Peter. After waiting two full minutes, she asks them to write down their answer on a piece of paper. She then asks if two students would like to act out what they would have done. Ernie, who prides himself in being glib and cocky, volunteers to play Peter. Roberta, a rather quiet child, volunteers to be the detective. They come to the front of the room and begin their play. Roberta grabs Ernie's arm and says, "Hey, boy, why did you steal that baseball?" Ernie responds, "I did not steal anything. The ball was in this box and I paid the price that is printed on it." Roberta says angrily, "You are a liar. You changed the box!" Ernie retorts, "I did not! I paid the price on the box. Prove that I didn't."

Miss Jansen stops the scene and asks Roberta, "You think that Peter was wrong to pay for that ball?" She turns to Ernie and asks, "What is another way that Peter might have acted?" Ernie replies, "He could just put the blame on Bob; after all, Bob made him do it." Miss Jansen turns to the class and asks, "How much is Bob to blame and how much is Peter to blame?" She then says to Roberta and Ernie, "OK, you two sit down. Let's have two more students come up and show us a different way that this scene could be portrayed."

The reader might recognize the above classroom lesson as a values-clarification exercise. Miss Jansen is attempting to provide students with activities that allow them to take an individual look at their own ways of behaving. Such activities help them explore their attitudes, aspirations, purposes, interests, and behaviors. Additionally, they learn to understand what some of the alternative values are that other people possess. Such a process enables students to consciously choose a future course of action from a selection of alternatives.

A value is defined by Raths, Harmin, and Simon as the outcome of a three-part process whereby the student is engaged in

Choosing:

1. freely
2. from alternatives
3. after thoughtful consideration of the consequences of each alternative

Prizing:

4. cherishing, being happy with the choice
5. willing to affirm the choice publicly

Acting:

6. doing something with the choice
7. repeatedly, in some pattern of life[1]

What does all this have to do with disruptive behavior in the classroom? Many teachers unwittingly give us the answer. It is common to hear a frustrated teacher lament the unscrupulous behavior of a student with such statements as "Kids today have no values. They have no sense of right or wrong." Louis Raths, Sidney Simon, and Merrill Harmin would agree with such thinking. They view the causes of much misbehavior as the result of a student not knowing or not thinking about his or her values and therefore not being able to live in accord with a guide of personal judgments.

Louis E. Raths, who developed the theoretical basis for today's popular techniques in values clarification, delineated three types of misbehavior. There is misbehavior that results from 1) a student's mental or physical capabilities, 2) a student's emotional experiences, and 3) a student's lack of values. For example, a student who bullies others or outsmarts others is taking advantage of his or her physical or mental assets. The student who cringes with fear every time he or she is corrected might be reliving the emotional trauma of being severely scared or beaten as a child. On the other hand, there are students who cheat, lie, or steal who do so because they do not possess any values criteria that would suggest that what they are doing is wrong. As Raths, Harmin, and Simon put it:

> We have found that several kinds of problems children often exhibit in school and at home are profitably seen as being caused by values, or, more precisely, by a lack of values. To put this another way, we have found that, when children with certain behavior problems are given value experiences of a particular kind, those problems often ease in intensity and/or frequency. In short, there is strong support for the notion that values must be added to the possible explanations of children's behavior problems.[2]

The students who can be most helped through values-clarification techniques are those who are very *apathetic, flighty, uncertain,* or *inconsistent,* or who are *drifters, overconformers, overdissenters,* or *role players.*"[3]

Unlike the other behavior management models in this book, the values-clarification model does not provide immediate steps for the teacher to take when dealing with a student engaged in a disruptive act. Rather, values clarification is a technique to be used over a long period of time. Those students who misbehave due to a "values vacuum" need the frequent and ongoing opportunities to be engaged in values activities. One does not acquire or change values from one minute to the next. It is only after much time and much exploration that change comes about. For these reasons, the reader should keep in mind that the values-clarification model is proposed to be helpful over the "long run," and the reader will need to consider other models in this book for remedying immediate disruptive situations.

Teacher as Clarifier and Non-Interventionist

The role of the teacher is to guide students through an exploration of their own values. This is done through informal teacher and student verbal exchanges as well as formal group exercises. The teacher must remain nonjudgmental and not press a student to accept the teacher's own values. The values-clarification authors believe that values are, by their very nature, personal. If a student is to act according to a private code of behavior, then the student needs to internalize that code by his or her own free will. Forcing one to accept a teacher's values is a losing proposition, as the student will rebel, neglect, and not be committed to such an external imposition. The Non-Interventionist's faith in the student's ability to make wise and productive choices permeates all the writings of the values clarificationists. As Raths, Harmin, and Simon wrote:

> . . . we have presented a view of the concept of value that is based on a particular notion of human potential, one which emphasizes man's capacity for intelligent, self-directed behavior.[4]

The teacher's role as a Non-Interventionist who believes in the student's ability to choose wisely is an active one. The teacher must set up situations that make a student look at his or her own present values, consider alternatives, and make future choices. It is those procedures for setting up such situations that we will explain along the Teacher Behavior Continuum. It is mainly in the categories of *Visually Looking On, Questioning,* and *Modeling* that the teacher receives the most help.

Values Clarification and the Teacher Behavior Continuum

Let's introduce a typical student misbehavior that might be the result of a lack of values.

> Simmie is an eleven-year-old girl who comes from a broken home. She lives with her Dad. Her other brothers and sisters live with their mother in another state. Simmie has to fend for herself, as her Dad works nights and sleeps during the day. She usually sees her father only a few minutes each day. Her behavior in school is erratic. Some days she works attentively and is a "model" student; on other days she is "off in her own world"—spacy, dreamy, and inattentive. She is mostly calm and aloof with other students, but once in a while she completely "flies off the handle," screaming obscenities and gouging others with teeth and fingernails.

As we explain the values-clarification procedures along the Teacher Behavior Continuum, we will include specific applications to Simmie that will help to clarify her values and eventually improve her behavior. Let's begin.

Visually Looking On

The teacher needs to be aware of spontaneous moments when students indicate their existing values. In such one-to-one contacts, the teacher needs to listen carefully to what the student is saying before moving into *questions*. Indicators[5] of a student's values are expressions of:

1. Attitudes—"I think that . . . ," "I don't feel that . . ."
2. Aspirations—"Some day, I want to be . . . ," "When I get older . . ."
3. Purposes—"When I finish this, I'm going to buy a . . . ," "I want to make a . . ."
4. Interest—"It feels great when I'm . . . ," "I love doing . . ."
5. Activities—"After school, I do . . ." "On vacations, I spend my time . . ."

When the teacher *visually looks on* and hears a student making such statements, he or she can be prepared to probe the student's underlying values. The teacher needs to keep in mind the seven-step criteria of a true value: 1) choosing freely, 2) choosing from alternatives, 3) choosing after thoughtful consideration of the consequences of each alternative, 4) prizing and cherishing, being happy with the choice, 5) willing to affirm the choice publicly, 6) acting and doing something with the choice, 7) acting repeatedly in some pattern of life.

> Simmie often comes to school and strikes up a conversation with Lucerne. Their teacher, Mr. Jordan, has often overheard her talking about how "out of sight" various Hollywood male movie stars are and that some day she "would love to live in California and learn to surfboard." The teacher takes such statements as *value indicators* of interest (male movie stars), aspirations (live in California), and activities (learn surfing).

Nondirective Statements

Nondirective statements are not delineated by the values clarificationists. Yet, in working with students, it is important to listen to their opinions and ideas and not to interject with one's own. When a student talks, the teacher should really listen (similar to Gordon's "active listening"), and to do so, he or she can use nondirective statements to paraphrase and encourage a student to continue.

> One morning Simmie passes the teacher at the door and says, "Wow, am I glad to be here at school." Mr. Jordan looks directly at her and says, "You are glad to be at school." Simmie replies, "You betcha, it's such a hassle getting out of the house without waking Dad and getting yelled at. I wish we had a bigger house." The teacher listens and replies, "You want to live in a larger house so you won't need to bother your dad." Simmie looks up and says, "No, not exactly. It's not Dad; it's just that the house is so crummy and messy. I don't want to talk about it." With that she breaks the conversation and sits down. Mr. Jordan returns to preparing himself for class.

It is important to note that the teacher did not press Simmie beyond her wishes to talk. When the student refuses to initiate conversation or asks to go no further, the discussion is at least temporarily halted. On many occasions a teacher can help a student think of his or her values by a simple nondirective statement (or a question) and leave it at that.

The teacher must take care not to interject his or her own thoughts and opinions. Nothing would have turned Simmie away further from the values-clarification process than after saying, "I wish we had a bigger house," Mr. Jordan had said, "Oh, I know. We all like bigger things, but we are too materialistic in this society. We should be happy with what we have." Such an interjected "pearl" might make the teacher feel like the "fountain of wisdom," but it would have left Simmie with the feeling that the teacher "has all the answers and what I think is unimportant."

Questions

Perhaps the most important tool that the values-clarifying teacher has is an abundance of questions to ask. If the student, in either an individual or group situation, indicates a willingness to continue the conversation, the teacher can formulate questions around the seven-step criteria of a value.[6]

1. *Choosing freely*
   —Where do you suppose you first got that idea?
   —How long have you felt that way?
   —Is there any rebellion in your choice?
   —How many years will you give to it? What will you do if you're not good enough?
2. *Choosing from alternatives*
   —What else did you consider before you picked this?
   —How long did you look around before you decided?
   —Did you consider another possible alternative?
3. *Choosing thoughtfully and reflectively*
   —What would be the consequences of each alternative available?
   —Have you thought about this very much?
   —Just what is good about this choice?
4. *Prizing and cherishing*
   —Are you glad you feel that way?
   —How long have you wanted it?
   —What good is it?

5. *Affirming*
   —Would you tell the class the way you feel some time?
   —Would you be willing to sign a petition supporting that idea?
   —Do people know you feel that way?
6. *Acting upon choices*
   —What are your first steps, second steps, and so on?
   —Have you made any plans to do more than you already have done?
   —Where will this lead you? How far are you willing to go?
7. *Repeating*
   —What are your plans for doing more?
   —Has it been worth the time and effort?
   —How long do you think you will continue?

Mr. Jordan has given class instructions to complete the sentence, "If I had three wishes to be granted, I would ask for. . . ." After waiting five minutes, he asks if anyone would like to share their answer. Simmie responds immediately.

Simmie: 1) Be a movie star, 2) marry a handsome actor, and 3) live in Hollywood."

Mr. Jordan: "Where do you suppose you got those ideas?" (Choosing freely.)

Simmie: "From watching movies and reading magazines."

Mr. Jordan: "Are there other things that you have thought about?" (Choosing from alternatives.)

Simmie: "Yeah, once I was going to be a high-fashion model, but I'm not tall enough."

Mr. Jordan: "What is so good about being a movie star, marrying someone handsome, and living in Hollywood?" (Prizing and cherishing.)

Simmie: "I'd be famous and rich."

Mr. Jordan: "Could you be famous and rich doing something else?" (Choosing thoughtfully and reflectively.)

Simmie: "Yeah, I guess so. I don't know doing what."

Mr. Jordan: (to the class) "Does anyone have any other ways that someone could become famous and rich?" (Choosing from alternatives.)

From this dialogue, the reader should get a sense of how Mr. Jordan is using questions to probe and explore the validity of Simmie's professed value. The teacher does not use the seven categories of questions in any rigid or all-inclusive manner. Rather, questions are to be used to probe a particular aspect of values at a time. There will be occasions when one will use a single kind of question as well as occasions when one will use all seven. The teacher will, with a student, eventually move into the final consideration of a true value: Is the student willing to act upon it (acting upon choices and repeating)? For example, is Simmie willing to work at being an actress, to take drama lessons, write scripts, practice diction, and so forth? If not, then she does not possess a true value and must look at the other choices open to her.

Directive Statements

When a teacher is engaged in values clarification, he or she should avoid the use of directive statements. If a student asks a teacher for his or her opinion, then the teacher should respond freely. However, this is quite different from telling the student what he or she should believe. At times an adult will, in actuality, be making a directive statement under the guise of questioning. For example, questions such as, "Don't you think that people should never do that?" or "You can't possibly believe that is proper behavior, can you?" are value-laden. They are thinly veiled attempts to have the student comply with the teacher's views. All such value influences (questions or directive statements) are not designed to facilitate a student's own thinking.

Modeling

The use of the entire class for the discussion of individual values is an invaluable tool for value formation. Remember that part of the criteria for value clarification is choosing from alternatives, being knowledgeable about consequences, and choosing freely. If a student is to truly form his or her own standards of conduct, the student must be aware of what the choices are in formulating those standards. By doing values-clarification exercises in a group, the student can listen to differing points of view and therefore have a greater source of information upon which to base the most rational decision. For these reasons, formal exercises for the teacher to use for the entire class are suggested. The teacher provides instructions, allows the individual student to reflect or write down his or her thoughts, and then asks if anyone would like to share their thinking. Students are not coerced to speak out. A quiet student who does not participate is still hearing various ideas and eventually might choose one *(modeling)* as his or her own.

We have already seen Mr. Jordan use such an approach by asking the class to complete the sentence, "If I had three wishes. . . ." A few days later he asks the class to rank in order[7] the following statements:

1. I would rather live
   _______ in the country

_______ in the suburbs

_______ in the middle of a large city

2. Which would you *most* not want to be?

_______ poor

_______ sickly

_______ ugly

After the students have made their rankings, he asks if anyone would discuss ranking for statement number two. Many hands are raised and a lively debate ensues among those who would least want to be poor, sickly or ugly. This time Simmie does not participate. Instead, she intently listens to the most attractive girl in the class explain why she would least want to be sickly. The girl explains, "Your health is most important. If you feel good, then you can always do something later on about being poor or ugly, but if you're sick, it keeps you from doing anything. Besides, look at all the poor or ugly people who became great. Eleanor Roosevelt and Winston Churchill weren't any great shakes to look at. Look at how poor so many famous actors and actresses were when they began. People such as Elizabeth Taylor, Paul Newman, and Woody Allen made it because they were healthy and could work hard. You gotta be concerned about your health first." Simmie shakes her head in disapproval throughout the girl's explanation, yet she listens to every word. . . .

There are literally hundreds of different values-clarification exercises that have been written for teachers to use. They can be found in the reference books at the end of this chapter. Some of them are listed here as examples.

- I Urge Telegrams:[8] The student writes an imaginative telegram to someone whom he or she wants to influence.
- What's in Your Wallet?[9] The student takes out three items that show different things that he or she values. The student can voluntarily explain or write down his or her choices.
- I Am the Jury:[10] The student listens to a case involving a brilliant honor student who is caught selling one five-dollar bag of marijuana. The listener has to decide on the penalty and give reasons for the choice.
- Your Personal Coat of Arms:[11] The student draws and writes key words for his or her own coat of arms that include the most significant event in life, the greatest achievement, how he or she would want to be remembered, and so forth.

Students respond to various activities in many ways. There are exercises that involve ranking, sorting, completion of sentences, composition writing, role playing, formal discussions, public interviews, and checklists. The ultimate purpose is the same: to allow students to become actively involved in determining their past, present, and future values.

Reinforcement, Physical Intervention, and Isolation

It should be obvious that teacher behaviors that shape and control students are antithetical to values clarification and are not to be used.

What Happened to Simmie?

The reader might feel that he or she has been left hanging on the outcome of values clarification for Simmie. Did Simmie become more in control and less erratic in her school behavior? Did she decide to become an actress and to work hard for it? Or, did she change her values and become content with improving her present homelife? Well, as the television "soap opera" announcer tells the waiting audience, "Tune in tomorrow for these answers and more." We, as teachers, will not find immediate and dramatic changes in our students. Values take a long time to change, and we should not look for results until after continuing such techniques over a lengthy period.

This might seem awfully long to wait, but the values clarificationists point out that if teachers expect academic skills to be attained slowly, then so should they expect social skills to be learned slowly. A student undergoes literally hundreds of reading activities before being expected to read. A student similarly needs numerous values activities before being able to think and behave in ways that are different. Returning to Simmie, we will have to wait before seeing what changes have resulted.

Summary

Briefly we can summarize teacher behaviors related to values clarification on the Teacher Behavior Continuum in Figure 5–1.

The teacher should a) avoid *directive statements* that judge, influence, and impose teacher values and b) avoid all teacher control in the forms of *reinforcement, physical intervention,* and *isolation*. The teacher overtly should 1) look and listen for *(visually looking on)* value indicators from the student. The teacher should 2) listen carefully, paraphrasing or repeating the student's thoughts *(nondirective statements)*. After listening, if the student is receptive, the teacher can 3) ask *questions* that probe the seven elements of a true value. The exposure and modeling of alternative values are brought about by the teacher's using 4) formal group exercises.

Ct ———————————————————————————————— cT

Visually Looking On	Nondirective Statements	Questions	Directive Statements	Modeling	Reinforcement	Physical Intervention and Isolation
1) Look for value indicators—attitudes, aspirations, purposes, interest, activities	2) Active Listening, paraphase student's thoughts	3) Probe for true value —choose freely? —choose from alternatives? —choose thoughtfully & reflectively? —prizing & cherishing? —affirming? —acting? —repeating?	A) Avoid judging, influencing or imposing teacher values.	4) Group exercises; i.e., —ranking —sorting —role playing —discussing dilemas	B) Avoid	

Valuing Model
Authors—Louis E. Raths, Sidney Simon, Robert Hawley, and others

[letters] —covert behaviors (numbers)—overt behaviors

FIGURE 5–1. *Teacher Behavior Continuum (TBC)*

Notes

1. Louis E. Raths, Merrill Harmin, and Sidney B. Simon, *Values and Teaching* (Columbus: Charles E. Merrill Publishing, 1966), p. 30.
2. Raths, Harmin, and Simon, *Values and Teaching*, p. 4.
3. Raths, Harmin, and Simon, *Values and Teaching*, p. 7
4. Raths, Harmin, and Simon, *Values and Teaching*, p. 46.
5. Raths, Harmin, and Simon, *Values and Teaching*, pp. 65–79.
6. Raths, Harmin, and Simon, *Values and Teaching*, p. 63.
7. Sidney B. Simon, Leland W. Howe, and Howard Kirschenbaum, *Values Clarification: A Handbook of Practical Strategies for Teachers and Students* (New York: Hart Publishing, 1972), pp. 58–75.
8. Simon, Howe, and Kirschenbaum, *Values Clarification: A Handbook of Practical Strategies for Teachers and Students*, p. 246.
9. Simon, Howe, and Kirschenbaum, *Values Clarification*, p. 329.
10. Robert C. Hawley, *Value Exploration Through Role Playing* (New York: Hart Publishing, 1975), p. 93.
11. Sidney B. Simon, Robert C. Hawley, and David D. Britton, *Composition for Personal Growth: Values Clarification Through Writing* (Hart Publishing, 1973), p. 58.

References

Hawley, Robert C. *Value Exploration Through Role Playing*. New York: Hart Publishing, 1975.

Raths, Louis E., Harmin, Merrill, and Simon, Sidney B. *Values and Teaching*, p. 30. Columbus: Charles E. Merrill Publishing, 1966.

Simon, Sidney B., Hawley, Robert C., and Britton, David D. *Composition for Personal Growth: Values Clarification Through Writing*. New York: Hart Publishing, 1973.

Simon, Sidney B., Howe, Leland W., and Kirschenbaum, Howard. *Values Clarification: A Handbook of Practical Strategies for Teachers and Students*, pp. 58–75. New York: Hart Publishing, 1972.

For additional materials and workshops offered, write to the Adirondack Mountain Humanistic Education Center, Upper Jay, New York 12987.

Instructional Media

Films

Title: Using Values Clarification

Author: Sidney Simon

Time: 29 minutes Color

Rental Fee: $45 per week Purchase Price:

Company: Media Five
3211 Cahuenga Boulevard, West
Los Angeles, California 90068

Synopsis: Discussion and demonstration of the development and meaning as well as strategies of values clarification. Shows how teachers are making valuing strategies a regular part of the school day.

Title: Values Clarification in the Classroom

Author: Sidney Simon

Time: 30 minutes Color

Rental Fee: $100 (Leader's manual with 25 teacher packets for in-service workshops)

Company: Media Five
3211 Cahuenga Boulevard, West
Los Angeles, California 90068

Synopsis: Provides background for utilizing the values clarification approach in the classroom.

Title: Beginning Values Clarification

Author: Sidney Simon

Time: 30 minutes Color

Rental Fee: $100 (Leader's manual with 25 teacher packets for in-service workshop materials)

Company: Media Five
3211 Cahuenga Boulevard, West
Los Angeles, California 90068

Synopsis: Provides background for the values clarification approach in the classroom.

Title: The New Focus on Values and Morality

Time: 29 minutes Color

Rental Fee: $45 per week Purchase Price: $395

Company: Media Five
3211 Cahuenga Boulevard, West
Los Angeles, California 90068

Synopsis: Introduces ideas, people, and practices in the morals/values area. Visits to elementary and secondary classes where strategies are in use.

Title:	Values, Identity, Responsibility		
Time:	29 minutes	Color	
Rental Fee:	$45 per week	Purchase Price:	$395
Company:	Media Five 3211 Cahuenga Boulevard, West Los Angeles, California 90068		
Synopsis:	Underlines the importance of communication in a child's affective development. Identity and responsibility are seen as the keys to effectively deal with student concerns and values issues.		

Title:	Teaching Morals and Values		
Author:	Madeline Hunter		
Time:	29 minutes	Color	
Rental Fee:	$45 per week	Purchase Price:	$395
Company:	Media Five 3211 Cahuenga Boulevard, West Los Angeles, California 90068		
Synopsis:	Illustrates a staff seminar on the teacher's role in the area of values and morality.		

Title:	Beginning Values Clarification		
Author:	Louis Raths		
Time:	29 minutes	Color	
Rental Fee:	$45 per week	Purchase Price:	$395
Company:	Media Five 3211 Cahuenga Boulevard, West Los Angeles, California 90068		
Synopsis:	A primer on values clarification covering three levels of education: facts, concepts, and values. Raths provides an explanation of the genesis of values clarification; Sidney Simon, Merrill Harmin, and Howard Kirschenbaum discuss and demonstrate classroom techniques.		

Title:	Values Clarification in the Classroom		
Time:	29 minutes	Color	
Rental Fee:	$45 per week	Purchase Price:	$395
Company:	Media Five 3211 Cahuenga Boulevard, West Los Angeles, California 90068		

Synopsis: Demonstrates values clarification teaching styles by Merrill Harmin. Description of theory-to-practice aspects of values clarification by Raths with others explaining how to raise issues, stimulate thinking, and be nonjudgmental.

Title: Finding Values Through Simulation Games

Time: 29 minutes Color

Synopsis: Depicts a twelfth-grade class playing the simulation game, "Star Power." Garry Shirts, the game creator, points out the values discoveries and discusses the use of simulation games for values development from the fourth grade on.

6

The Social Discipline Model of Rudolf Dreikurs

It is the first day of winter semester and Mr. Garcia is casually observing his new class of students entering the room for third-period chemistry class. He finds nothing particularly distinctive about this new group until Ronald appears. This student is dressed in faded blue jeans that are covered with sign-patches expounding such messages as "luv," "keep on trucking," and "far out." Even more noticeable are the two patches running across the seat of the pants with the words "screw you" on one hip pocket, and "Mother f____ker" on the other. The rest of Ronald's attire includes a T-shirt and a western-style hat pulled down over his eyes. In order for him to see while walking, he has to lead with his chin and look out over his nose.

Mr. Garcia gradually loses sight of Ronald as he visually skims the remaining members of the classroom, but suddenly he hears a girl's scream, another student's laugh, and the classroom quiet. Everyone's attention focuses on Ronald, who is slouched down in his seat with his hat pulled over his face. The class glances from the teacher to Ronald and back to the teacher. Seeing that neither the teacher nor Ronald is going to make any further move, the class returns to their chatting. A few minutes later Mr. Garcia begins reading through the class roster, calling each student's name and receiving in return a proper acknowledgment such as "I'm here." When he calls out "Ronald Foster" the response is, "OK, Keep cool, Teacher-o!" which breaks up the class with laughter. Mr. Garcia ignores

"Mr. Baker has a little problem with defensiveness."

Clem Scalzitti, from *Phi Delta Kappan*

this response, finishes calling the roll, and finally introduces himself and the content of the course. He turns his back to the class and begins to write the name of the textbook across the chalkboard. Before he can finish, the same girlish scream is heard, but this time with such intensity that it signals something more serious. The girl seated in front of Ronald jumps to her feet, crosses her arms across her chest, and runs frantically to the classroom door. As she passes before Mr. Garcia and the front of the class, everyone can see that her bra is open in the back. A few nervous giggles come from the class, and now all eyes focus on Ronald and then, unfortunately, *back to Mr. Garcia.*

Mr. Garcia is quite obviously "on the spot." It is the beginning of the semester, he faces a troublesome male student, a distraught female student, and a class of thirty-one teenagers waiting to see what will transpire. What specific steps should he take to defuse this situation, get the class back on track, help the girl, and eventually aid Ronald in improving his behavior? What would you do? We will explain Rudolf Dreikurs's techniques as we apply them to Mr. Garcia's treatment of Ronald. As the explanation unfolds, the reader will see a particular application of teacher treatment to the category of student misbehavior that Ronald fits as well as Dreikurs's applications to three other common categories of misbehavior, as identified by him.

Dreikurs and Alfred Adler's Social Theory

Dreikurs's writings flow out of the work of the noted social psychologist Alfred Adler. Adler believed that the central motivation of all humans is to belong and be accepted by others. Man is foremost a social animal. Books written by Dreikurs and his various associates *(Children: The Challenge, Logical Consequences, Encouraging Children to Learn, Psychology in the Classroom,* and *Discipline Without Tears)* all have a common bond with Adler. This bond is that all behavior, including misbehavior, is orderly, purposeful, and directed towards achieving social recognition.[1] Each action taken by such students as Ronald Foster is goal-directed. The "inner" goal results in the "outward" behavior. The teacher must have a student like Ronald recognize his "inner" goal and then help the student to change to the more appropriate goal of learning how to belong with others. This is the rationale for placing Dreikurs with the Interactionalists. He believes in an underlying cause for misbehavior (similar to the Non-Interventionists), yet he believes that its correction is the result of a teacher actively showing a student how to belong.

When a student is unsuccessful in obtaining social acceptance (sometimes as early as his or her infant or toddler years at home), a pattern of misbehavior begins. He or she is left with the recourse of trying to fulfill inner needs by annoying, destructive, hostile, or helpless behavior. If we, as teachers, can help misbehaving students understand their mistaken, faulty goals and provide them with avenues for group acceptance, then such students will rationally change their own behaviors. These subconscious goals that motivate misbehavior are 1) *Attention-Getting,* 2) *Power and Control,* 3) *Revenge* and 4) *Helplessness.*[2]

1. Attention-Getting: This is evident when a student is constantly looking to belong and be recognized in the class. Instead of receiving such recognition through productive work, often a student will resort to acting in ways that demand incessant praise or criticism. Both praise and criticism of an incessant nature are equally undesirable.

2. Power and Control: This is a goal for a student who feels inferior, who feels unable to measure up to the expectations of others or of self. It makes no difference whether the student is actually handicapped in some way or has only a false perception of being inferior. In either case, the youngster will try to remedy this perception of inferiority by trying to get his or her own way, by being the boss, by forcing himself or herself onto others, or by bragging or clowning.

3. Revenge: This is a goal for the student who feels unable to gain attention or power. This student sees himself or herself as having unequal status because of what others have done to him or her. This student places the blame for his or her plight on those outside. The student feels hurt by others and compensates by following the injunction of an "eye for an eye." In other words, "If I'm hurting, then I have the right to make others hurt." The student goes beyond the desire for attention and power, beyond the desire to win. He or she resorts to achieving status, not by merely winning over others, but by beating others with maliciousness and humiliation.

4. *Helplessness or Inadequacy:* The student operating with this goal is the most pathetic. He or she has given up on the possibility of being a member or of gaining any status in the group. This student not only feels uncared for, unequal, and wrongfully treated but also feels incapable of doing anything (either constructively or destructively) about it. The student has accepted the feeling of being a nobody and no longer cares what happens.

With this beginning understanding of Dreikurs, let us move to the Teacher Behavior Continuum with Mr. Garcia and Ronald Foster.

Dreikurs's Methods and the Teacher Behavior Continuum

To begin, the teacher must determine which of the four faulty goals is motivating the student. This determination is basically a four-step process, as follows:

1. The teacher observes and collects information about the student in situations involving peers and family.
2. Once the teacher has gathered information about the student, he or she can then hypothesize or guess which of the underlying goals is held by the student.
3. This goal can be verified by the teacher by reflecting on what feelings arise within the teacher as a result of the student's behavior.
4. Final verification is achieved by confronting the student with a series of four questions and looking for the student's recognition reflex.

In carrying out this procedure, the teacher moves through *Visually Looking On, Questions, Directive Statements,* and back to *Questions*.

Visually Looking On

Mr. Garcia, in the immediate situation with thirty-one pairs of eyes peering at him, disinvolves himself emotionally from Ronald's behavior. He has noted the first impression of rudeness, braggadocio, and flashiness that Ronald has created. Mr. Garcia makes a mental note to himself to search for more information by looking at school records, talking to former teachers, and possibly making a home visit. For now, though, with limited information, he suspects that Ronald's goal might be attention-getting, power, or revenge. It certainly is not helplessness!

It is important to remain calm during the beginning encounter with a student operating under any of the faulty goals, and not to give the student what he or she seeks. For example, the worst thing Mr. Garcia could do would be to call out loudly and angrily to Ronald. To do so would give Ronald the attention he seeks (attention-getting), or it would accelerate the battle of who will win out (power), or it would drive Ronald into physically lashing out (revenge).

Mr. Garcia can remain calm because he knows rationally that Ronald's behavior is not directed personally at him but is simply the student's previously learned mode of responding in groups. Of course, a quite human reaction from a teacher would be to explode, but this urge must be held in check. Examining this emotional urge or feeling toward the student will be most helpful in narrowing down and identifying the student's goal.

Questions (covert)

Now Mr. Garcia can capitalize on the inner emotion that Ronald's behavior has evoked. Dreikurs suggests that teachers covertly ask themselves four questions related to the goals.[3]

1. Do I feel annoyed? If so, he or she might have reason to suspect *Attention-Getting* as a goal.
2. Do I feel beaten or intimidated? If so, he or she might have reason to suspect *Power* as a goal.
3. Do I feel wronged or hurt? If so, he or she might have reason to suspect *Revenge* as a goal.
4. Do I feel incapable of reaching the child in any way? If so, he or she might have reason to suspect *Helplessness* as the goal. Mr. Garcia analyzes his feeling as "annoyed," to say the least, and even slightly intimidated, which suggests that Ronald's goal might be attention-getting or power.

If the teacher had given free rein to his first impulses, let us see what Ronald's probable responses would have been. If Mr. Garcia had yelled at him, Ronald might have responded with, "That's cool, daddy-o. Don't get all upset; you are losing your head over nothing." In other words, if Ronald's goal was *power,* he would have won at that point. He would have "shown up" Mr. Garcia in front of the class as a teacher who becomes easily flustered while he, a seventeen-year-old student, was more of a man, with calm and collected reactions. If Ronald's goal was to get *attention,* he would have responded in a different way. Mr. Garcia's yells might have caused Ronald to sheepishly put his head down and grin to himself. The rest of the class would be observing Ronald, and as soon as Mr. Garcia turned away, Ronald's head would be back up, face smiling, and looking around to make sure that everyone had seen him. In both cases, Mr. Garcia's primary reaction would have done little to prevent numerous future occurrences. Mr. Garcia knows he can't play into the student's scheme and is ready now to take specific action. He goes with a guess that *attention-getting* is Ronald's primary goal.

Directive Statements

The previous reflective and covert behaviors of *visually looking on* and *questions* were primarily enacted to gather information, to narrow down and identify the student's possible goal, and to make a tentative plan for action. A teacher trained in Dreikurs' approach would take only a split second from first witnessing the girl running out of the classroom to begin action with Ronald.

Having identified attention-getting as Ronald's underlying goal, Mr. Garcia acts in a way that deprives Ronald of the attention related to his misbehavior. Mr. Garcia turns to the girl and quietly tells her to come back in the classroom when she is ready and to take another seat away from Ronald. He then turns to the class and states, "Class, I would like to introduce you to some of the laboratory equipment you will be using this year. In a few minutes I would like you to break up into groups of four people and gather around the lab tables at the back of the room. When you get settled, open to the first page of your lab manual, where you will find pictures of the various kinds of equipment. As a group, see if you can first learn the equipment names, then I will join each group briefly to demonstrate how to use some of the more dangerous equipment, such as the Bunsen burner. OK, class, find your groups of four and move to your tables." Turning to Ronald, he adds, "Oh, Ronald Foster, your behavior has told me that you are not ready to work with others. I want you to remain in your seat. When you think you can join a group without being disruptive, you may do so."

Having attended to the class, Mr. Garcia gives Ronald a *directive statement*. He has told Ronald that he can join the group if and when he is ready to contribute in an appropriate way. This is an example of a teacher applying *logical consequences,* rather than punishment. (We will explain this difference more fully in the section on reinforcement. For now, let us say that Mr. Garcia has employed the loss of the student's right to engage in an activity as a result of behavior that would be counterproductive to accomplishing that activity as a logical consequence.) Before Mr. Garcia can conclude definitely that attention-getting is Ronald's goal and then continue with a long-range plan based on that goal identification, he needs further verification. He can achieve this by returning to overt questioning with Ronald.

Questions (overt)

Ronald has stayed by himself, slouched down with his hat over his face for nearly half the period. This is a further sign that Mr. Garcia has correctly identified Ronald's goal. If Ronald had wanted power, he would have continued to defy the teacher's rules. If Ronald had wanted revenge, he would have physically retaliated against the girl or teacher.

Mr. Garcia eyes Ronald slowly getting out of his seat and moving towards the lab table. There is only one spot open in the groups of four, and he heads towards that spot. When this group of three notices that he is ready to join them, one of the girls at the table (the very one that Ronald bothered) begins to complain and shout, "No, No, you don't! You're not joining our table, turkey." Ronald then turns to another nearby group and is greeted with, "You're not coming into our group. There is dangerous stuff here—you'll get us killed!" With a parting shot, "You're all a bunch of jerks," Ronald returns to his desk. Mr. Garcia moves towards him, takes a seat nearby, and in a voice that cannot be heard by anyone else begins to question Ronald.

Teacher: "Do you know why you acted like you did this morning?" *(confronting)*

Ronald: (Simply shrugs his shoulders)

Teacher: "I have some ideas. Would you like to know?"

Ronald: (Gives a yes nod)

Teacher: "Could you want special attention?" *(verifying)*

Ronald: For the first time his eyes look directly at Mr. Garcia, and he gives a slight smile. *(recognition reflex)*

During a discussion in a calm setting, Dreikurs proposes that the teacher do as Mr. Garcia has done.[4] The teacher should ask the student if he or she is interested in knowing why he or she behaves as he or she does. If the student does not resist, the teacher asks four sequential questions. Dreikurs listed them as:

(Attention) 1. Could it be that you want special attention?

(Power) 2. Could it be that you want your own way and hope to be boss?

(Revenge) 3. Could it be that you want to hurt others as much as you feel hurt by them?

(Helplessness) 4. Could it be that you want to be left alone?[5]

After the teacher asks each of these questions, he or she looks *(visually looking on)* for behavioral verification. If the student smiles, laughs, looks up suddenly, moves his or her shoulders, or shows other signs of response to the implied goal, then the teacher has conclusive evidence that his or her hypothesis is correct and treatment can proceed. The teacher formulates a plan and returns to appropriate *directive statements*.

Directive Statements

Now that Ronald has given the "recognition reflex" to question number one, Mr. Garcia can be confident that *attention* is his goal. Mr. Garcia's task now becomes one of finding ways for Ronald to receive attention through constructive social behavior. In other words, he needs to give Ronald the attention that he craves. Following are descriptions of treatment for each of the four goals that correspond with Dreikurs' prescriptive chart for teachers.[6]

Attention: A student who seeks attention should not receive it when he or she acts up. To give attention to the student for inappropriate behavior would be playing into the student's plan and would not help the student to learn how to behave productively in the group. Instead, the teacher might do some of the following:

- Tell the student that he or she will be talked to three times each morning. The teacher then initiates conversation with the student at three times that are divorced from any misbehavior.
- Set aside a period of time when the student will be listened to by everyone in the class. He or she may tell a story, a joke, or share something at a designated time each day.

Power: A student who wishes to possess power should not be able to engage the teacher in a struggle. The teacher who falls for this "bait" and gets pulled into the battle is merely continuing the excitement and challenge for the student. The student becomes increasingly bolder and pleased with trying to test the teacher. The teacher should attempt to remove the issue of power altogether and force the student to look for some other goal for behaving. Some examples of a teacher disengaging from a power struggle would be:

- When the student defies the teacher, the teacher merely says, "I cannot force you to do this. If you will not work on your paper, then choose to do something else that is quiet. Later, you can tell me when you will get your work done (at recess, at home, in the morning, and so forth)."
- Give the student power by allowing him or her to be lunch monitor, take messages to the office, collect homework, take attendance, be group leader, and the like.

Revenge: In this case, the teacher is dealing with a more difficult task. A student who feels hurt and wishes to retaliate must be handled in a caring, affectionate manner. It is probable that this student appears unloving and uncaring, and is very hard to "warm up to." But this is exactly what the student needs, to feel cared for. The teacher might show such care by:

- Saying, when the student attempts to hurt someone else, "I cannot let you hurt anyone, and I don't want to see you get hurt. I care for you and want to help you. How can I help you solve this problem?"

- Having special moments with the student. Take him or her out to lunch or to an after-school event, or even a visit to your home. Have frequent private, friendly conversations. Be sure to greet the student with a smile and a cheerful "hello" each day.

Helplessness: The student who shows inadequacy or helplessness is the most discouraged. He or she has lost all initiative of ever trying to belong to the group. The teacher must exercise great patience and attempt to show the child that he or she is capable. Some practices that might help a helpless student would be:

- To allow the student to bring in a favorite project or hobby from home that he or she can work on in school (building miniature cars, embroidery, coin collections, and the like).
- To bring in a project for the child to do in school from which he or she will experience success and be able to show the rest of the class his or her achievement (a walkie-talkie kit, painting by numbers, building a stereo component, learning Morse code, and so on).
- To respond to a despairing student who might throw his or her papers, pencils, or books with, "You are trying hard and it is difficult to learn to write (spell, divide, compose, and so forth). I know that you are going to improve and learn. Let's pick up these papers and try again."

Let us see how Mr. Garcia takes the general guidelines for the attention-getting student and develops a unique treatment for Ronald.

After questioning the student, Mr. Garcia continues his conversation. He discovers that during the summer Ronald works on a ranch in Montana (the reason for the cowboy hat). One of his hobbies over the past three years has been collecting belt buckles. His collection currently contains over two hundred different types, one of which he is wearing. Mr. Garcia asks him if he knows what metal is in the belt buckle. Ronald does not know.

Mr. Garcia capitalizes on Ronald's interest in buckles by telling him that during this semester the class will be learning a great deal about various metals. He further tells Ronald that, after he learns to use the equipment safely and understands the general principles of chemistry, he can melt, combine, and cast metals to make his own belt buckle. Ronald might also learn how to control various acids and then burn designs into the metal. In fact, to help interest the other students in the chemistry of metals, Ronald is told he might bring his buckle collection in to share with the class. As can be seen, Mr. Garcia is finding a socially acceptable way for Ronald to receive attention.

Ronald is obviously interested, but he jars Mr. Garcia back to the immediate situation with a sarcastic, "Well, teach, this sounds groovy but there's one big problem. I can't do all these neat things without equipment, and no one wants me in their group. What do you suggest? Maybe you'll buy me my own laboratory?" Mr. Garcia, as a Dreikurs teacher, knows that he must capitalize on using the group of students as a *model* to help Ronald to adjust.

Modeling

Mr. Garcia informs Ronald that at the end of class today, and on every Friday, there will be a short class council meeting to discuss problems that are of concern to the members of the class. He adds that Ronald could bring up his problem at that time and see what he and the class might work out.

Dreikurs believes that Western schools and classrooms, as part of a democratic society, need to be models or laboratories of that society.[7] In other words, students need to practice democratic principles in school in order to learn how to contribute later to society as a whole. The central process for carrying out this modeling of democracy is the use of the class meeting, which Mr. Garcia refers to as the class council. Regular meetings should be held to discuss everyday occurrences as well as long-range policies. We will see in the next chapter how a fellow Interactionalist, William Glasser, has further refined and elaborated on this concept of classroom meetings.

Meetings can be conducted informally without a designated leader, or formally with a rotating president, recorder, and treasurer. Voting should be avoided as it has a tendency to alienate the minority. Instead, decisions should be made through arriving at a consensus of all members. When many people agree with a decision, peer pressure tends to influence the one or two "holdouts" and thus make the decision unanimous. (We see this at political party conventions. After a hard battle among several candidates, one individual finally emerges a winner and all opposition evaporates. A united party once again emerges.) Let's see how Mr. Garcia capitalizes on the group process.

Mr. Garcia calls the class back to their seats and tells them that, in his classes, he always has a class council meeting on Fridays for the last twenty minutes of the period. However, since this is the first week of a new semester and they have a lot of problems to work out, they will have a meeting every day this week, beginning today. The class is then encouraged to begin an open general discussion. One or two students bring up different problems pertaining to missing lab equipment, how they are going to be graded, and whether the lab could be open during their free period after lunch. Finally, Ronald raises his hand, and everyone turns to look at him. "I have no equipment, and I'm in no group." The girl whom he previously embarrassed shouts, "Serves you right." Mr. Garcia interjects, "What Ronald has done is in the past. What can we do about his not having a group to join?" The class begins in earnest to discuss the issue. Most students express the feeling that if Ronald has no equipment then he cannot pass the course and that would be unfair. Some members ask the three-member group if they would let

Ronald into their group. Again, the girl that had been embarrassed states, "No way! He will bug us and keep us from our work. Those chemicals are dangerous!" However, the other two members of the group say that they would be willing to work with him on a trial basis. Finally, after much discussion, it is decided that the girl will change places with a student in another group and Ronald would now have three people with whom he could work at the laboratory table. Ronald appears greatly relieved to hear this decision.

Up to this point, everything seems to have been resolved. But what happens if Ronald continues to misbehave? What recourse does the teacher or class have? We need to look at Dreikurs's interpretation of *logical consequences* to answer these questions.

Reinforcement

Dreikurs does not believe in the Interventionists' use of punishment (negative reinforcement) or praise (positive reinforcement). Instead he substitutes *natural/logical consequences* and the process of *encouragement*. Let us explain each as it applies to Ronald.

Natural/Logical Consequences: If Ronald should create a commotion after becoming accepted in the group, he could be disciplined as a result of some of the following logical consequences:

Generally,

- Have the group of three decide what should be done with Ronald.
- Have Ronald work alone and have him use the laboratory equipment on his own time (at lunch, study hall, after school).
- Bring Ronald's misbehavior back to the entire class in a classroom meeting to decide on future consequences.

Specifically,

- If Ronald has been causing a disturbance by poking students with a pencil, take away all of his pencils and tell Ronald that whenever he needs to write he'll have to come to the teacher's desk to ask for a pencil.
- If Ronald has been constantly moving out of his chair and distracting others, tell Ronald that he does not seem to need a chair and take it away from him. Let him stand until he requests to have it back and agrees to stay in it.

A *natural* consequence is defined as that which happens as a result of one's behavior. If a student is rushing to get into line and trips and falls, we call this a natural consequence. On the other hand, if a student is rushing and pushing others in order to be first in line and is removed by the teacher to a place at the end of the line, then this would be identified as a *logical* consequence. In other words, a natural consequence is an inevitable occurrence that happens by itself, while a logical consequence is arranged but directly related to the preceding behavior. Dreikurs believes that, in a democratic society and in a democratic classroom, students must be responsible for how they behave. There is no room for autocratic punishment, as such punishment further alienates and discourages a child. Extensive punishment serves as a force to drive a student toward the goal of revenge. Punishment (or negative reinforcement) is not seen as being logically related to a student's behavior. It is inflicted as a reaction to personal dissatisfaction felt by the teacher. Punishment says to the student, "You had better behave or I (the teacher) will make life miserable for you." If the student does "knuckle under," it is because of the power of the teacher and not because the student has learned how to be a proactive member of the group. If one accepts Dreikurs's definition of human behavior as a purposeful attempt to belong, then a teacher who uses punishment blocks a student's purpose. Punishment "plays back" into the student's misdirected goals. It gives attention, enhances the power struggle, stimulates further revenge, and keeps the helpless child in his or her place.

Additionally, Dreikurs rather pragmatically points out that, in today's age of equal rights and militancy, students are not easily coerced by the use of authoritarian power. Not only does punishment thwart a student's ambition, but it simply does not work.[8] Let us further explore the operational distinction between punishment (negative reinforcement) and natural/logical consequences. Sending a student home with a note, keeping him or her after school, paddling, scolding, ridiculing, or standing the student in a corner are all forms of physical or psychological punishment. The teacher's actions are aimed at hurting the child or making him or her feel badly. Punishment is the teacher's vengeance for a committed crime. On the other hand, students who clean up the mess they created, who are put at the end of line for shoving, who miss recess because of tardiness with their assigned work, or who are barred from using certain materials until they choose to use them properly are all actually involved in the effects of logical consequences. Logical consequences are not always easy to tailor to every disruptive action. However, it is the teacher's task to arrange the situation that follows the disruption in a way that the student can see a relationship between the consequences and his or her behavior. (This is a further break from the Non-Interventionists' position, particularly Gordon's, who would criticize logical consequences as being false, contrived, and manipulative.)

Finally, it is important to note the differences in a teacher's attitude and manner in the application of logical consequences as opposed to the act of punishment. Two teachers might arrive at the same solution for a problem caused by a child's behavior, but one will be an example of logical consequences and the other will be an example of punishment. Sounds confusing, but it really isn't! During quiet work time, Sue Ann continually pokes Ernie with a pencil. One teacher, Mr.

Matter-of-Fact, tells Sue Ann, "Sue Ann, if you continue to poke Ernie then you will have to give me all your pencils. I'll give them back to you at recess when the rest of the class is outdoors. Then you can finish your work without bothering anyone." The other teacher, Mr. How-Dare-You, says, "Sue Ann, I have told you a thousand times not to do that. Can't you understand anything? If I catch you once more I'll take all your pencils away and you'll stay in at recess. Maybe being alone is the only way that you can work!" Mr. Matter-of-Fact has calmly told the student to use the pencil correctly or give it up. Mr. How-Dare-You acts as though he has been personally affronted and that Sue Ann's misbehavior is a direct challenge to his authority. He tries to hammer her down by scolding, questioning her competence, and challenging her. The same outcome has occurred, the student has had the pencil confiscated, but Mr. Matter-of-Fact has used logical consequences and Mr. How-Dare-You has applied punishment.

Encouragement: At the same time that the class and Mr. Garcia are applying logical consequences to Ronald's behavior, Mr. Garcia is also using the encouragement process. Mr. Garcia asks Ronald to keep inventory of all laboratory equipment and to prepare an order of new supplies for the class. He makes sure that Ronald brings in his belt buckle collection. Mr. Garcia also makes a mental note to greet Ronald warmly each day.

The encouragement process is an attitude taken with a misbehaving student that results in a climate of respect and optimism.[9] One must remember that a student whose goal is attention feels stifled by authority, and may retreat to the even more destructive goal of *power*. When that goal is "beaten down" by an overbearing, punitive teacher, the student may then resort to the goal of *revenge* to retaliate. When revenge is crushed by even more coercive means, we may finally have the most pathetic result, a student who has simply given up and has internalized the goal of *helplessness*. This lowering of goals is the result of a student becoming further discouraged. Not only does the student retreat further back into gloom and despair, but so does the teacher. The vicious cycle compounds the problem.

The role of the teacher is to stop this dissipation of hope by using encouragement. This is accomplished by such teacher-actions as:

- *Emphasizing improvement rather than a perfect product.*
- *Criticizing the student's actions, but not the student;* i.e., "I like you but I don't like to hear you shouting."
- *Keeping the student in a group with other students who are willing to help.* Determine those peers who are most accepting and tolerant of the student in question. Sit the student with them and arrange for him or her to work with them in groups. Find a companion or friend for the student.
- *Refraining from having the student compete against others.* Do not compare the student to others ("Why can't you behave like Rufus?") or con-

stantly single out for praise others who outperform the youngster. Deemphasize grades; try to grade the student on effort, not his or her rank in relation to others. Avoid contests for the best-behaved student or citizen of the week, where the student has little chance of winning.

Dreikurs believes that the provision of positive reinforcement is generally not a desirable method. Encouragement is much broader than the Interventionists' use of verbal praise, material or situational rewards as conditioning to achieve appropriate behavior. In 1963, Dinkmeyer and Dreikurs wrote:

> Unfortunately, even the well meaning and sincere educator may often fail to convey much needed encouragement if he tries to express his approval through praise . . . Praise may have a discouraging effect in the long run, since the child may depend on it constantly and never be quite sure whether he will merit another expression of special approval and get it.[10]

Dinkmeyer and Dreikurs are not saying that praise should be totally avoided, but what they are suggesting is that too much praise makes a child dependent on the teacher. The student who is "won over" by the teacher to work quietly due to the teacher's praise ("Oh look at Hillary! What a fine student to be working so quietly! I am so proud that you're being so quiet.") has not learned social behavior. Instead of learning how to act out of consideration for others, the child instead is learning how to act for purposes of receiving the teacher's special compliments and dispensations. In other words, the child behaves well, but for all the wrong reasons. If the teacher is removed from the scene, the child's behavior will deteriorate. The child needs to internalize the correct motivation for being well behaved (acting as a productive member of the group), in order for it to be lasting.

In addition, the child who sees himself or herself as a failure and is motivated by *revenge* or *helplessness* will tend to disbelieve the authenticity of the teacher's words. A child who refuses to work and "gives up" on carrying out any order might have reason to speculate on why the teacher makes such an effort to praise him or her ("Oh, Sam, look what a good job you did! You make me so pleased when you hang your coat up!" Or, "Margie, it's great the way that you answered that question!"). The student will in effect believe that the teacher is overcompensating and that he or she is being singled out because he or she is indeed inferior. The child might think, "Why make such a big deal about hanging my coat up or answering a simple question? The teacher must think I'm a real nincompoop (idiot, jerk, bozo, and so on)." Thus the opposite effect of what the teacher intended will result, a further sign that reaffirms the child's inferiority. In this vein of thought, Dreikurs and Grey wrote that there is a fundamental difference between the act of reward and the act of encouragement. Few realize that, at times, success can be very discouraging. The child may conclude that, although success was achieved once, it could not happen again. The student's recent "success" may become a threat to his or her future ability to succeed. But what is worse, such an event often conveys to the child the assumption, which actually is shared by most of his or her teachers and fellow students, that he or she is worthwhile only when he or she is successful.[11]

What we have, then, is the premise that praise or other forms of reward seem to heighten a child's anxiety to have to always "measure up." It puts constraints on a child who feels such pressure. He or she feels comfortable only when being successful. The discomfort with being unsuccessful discourages a child further from feelings of being accepted and of being an acceptable person. He or she feels accepted only when successful, but not when other than success occurs as a result of efforts expended. The child who needs to learn to be a member must learn to accept his or her individual self as being a person capable of both success and failure but, despite outcomes, who is still worthy of being loved and accepted by others.

A child who is always dependent on being rewarded for what he or she does is in a bind when it comes to taking a risk. The child who is learning how to belong must be encouraged to try new ways of behaving. The student who learns that it is safe and rewarding to be meek and passive will not easily venture into the unknown by being assertive and active. He or she won't venture into untried areas. This is the danger of having "success proof" programs or "praise laden" teachers.

The teacher must not stress the concept of success but, instead, promote a climate of always accepting the student as worthwhile. This happens when a teacher uses encouragement rather than such reinforcement as praise.

Following are two contrasting lists that give examples of praise versus encouragement. Praise focuses on the teacher being pleased by the child and on the child achieving a completed product. Conversely, encouragement focuses on the student and on the process of the student trying.

Praise	*Encouragement*
1) "I (teacher) like what you have done."	1) "You're trying harder."
2) "Great job! What a smart person."	2) "You must be happy with . . . (playing that game, being with others, and so on)."
3) "You get a star (token, free time) for doing that."	3) "It must be a good feeling to know you're doing well."
4) "I'm going to tell everyone how proud I am of you."	4) "You have every reason to be proud."

Physical Intervention and Isolation

Forms of teacher intervention such as paddling or shaking a student would be rejected by Dreikurs. Such treatment would be seen as a form of punishment that would drive a student further away from social cooperation. Pain experienced as a natural consequence (without the possibility of serious harm) could be allowed. Some examples of this might be the student who rushes to be first in line and in his or her haste falls and is bruised, or the student who repeatedly provokes the classroom gerbil and is bitten. On the other hand, there are some natural consequences that might eventuate when a student precariously tilts back in his or her chair, or when a "ninety-pound weakling" begins to taunt and enrage a two-hundred-and-fifty-pound high-school football tackle. These could be dangerous consequences, and the teacher would be wise to prevent them from occurring. It is important to note that a teacher should carefully judge the natural consequence before deciding to act or not to act in a given situation.

The use of isolation must also be judiciously used by the teacher. Dreikurs advocates the use of isolation only as a logical consequence. We saw that Ronald was isolated temporarily by Mr. Garcia when his behavior was immediately disruptive of others. However, Ronald was given the opportunity to join the group once he decided that he wished to belong.

It is obvious that if being part of a group is the ultimate goal for all individuals, then each person needs to learn to relate successfully to others. One only learns such relationships by practicing appropriate behaviors with others. One does not learn cooperation by being lectured to or having to sit by oneself. For these reasons, instead of relying on isolation, the teacher is required to look constantly for ways to encourage attachments between the offending child and other members of the class.

Summary

We have positioned Dreikurs as the initial example of our Interactionalists for three reasons. First, closely aligned with the Non-Interventionists, he has an optimistic belief in the child's rational capacities. Second, unlike the Non-Interventionists, he believes that such a development must occur in a social milieu where adults or peers need to intervene and redirect the child's misplaced goals. Third, Dreikurs instructs the teacher to use specific actions to redirect the child's misdirected goal. The use of such actions is much more assertive than the Non-Interventionists' nonjudgmental approaches. Dreikurs has the teacher use strategies that personally combat the child's game and aim to consciously pull the group to his or her side. The teacher then arranges *logical consequences* for the offending student to experience. Dreikurs believes that every student can attain his or her place in life but needs the active help of the adult. His approaches therefore are more intrusive than the Non-Interventionists', but could hardly be described as the shaping mechanisms of the Interventionists.

Looking at Figure 6–1, we can now identify the covert and overt behaviors of a teacher using this model. The teacher begins by covertly observing and col-

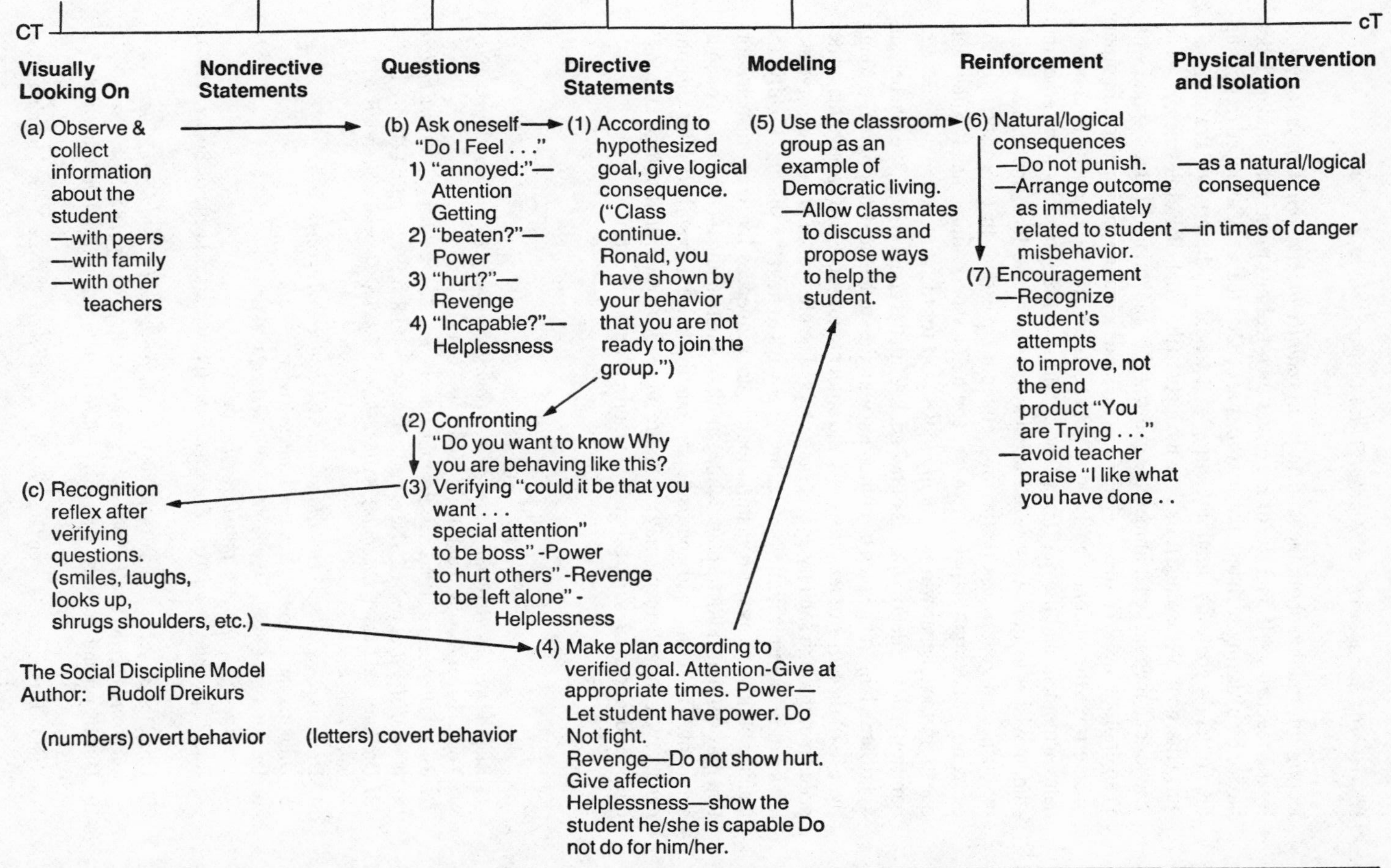

CT
cT
Visually Looking On
Nondirective Statements
Questions
Directive Statements
Modeling
Reinforcement
Physical Intervention and Isolation
(a) Observe & collect information about the student —with peers —with family —with other teachers
(b) Ask oneself "Do I Feel . . ." 1) "annoyed:"— Attention Getting 2) "beaten?"— Power 3) "hurt?"— Revenge 4) "Incapable?"— Helplessness
(1) According to hypothesized goal, give logical consequence. ("Class continue. Ronald, you have shown by your behavior that you are not ready to join the group.")
(5) Use the classroom group as an example of Democratic living. —Allow classmates to discuss and propose ways to help the student.
(6) Natural/logical consequences —Do not punish. —Arrange outcome as immediately related to student misbehavior.
(7) Encouragement —Recognize student's attempts to improve, not the end product "You are Trying . . ." —avoid teacher praise "I like what you have done . .
—as a natural/logical consequence
—in times of danger
(2) Confronting "Do you want to know Why you are behaving like this?
(3) Verifying "could it be that you want . . . special attention" to be boss" -Power to hurt others" -Revenge to be left alone" - Helplessness
(c) Recognition reflex after verifying questions. (smiles, laughs, looks up, shrugs shoulders, etc.)
(4) Make plan according to verified goal. Attention-Give at appropriate times. Power— Let student have power. Do Not fight. Revenge—Do not show hurt. Give affection Helplessness—show the student he/she is capable Do not do for him/her.
The Social Discipline Model
Author: Rudolf Dreikurs
(numbers) overt behavior
(letters) covert behavior

FIGURE 6–1. *Teacher Behavior Continuum (TBC)*

lecting information about the student by a) *visually looking on*. This is followed by the teacher's self-analysis of his or her own feelings toward the student's behavior by b) asking such internal *questions* as, "Do I feel . . . annoyed (reflecting the student's goal of Attention Getting), . . . beaten (the goal of Power), . . . hurt (the goal of Revenge), or . . . incapable (the goal of Helplessness)." The teacher can then make an immediate guess at the student's goal and respond with 1) an appropriate *directive statement* that includes a logical consequence. In order to determine the student's goal and to plan accordingly, the teacher will choose a calmer moment and use *questions* that 2) confront the student as to whether the student wishes to know why he or she behaves as he or she does, and then 3) verify the suspected goal by asking the four sequential questions that correspond to the elements of attention, power, revenge, and helplessness. Immediately after each question, the teacher will be *visually looking on* for the student to exhibit a "recognition reflex" identifying his or her goal. With the goal verified, the teacher can 4) initiate a long-range plan by conferring with the student and describing, through the use of *directive statements*, how the student can successfully have his or her needs met through socially appropriate ways. The classroom group can serve as a *model* of democratic living by 5) proposing ways to help the student. Finally, the teacher builds the use of 6) natural/logical consequences for those misbehaviors that may continue into the plan, while simultaneously using the process of encouragement. This combined approach prevents the student from becoming discouraged, even though there may be future instances when natural/logical consequences occur as a result of socially inappropriate behavior.

Notes

1. Rudolf Dreikurs, *Psychology in the Classroom: A Manual for Teachers*, 2nd ed. (New York: Harper & Row, Publishers, 1968), pp. 16–17.
2. Rudolf Dreikurs and Pearl Cassel, *Discipline Without Tears: What to Do with Children Who Misbehave*, rev. ed. (New York: Hawthorn Books, 1972), pp. 34–41.
3. Dreikurs and Cassel, *Discipline Without Tears: What to Do with Children Who Misbehave*, p. 41.
4. Dreikurs, *Psychology in the Classroom: A Manual for Teachers*, p. 55.
5. Dreikurs and Cassell, *Discipline Without Tears*, p. 42.
6. Dreikurs and Cassel, *Discipline Without Tears*, p. 44.
7. Dreikurs, *Psychology in the Classroom*, pp. 71–73.
8. Rudolf Dreikurs, *Children: The Challenge* (New York: Hawthorn Books, 1964), p. 76.
9. Don Dinkmeyer and Rudolf Dreikurs, *Encouraging Children to Learn: The Encouragement Process* (Englewood Cliffs: Prentice-Hall, 1963), pp. 45–56.
10. Dinkmeyer and Dreikurs, *Encouraging Children to Learn: The Encouragement Process*, p. 121.
11. Rudolf Dreikurs and Loren Grey, *Logical Consequences* (New York: Meredith Press, 1968), p. 157.

References

Dinkmeyer, Don, and Dreikurs, Rudolf. *Encouraging Children to Learn: The Encouragement Process.* Englewood Cliffs: Prentice-Hall, 1963.

Dreikurs, Rudolf. *Children: The Challenge.* New York: Hawthorn Books, 1964.

Dreikurs, Rudolf. *Psychology in the Classroom: A Manual for Teachers.* Second Edition. New York: Harper & Row, Publishers, 1968.

Dreikurs, Rudolf, and Cassel, Pearl. *Discipline Without Tears: What to Do with Children Who Misbehave,* rev. ed. New York: Hawthorn Books, 1972.

Dreikurs, Rudolf, and Grey, Loren. *Logical Consequences.* New York: Meredith Press, 1968.

Instructional Media

Films

Title: Individual Psychology in Counseling and Education
Part I. Rudolf Dreikurs

Time: 35 minutes Color

Company: American Personnel and Guidance Association
1107 New Hampshire Avenue
Washington, D.C. 20009

Synopsis: Examines the background and basic concepts of individual psychology and emphasizes that the term "individual" stands for uniqueness of the individual as well as for his or her individuality. Provides an overview of Alfred Adler's concepts; discusses the role of emotions, and relationship of emotions to personal intentions; and presents the optimism of the Adlerian position, specifically that it sees in every human being the immediate potential for being different.

Title: Individual Psychology in Counseling & Education
Part II

Time: 35 minutes Color

Rental Fee: $25 Purchase Price: $250

Company: American Personnel and Guidance Association
1107 New Hampshire Avenue
Washington, D.C. 20009

Synopsis: Explores some of Adler's major contributions on the concept of holism, the use of early recollections, and the idea of social interest or the feeling of belonging. He compares individual psychology with other theoretical approaches, and stresses educating teachers, counselors, and parents in personality development and understanding children.

Title:	Individual Psychology: A Demonstration with a Parent, a Teacher and a Child, Parts I & II.		
Author:	Dreikurs		
Time:	70 minutes (Two Reels)	Color	
Rental Fee:	$40 per day	Purchase Price:	$400
Company:	American Personnel and Guidance Association 1107 New Hampshire Avenue Washington, D.C. 20009		
Synopsis:	Demonstrates, through interviews with a "problem" child, his mother, and his teacher, how individual psychology can be applied to normal situations in counseling and education. Then he sums up what he sought to accomplish and what the central points were in the demonstration.		

7

The Reality Model of William Glasser

Sara sits nervously waiting in the administration office of the middle school. She shuffles her feet, keeps her head down, and turns away from anyone who might enter the room. Mrs. Washington, her eighth-grade teacher, has sent her with a note to see the principal.

The moment arrives when the secretary beckons to Sara, indicating that the principal is ready to see her now. The secretary swings open the door to the inner office, and Sara slowly shuffles into the room. Keeping her eyes averted, she hands the principal the note. Ms. Powers reads it through carefully, pauses, and then says to Sara, "Mrs. Washington would like to meet with us before we decide about what should be done about your behavior. Recess is in a few minutes, so we will wait. Please go back to the other room and wait."

The note from Mrs. Washington read:

> Ms. Powers
>
> As you know, Sara has a tendency to not hear the directions that she does not want to follow. Last week we made a plan where she agreed to respond to all my directions (put away personal belongings, stop talking, line up, and so on) within fifteen seconds. Each day that she complied I agreed to let her have the *privilege* of reading her favorite "Movie Glamour" magazine. However she also agreed that if she did not comply then she would have to do extra school work during the period allocated for her "privilege" time.
>
> Well, today, Sara continued talking and wisecracking while I was trying to get class started. I told her three times to stop, yet she just pretended not to

hear. I told her that she was responsible for her behavior and therefore would have to take the agreed upon consequences of extra work. Well, when the last ten minutes of class came, she took out her movie magazines and refused to do the work that we had agreed upon. I told her that if she broke her commitment she would have to go to the principal's office.

I would appreciate your not discussing anything with Sara until I get there. Let's continue with Glasser's approach of ''starting fresh'' and drawing up another *contract* with which all three of us can agree. I'll be there after class at 10:45.

Mrs. Washington

Both the principal and teacher are well versed in William Glasser's approach to discipline. Upon Mrs. Washington's arrival, she and Sara move into Ms. Power's office. They seat themselves in a semicircle, facing each other.

Ms. Powers begins, ''Sara, what happened? What were you doing to be sent to me?''

Sara says, ''The other kids were bothering me. I could not hear the teacher.''

Ms. Powers replies, ''No, Sara, I didn't ask that. I want to know about what you were doing. How is your behavior in class helping you?''

Sara stares back and says, ''I guess my not listening doesn't help me much.''

Ms. Powers continues to press. She asks, ''What rules are you breaking?''

Sara mumbles, ''Oh, I'm supposed to listen to the teacher and put away my stuff and stop talking when she tells me to. But really, Gloria was making me talk.''

Ms. Powers disregards Sara's last comment and says, ''What are you going to do about *your* behavior? Mrs. Washington and I want to help you to enjoy school, and we will work with you, but *you* are going to have to make another plan to improve yourself. It has to be a plan with which we all can be comfortable. Do you have some ideas?''

Sara replies, ''Yeah, I'll do the same plan I had before about the magazines.''

Mrs. Washington enters the conversation. Addressing Sara, she says, ''We have already tried that plan and you did not do what you agreed to do when we made that contract. We could try again but I want you to think it out so that the next time it will work. Ms. Powers should be part of the new contract.''

Sara speaks, ''You all decide. That'll be all right with me.''

Ms. Powers interjects, ''No, Sara, we are not going to be responsible for your behavior; only you can be responsible. We'll help you after you've decided what your plan will be. You are to stay in the in-school isolation room until you've made your plan. See me when you've decided that you have a plan that works.''

Sara spends the remainder of the day in a comfortable but small room, isolated at the end of the corridor. At the end of the day she tells Ms. Powers and Mrs. Washington that she has a plan written out for them. They all read it and, after a little help with the wording, finally agree upon the following:

Sara's Plan Thursday, February 17

I, Sara Orton, agree to listen to the teacher's directions and to do what she says.

If the teacher, Mrs. Washington, does not have to repeat her directions to me for an entire day, then I can have the privilege of being named the "Office Helper" and going to Ms. Power's office to answer the school phone during the next lunch time.

If the teacher only has to repeat directions to me twice during the day, then I can have the privilege of ten free minutes to read my magazines, but I can't hold the job of "Office Helper."

If the teacher has to repeat directions to me more than twice, then no magazines and no phone.

I agree to carry out this plan for one week and report to Ms. Powers next Friday on how I'm doing.

Signed,
Sara Orton

Witnessed by,
Mrs. Washington
Ms. Powers

Glasser and Reality Therapy

What the preceding case has illustrated are some of the steps of "Reality Therapy," as espoused by William Glasser. Glasser is a psychiatrist who was trained in and later broke from Freudian psychoanalysis. He believed that the traditional clinical approach of working with disturbed patients was seriously deficient. He believed that Freudian and play therapy encouraged dependence. He believed that the approach of allowing a person to give free vent to his or her emotions and to dissect and analyze his or her personal history, with the psychoanalyst then giving interpretations and labels to the individual's inner conflicts, was an inefficient one and did not help patients live in the real world. He believed that individuals who were escaping reality by behaving in inappropriate ways did not need to find a rationale and defense for their illogical behavior. Instead, people must be helped to acknowledge their behavior as being irresponsible and then to take action to make it more logical and productive. As a psychiatrist, Glasser does not believe in working with the unconscious, or of being nonjudgmentally accepting (such as the Non-Interventionists believe) of a person's action. His statement, stripped to its essentials, is that human beings must live in a world of other human beings. Each individual must satisfy his or her own needs in a way that does not infringe upon another's.[1] He clearly states that individuals are each responsible for their own actions and, regardless of how disturbed or dependent they claim to be, people must bear the consequences for their own behavior and make a commitment to act in a responsible manner toward others.

This might read as a rather harsh manner of treating inappropriate behavior, but Glasser's work and writings are not cold and dictatorial. Rather, the reverse is true. He has applied his psychiatric concepts of Reality Therapy to work with delinquent girls (as cited in *Reality Therapy*) and to work with children in public schools (as cited in *Schools Without Failure*). In both settings, he is found to be one who practices and advocates for others a personal and caring relationship with misbehaving students. He sees the establishment of care and warmth as a necessary human prerequisite for an individual who hopes to begin to come to grips with the sometimes awesome responsibility of being planner, manager, and executor of one's own actions.

Glasser's Methods and the Teacher Behavior Continuum

Visually Looking On

Visually looking on is not in the Glasser model as a specific overt step by a teacher in working with a child, as it is with the Non-Interventionists. Rather, Glasser asks the teacher to covertly assess the situation. This is a three-part process. As the teacher, one needs to:

1. Reflect on your past behavior with this student.
2. Start with a fresh approach. (If your actions haven't been successful in the past, why think that they will work in the future?)
3. Expect a better tomorrow. (Since the past has not been effective, the teacher can be optimistic. After all, the situation can hardly get much worse!)

Nondirective Statements

Again, Glasser is too much of an Interactionalist to use this central behavior of the Non-Interventionists. He does not agree with empathetic, all-supportive acceptance of the child. He makes this quite apparent when he discusses one of his first cases as an intern with an emotionally disturbed young boy. After weeks of using play-therapy steps of visually looking on and nondirective statements, he became increasingly frustrated with the child's continuing egocentric and destructive behavior. Finally he wrote:

> I began a kind of Reality Therapy. I told him (the child) to shut up and for once in his life to listen to what someone had to say. I informed him that the play was over, and that we would sit and talk in an adult fashion, or if we walked we would walk as adults. I explained clearly that I would not tolerate any running away or even any impolite behavior while we were walking. He

would have to be courteous and try to converse with me when I talked to him. He was to tell me everything he did and I would help him decide whether it was right or wrong.[2]

Directive Statements

As is evident in the previous quote, Glasser believes in defining clear boundaries of acceptable behavior. Further, he suggests that the teacher's role is to enforce and encounter, with *directive statements* or commands, the student who transgresses. When a child steps out of line, the teacher confronts the student and tells that student to stop transgressing. Examples of such directive statements might include:

—"Johnny, put that ruler down and get back to work."

—"Felix, if you are going to talk you must first raise your hand."

—"Selena, this is quiet reading time, so open your book and begin reading."

—"Antonio, give me that slingshot. A slingshot is not to be used around people or animals that can be hurt by it."

—"Johanna, keep your hands off that mural! It was just painted and must dry."

The teacher does not berate the student with such warnings as "Don't you dare do that again," or insults like, "You are acting like a little baby!" or such negative speculations as, "There must be something wrong with you to act that way." Instead, Glasser wishes the teacher to express directly the misbehavior and then to follow with a description of an appropriate behavior. The issue at stake is the student's *irresponsible* behavior. Therefore, the teacher needs to tell the student in effect to stop the wrong, irresponsible behavior and to act correctly and responsibly. If this does not achieve results, then the teacher is to follow such directive statements with questions.

Questions

The teacher frames *questions* for the student to make the child think rationally about his or her actions and eventually verbalize concerning these irresponsible behaviors. The teacher might confront the offending child at the time of disruption with a question such as, "What are you doing?"

The teacher is not interested in excuses or reasons; he or she simply wants the child to verbalize what is happening. The teacher is not to ask the student *why* he or she is doing something. A "why" question simply gives the student the opportunity to disown the behavior with such excuses as "Oh, I was mad (tired, or hungry)," "He made me do it," "They're always picking on me," and so on.

We saw how Ms. Powers avoided a "why" question, yet Sara still wanted to rationalize her behavior with "But Gloria made me. . . ." Ms. Powers would not accept such excuses. The confronting adult attempts to keep the student's discussion of the problem within the present, in order to get the issue of misbehavior out on the table, and then presses for a plan to be made.

After the question, "What are you doing?" the teacher asks the child to tell in what ways this behavior fulfills the child's needs. For example: *"How does (spitting, fighting, coming in late, and so forth) help you?"*

The student is thus asked to think of the consequences of his or her own actions. Usually the student will not be able to give a ready answer. The last objective of the teacher is to press for a plan or contract and commitment by the student by asking, *"What are you going to do about your behavior?"* or *"What is your plan going to be so that you don't break that rule again?"* These questions are crucial to reality therapy because they force responsibility back on the student. Many students get into a "cat-and-mouse" game with their teachers by constantly challenging the teacher to do something. By turning this challenge for action back to the student, there is no game left to play. Now the student's irresponsible actions will be dealt with according to the student's own plan. They will not be dealt with according to the dictates of an adult who has been forced to play supervisor. It is not the teacher who is responsible for the child's behavior, but the child who is responsible for that behavior. This does not mean that the teacher is passive in the student/teacher interaction; rather, the teacher becomes an active partner with the student in making a plan and then provides the student with the help necessary to implement the plan, which reflects the student's own feelings and thoughts.

Modeling

Glasser does not address this behavior as a specific step in working with a disruptive child. He would, however, surely agree that a teacher should set an example of being responsible to others and of being committed to carry out any stated pledge to students.

Reinforcement

Reinforcement is not advocated by Glasser in terms of schedules and concrete rewards, as seen by the Interventionists. Yet he does agree with the use of reinforcement as it applies to the loss of privileges for breaking one's plan or contract. In this respect, he and Dreikurs are in agreement. A student needs to have logical consequences follow his or her behavior, whether that behavior be positive or negative. The student is encouraged to decide what those privileges or negative results should be.

It is not for the teacher to impose his or her praise or punishment, because, in so doing, the teacher lets the student off the hook. Rather, the student must accept the natural repercussions of the misbehavior and should not be shielded from them. If the student does not respond to the question, "What are you going to do about it?" then the teacher can help by suggesting a plan that the student can agree to, or by sending the student away until he or she comes up with an acceptable alternative plan. Once a plan is agreed upon, Glasser goes so far as to tell the teacher to *have the student sign a written pledge to honor his or her plan.*[3] *The student agrees in writing to lose the privileges if he or she should falter and break the agreement. Commitment* is Glasser's key word!

For example, a student named Hector had agreed to a plan with his teacher that he would not fight during the morning recess. Hector knew and agreed to the terms of the plan which meant that to fight would mean the loss of recess. If partaking in recess was, in fact, more reinforcing to Hector than the pleasure of fighting, then in time the teacher would expect that the loss of that privilege would rationally alter the student's behavior. Hector would be expected to eventually realize that his physical aggression was not helping him enjoy his prized outdoor activity, and that to fight would mean that he had broken his commitment. The message became simple, "If you really like to go outdoors, then behave in ways that will make going outdoors a certainty."

Of course, the reader might wonder how this strategy, which appears so foolproof in theory, would work with the student who could care less about recess or who never thinks about any of his or her actions in terms of the consequences they might have. Glasser would admit that the student who could care less will be a more difficult case to treat.[4] It is obvious that, to a student such as this, being able to play outdoors at recess is not sufficiently motivating. The student would rather fight and stay in than not fight and stay outdoors. So what do we do? The answer, which might well appear somewhat simplistic, is to merely find some other activity or situation that is more valued by the child than fighting. Some alternatives for younger children might be suggested by the teacher:

—awarding the job of classroom helper.
—granting free time for personal projects.
—permitting the child to work with the school custodian.
—allowing time to listen to records.
—making the child the "official" messenger to the school office for the day or week.

Some possibilities for older students might be the teacher granting permission for:

—free time for personal projects.
—listening to popular records.

—reading popular movie or sports magazines.

—playing a game (electric football, hockey, chess).

—watching television.

If it is determined that the student cannot engage in any activity that is more personally reinforcing than his or her misbehavior, then the problem falls into one of two categories. Either the classroom situation is in need of being drastically overhauled, or the student is beyond the help of the school.[5] In other words, if the child is experiencing no success and finds no relevance in what he or she is doing, then the teacher must stand back and assess the entire classroom curriculum and organization.

Glasser believes that misbehavior of most students results from the failure of teacher and schools to fulfill their needs. He believes that students want to experience success, they want to have feelings of self-worth, and they want to learn. In too many situations, students are obstructed by such practices as:

—grades that label a few as successful and many as failures.

—constant teacher lectures to be sat through passively.

—reading materials that are geared for the average student and are thus too hard for the slower ones and too easy for brighter students.

—classroom topics or subjects that are irrelevant to the students.

—too much memorizing and recitation of facts instead of discussions and experiments.

With such conditions, it is a wonder that more students don't misbehave. School for students in such classes is simply an unhappy, unsuccessful, irrelevant, and boring place to be. On the other hand, if the classroom is an exciting place for all but one student, and the teacher cannot find (after numerous times) any activities that interest this misbehaving child, then the teacher has further ground to suspect that the child's problems are beyond the scope of the immediate classroom. Such a student might need to be referred for outside psychological or social help.

There are some students who simply are unaware of consequences, and dealing with these youngsters is an easier matter. A student perhaps has always exploded with rage whenever his or her "feathers have been ruffled." The aftereffect of this temper may never have been consciously processed by the student. As this student is still liable for his or her actions, regardless of the internal degree of cognizance, it is therefore the teacher's role to:

a) raise the child's level of awareness by pointing out the immediate behavior and consequences.

b) commit the student to creating a signed plan.

c) enforce the natural consequence of loss of privileges if the plan is violated.

For example, it might take months of repetitive loss of recess before a child such as Hector (in the earlier illustration) becomes aware of what his behavior is doing to him. In time, with consistent application, the lesson cannot help but be learned. Glasser suggests that the teacher begin anew by (1) reflecting on past behavior, (2) starting fresh, and (3) expecting a better tomorrow. The student is given as many chances as have been agreed upon with the teacher.

Physical Intervention and Isolation

Physical Intervention: Glasser is not a believer in the teacher's use of physical control. He is certainly not an advocate of paddling or spanking. He has even more concern with the psychological damage that adults do to children by using humiliation and ridicule. He does not believe that any form of punishment, whether physical or psychological, is appropriate. He does not justify his position on moral grounds, but on the grounds that punishment simply is not effective. To paraphrase a statement he made to a group of school teachers and administrators, he said:

> If punishment really worked we should have no delinquents or criminals. After all, as children, most of today's convicts have been punished and abused frequently. If punishment worked then we should now have a perfect society. We obviously don't and we obviously need to look for other methods."[7]

Isolation: Glasser sees the use of isolation, not for the purposes of punishing a student, but instead, for providing a place for the student to sit quietly and think about a plan for re-entering the classroom milieu. When a student persists in breaking his or her commitment, or refuses to make one, then the student is removed to a place so that he or she can begin again. The first step of isolation takes place "in class." Glasser calls this "off to the castle." The student should be able to observe or listen to what is going on, but his or her placement should not interfere with the classroom routine. In the elementary school, such a place is easily made in the classroom; in the junior high or secondary school, such a place, if not available within the room, can be set up in close proximity (i.e., the hall). The student is told to stay in the designated area until he or she has made a plan to insure a successful return to the group. This plan, again, has to be agreeable to both student and teacher. If the student bothers others while in the isolation area or persists in acting out after returning to the classroom, then the teacher could move to the second step of isolation, which leads *away from the classroom to an "in-school" suspension room.*

The teacher would need to have the principal's and faculty's support to free the necessary space for such a purpose. If an extra room is not available, a large storage area or a seldom-used office would be suitable. The environment should provide a relaxing place that is physically apart from the busy school activities. Movement to this area means that the student is being treated in a realistic manner. Until he or she takes the responsibility to plan and implement acceptable behavior in the classroom, he or she cannot participate in such activities. Glasser would suggest that, after all, this is the basis for societal enforcement of reasonable law and order. If you break the rules, then you are removed from the larger society. During the periods of in-school suspension, the principal or guidance counselor will need to be involved, but the parents will not. The teacher need not be concerned with the student's past, home life, or what his or her parents can do about the student's behavior. The teacher is only concerned with what can be done within the context of school. Not until the teacher has to resort to out-of-school isolation is it essential to involve the parents. This does not mean that the teacher must keep parents ignorant of their child's behavior. However, it does mean that the teacher should not look to the child's home as a source for help. The student's problem is in school, and it is the school's responsibility to handle it.

The child needs to learn to live appropriately in a classroom and to deal with the immediate consequences of his or her behavior in that room. Therefore, sending warning notes home or asking parents to punish the child would make the parents responsible for a problem that is not theirs. In effect, making the parents accountable to "shape up" their youngster removes that responsibility from the school and, more importantly, from the child.

The next form of isolation is suspending the student from school. If the student cannot show minimal control in an in-school suspension, then out of the school he or she goes. The student can return when a plan is made.

Throughout each form of isolation (in-class, in-school, out-of-school), the teacher remains a helping person, one who is not afraid to tell the student where he or she has transgressed, one who is willing to ask pointed questions as to what the student is doing, and one who will encourage the student to commit himself or herself to a plan. The teacher never lets the child get away with breaking his or her commitment and the teacher never lets the student shift responsibility for his or her behavior to others. At the same time, the teacher is not a mechanistic enforcer of law and order. The teacher constantly tells the student, "I want to help you to become more in control of your own actions. I will talk, listen, give opinions and offer advice, but at the end it is you who have to make the decision and commitment. I cannot and will not do that for you." So, as can be seen, the teacher becomes personally involved with his or her student. The teacher cares, and that caring is clearly shown by the teacher never allowing the child to transcend the boundaries of the commitment that the child has made. The teacher remains as one who will enforce reality behavior and the student remains as one who must learn the meaning of that reality.

In fully explaining the mechanism of isolation, let us refer to our previous teacher behaviors of *questions* and *directive statements*. These teacher behaviors do not stop when isolation begins. Rather, the teacher continues to ask the student through each stage of isolation to reply to such questions as, "What are you doing?" "What rules are you breaking?" "In what ways is this behavior helping you?" "What are you going to do about it?" and "What is your plan?" The teacher also tells the student directly what his or her transgressions are and what the consequences of these behaviors are. Any interaction with the student should contain such direct confronting statements as, "Stop doing that!" "The rule is. . . ," "You are breaking the rules and therefore cannot be part of the group," "You cannot have back your privilege (or return to the group) until you tell me your plan," and "Don't give me any excuses, tell me what you did!" Therefore, questions and directive statements are interspersed throughout the process of isolation and are essential in aiding the child to become aware of his or her actions, the consequences involved, and the responsibilities that need to be met. Glasser also points out that there may well be a few students who will actually need to be referred to an outside agency, such as a treatment center for delinquent children, when they engage in types of criminal behavior and none of the previous steps have met with any success.

The Classroom Meeting

It would be a disservice to the reader to omit one of the major formats for applying the teacher behaviors of reality therapy. What Glasser is perhaps best known for among school practitioners is the classroom meeting.[8] This practice of holding regular meetings provides a structure for dealing with both an individual student's problems as well as for revising the overall organization and curriculum of the class. The teacher meets with the entire class on a regular basis. They always sit in a circle facing each other, usually on a rug, sometimes in chairs. The teacher stresses to the class that during this meeting there are no wrong answers, and that each child should feel free to express his or her ideas, opinions, and feelings. The teacher is expected to express his or her ideas, opinions, and feelings in the same manner. The students are told that they are to talk about the present and the future, not to dwell in the past. The teacher further adds that students are not "to put down" or use insulting terms when speaking to or about others.

Since there are no "wrong" answers, every child in the meeting has the opportunity to be successful. A child need not fear being corrected for what he or she says. The teacher *(visually looking on)* encourages everyone, with nods and words of approval, to speak, but does not force anyone who resists. The teacher may ask a student for his or her ideas, and if no reply is forthcoming, may say *(nondirective statement)* something like, "Well, you think about it and let me know if you come up with an idea that you would like to discuss. I'd like to hear it."

Glasser speaks of three types of meetings: 1) open-ended, 2) educational/diagnostic, and 3) problem-solving. Open-ended meetings are held for students to create their own fantasies and to explore imaginary problems; for example, "What would we do if we were stranded on the moon?" The educational/diagnostic meeting is one where the teacher discusses a curriculum topic in order to find out what students already know about it, what they don't know, and what further interests they might have (i.e., What is pollution? Where does it come from? Why is it a problem?). The teacher then uses that information to make curriculum decisions as to what aspects of the topic would be most essential to cover and what activities would be most relevant to the students. The third type of meeting is the problem-solving one, whereby the class focuses on a real problem that affects all of them. They clarify the problem, add information, propose alternative solutions, and finally commit themselves to a plan of action. Examples of such general problems might be:

- How the playground balls are to be distributed at recess.
- What to do about missing items in the class.
- How to cut down on asking the teacher questions when he or she is busy.
- What to do about name-calling among the students.
- What to do about the length of time it takes to get the whole class settled before starting the next lesson.
- What to do about the "graffiti" and littering problems in the restrooms.

Specific problems concerning individual students are also a topic for problem-solving meetings. The use of this kind of meeting as a vehicle for working with student misbehavior is an application that we would now like to discuss. Behaviors by an individual that would be relevant as topics for a classroom meeting might include:

—A student who "hogs" the playground equipment (balls, bats, frisbees, and the like).

—A student who physically pushes other students around.

—A student who constantly distracts others from working (by making loud noises, talking, and so forth).

—A student who takes items from others.

—A student who plays cruel "tricks" on others (locks children into closets, writes on other's homework, and so on).

—A student who tries to be boss all the time, who is always telling others what to do but will not accept any criticism of self.

As we have seen, integral to Glasser's approach is for a student to be made aware of and become responsible for the consequences of his or her actions. When a student has behaved in ways that are constantly disruptive to the majority of other students, and the problem has escalated from one that is solely between student and teacher, then Glasser believes that the student needs to be confronted and helped by the entire class. Therefore, the problem-solving classroom meeting is held, and the misbehaving student hears what others think of his or her behavior.

The teacher holds a firm rein on this type of meeting to insure that it does not become a name-calling free-for-all. The teacher explains the reason for the meeting, such as wanting to discuss a student who has been destroying other children's property. The teacher then suggests that, as a group, perhaps the class can help the student to act more appropriately.

1. The teacher asks each student to openly express what this student has recently done to interfere with him or her personally. The students are asked to tell that student, face-to-face, what those behaviors are and what effects they have had on them (emotionally and/or physically).
2. After all have had their chance to speak (including the teacher), the misbehaving student is given an opportunity to explain what others have done to interfere with him or her.

At this juncture, the meeting swiftly swings from "getting all the cards out on the table" to doing something constructively with the information that has been gleaned.

3. The teacher suggests that the class and the offending child might be able to offer some possible solutions to the problem, ones which would be agreeable to all. The teacher listens to all ideas and then asks the group to narrow down the alternative plans and ideas that were offered.
4. Finally, the child is asked to select a plan and commit himself or herself to it. At the same time, the members of the class (including the teacher) commit themselves to carrying out any actions that will help the child in implementing his or her plan.

The conclusion of such a meeting is the achievement of an agreed upon, manageable plan. The participants leave the meeting with a feeling of positive action.

The reader should notice that the *teacher's role in such a classroom meeting is identical to the role required in dealing with a child on a one-to-one basis*. The same techniques of *"what" questions* and *direct statements* are used to keep the discussion on target and within the boundaries of rules. All verbalizations are designed to help the class and child come to grips with the reality of behavior and for them to "get on" with a course of action. The offending child is kept in the "straitjacket" of responsibility, and, after a *plan* is agreed upon, the teacher remains as the enforcer of *logical consequences*. Breaking of such a commitment could result in the student being led through the three levels of isolation.

To many teachers, the use of a classroom meeting for the confrontation of a child by his or her peers seems to be a harsh approach. Many would feel that, for some children, there is the danger of emotional harm and the reinforcement of a child's negative self-concept in such a confrontation. Glasser is careful to point out that such a meeting needs to be carefully guided by the teacher to avoid any such destructive outcome.[9] The teacher needs to carefully move the discussion from the phase of eliciting peer perceptions to that of developing helpful solutions. The classroom meeting is purposefully used to show the offending child that he or she cannot act in an egocentric vacuum of being oblivious to the effects of his or her behavior on others. If the teacher shields the disruptive child from feedback from peers, then that child has little opportunity to explore the reasons for cooperative behavior. If the child is really bothering his or her peers, as well as the teacher, then the student needs to know this directly by those affected. If the student is to live with others, then there is nothing more realistic than for others to inform the student when his or her actions are transgressing on their rights. The meeting is not designed, or held, to blame or punish the child, but to *find solutions* that will help the child.

Summary

In the book, *Schools Without Failure,* Glasser goes beyond the specifics of working with disruptive, "unrealistic" students and addresses what he considers to be the major source for inappropriate behavior. In doing so, he speaks of covert behaviors that the teacher might use with such students. Students, as all humans, wish to fulfill their needs, and misbehavior can be explained as a person's unsuccessful attempt to succeed in these efforts. Glasser sees schools as institutions that breed failure and irrelevancy.[10] Most misbehaving students do not feel successful in school. They are not involved in what they learn, and therefore they erect a shield of defiance, apathy, and unconcern to protect them from the further hurt of inadequacy. Consequently, when a misbehaving student is expected to give up privileges (or successful experiences) as a result of wrong action, the student has none to give up and the defiant behavior continues. So, in these situations, Glasser tells the teacher to covertly use *visually looking on* with the student by:

a) observing the student and the situation.
b) assessing what the teacher himself or herself is currently doing and what success the student is having.
c) if necessary, starting fresh by reversing classroom organization and /or activities.

Only at this point, if failure continues, does the teacher begin the process of overt behaviors.

The central technique for the teacher to use is an approach that confronts the student and makes him or her responsible for his or her own behavior. A student, upon transgressing rules, is:

1. Confronted and told to stop. *(Directive Statements)*
2. Asked "What" questions. *(Questions)*
3. Pressed for a plan and commitment. *(Directive Statements)*
4. Faced with logical consequences that have been agreed upon. *(Reinforcement)*
5. Faced with failure to carry out commitment and plan—which results in class *isolation* ("off to the castle")—where steps 1, 2, 3, and 4 are repeated.
6. In the case of continual failure, placed in in-school *isolation* (principal's office or school isolation room), where principal repeats steps 1, 2, 3, 4, and 5.
7. If he or she persists in continual failure, placed in outside-of-school *isolation* (sent home); when the student returns, the teacher and principal repeat steps 1, 2, 3, 4, 5, and 6.
8. Referred to an outside agency if the previously cited steps fail.

William Glasser is an Interactionalist. He believes in the capability of each individual to be responsible, but he tempers that optimism with the need for an individual to learn the moral or acceptable boundaries necessary to live successfully in society. As he wrote:

> All students must be accepted as potentially capable, not as handicapped by their environment.[11] They do not decide, however, whether or not rules, once established should be enforced. They may choose to disobey the rules; this choice is open to all. But they then have to accept the consequences of their choice.[12]

Notes

1. William Glasser, *Reality Therapy: A New Approach to Psychiatry* (New York: Harper and Row, Publishers, 1975), p. 13.
2. Glasser, *Reality Therapy: A New Approach to Psychiatry*, p. 170.
3. William Glasser, *Schools Without Failure* (New York: Harper and Row, Publishers, 1969), p. 126.
4. William Glasser, "Disorders in Our Schools: Causes and Remedies," *Phi Delta Kappan*, January 1978, p. 331.

Ct						cT
Visually Looking On	**Nondirective Statements**	**Questions**	**Directive Statements**	**Modeling**	**Reinforcement**	**Physical Intervention and Isolation**
a) Observe —the student —the situation b) Assess —what the teacher is currently doing —what success the student is having c) Classroom reorganization and activities d) Move to overt behaviors —if step c does not work —if present teacher behaviors are unproductive		(2) "What" Questions "What are you doing?" "What are the rules?" "In what ways is your behavior helping you?" "What is your plan?"	**(1) Confront transgressor. "Stop that, the rule is . . ." (3) Press for a plan. "You must make a plan; I will help but you are responsible."		(4) Reap the consequences of plan.	(5) Off to the castle (Classroom Isolation) Repeat 1, 2, 3, 4 (6) Off to the office (with principal doing 1, 2, 3, 4) (7) Removal from school Repeat 1, 2, 3, 4, 5, 6. (8) Referral to outside agency.

The Reality Model
Author: William Glasser

(numbers) overt behavior
(letters) covert behavior

**Steps 1-4 can be carried out in class meetings

FIGURE 7–1. *Teacher Behavior Continuum (TBC)*

5. William Glasser, *Glasser's Approach to Discipline* (pamphlet published by Educator Training Center, Los Angeles, California), Step 10, pp. 8–9.
6. Glasser, *Glasser's Approach to Discipline,* Step 7, p. 6.
7. Glasser's presentation to the School Council of Ohio Study Group, (Delaware, Ohio: December 6, 1976).
8. Glasser, *Schools Without Failure,* Chapters 10 and 11.
9. Glasser, *Schools Without Failure,* p. 129.
10. Glasser, *Schools Without Failure,* Chapter 3.
11. Glasser, *Schools Without Failure,* p. 199.
12. Glasser, *Schools Without Failure,* p. 200.

References

Glasser, William. "Disorders in Our Schools: Causes and Remedies." *Phi Delta Kappan.* January 1978.

Glasser, William. *Glasser's Approach to Discipline.* Los Angeles: Educator Training Center.

Glasser, William. *Reality Therapy: A New Approach to Psychiatry.* New York: Harper and Row, Publishers, 1975.

Glasser, William. *Schools Without Failure.* New York: Harper and Row, Publishers, 1969.

For additional information contact the Educator Training Center, 2140 West Olympic Boulevard, Suite 518, Los Angeles, California 90006, (213) 386-2511.

Instructional Media

Filmstrips

Title: Glasser's Ten Steps to Discipline

Author: William Glasser

Two filmstrips with two cassettes with teacher's guide

Color

Purchase Price: $45

Company: Media Five
3211 Cahuenga Boulevard, West
Los Angeles, California 90068

Synopsis: Presents an illustration of the ten-step approach to all disciplinary problems, no matter how severe, with classroom scenes.

Title: The Reality Therapy Approach

Time: 29 minutes Color

Rental Fee: $45 per week Purchase Price: $395

Company: Media Five
3211 Cahuenga Boulevard, West
Los Angeles, California 90068

Synopsis: Documentary film of teachers successfully using concepts developed by Glasser to achieve effective school discipline. Explains the five-part approach to discipline and the seven steps of Reality Therapy.

Title: Dealing with Discipline Problems

Time: 29 minutes Color

Rental Fee: $45 per week Purchase Price: $375

Company: Media Five
3211 Cahuenga Boulevard, West
Los Angeles, California 90068

Synopsis: Teachers supply the commentary on what they are doing and why, often suggesting alternative ways of dealing with real-life situations. Filmed on location at model schools-without-failure, revealing how teachers apply success-concepts of Reality Therapy in everyday practice.

Title: The Reality of Success

Time: 28 minutes Color

Rental Fee: $40 per week Purchase Price: $395

Company: Media Five
3211 Cahuenga Boulevard, West
Los Angeles, California 90068

Synopsis: The film provides a background on Reality Therapy, helping problem students to achieve self-motivated, productive behavior. Pinpoints the value and importance of maintaining good personal relationships, dealing in the present, and getting the troubled child to make a value judgment and plan his or her improvement.

Title: Glasser on Discipline

Author: William Glasser

Time: 28 minutes Color

Rental Fee: $45 per week Purchase Price: $395

Company: Media Five
Cahuenga Boulevard, West
Los Angeles, California 90068

Synopsis: Details a successful approach to an old problem: school discipline. Glasser outlines five basic elements for achieving effective discipline in school.

Title: Roles and Goals in High School
Author: William Glasser
Time: 29 minutes Color
Rental Fee: $45 per week Purchase Price: $395
Company: Media Five
3211 Cahuenga Boulevard, West
Los Angeles, California 90068
Synopsis: Illustrates the relevance of Glasser's Identity Society and School-Without-Failure concepts in the high school milieu. Includes role-play with teachers and use of Reality Therapy to handle discipline problems.

Title: The Glasser Up-Date
Author: William Glasser
Time: 30 minutes Color
Purchase Price: $750

Four programs on ¾″ video cassettes, with two programs per cassette.

Company: Media Five
3211 Cahuenga Boulevard, West
Los Angeles, California 90068
Synopsis:

1. Basics for School and Life—Examines how to gain the strength needed to strive toward success.
2. The Problems of Weakness—Discusses the "acting out" and other weakness symptoms resulting in school disciplinary problems. Details the causes of student weakness that result in alcohol and drug abuse.
3. Eight Steps to Success—Provides the revised and updated approach to applying Reality Therapy to help students move toward personal responsibility and success in school.
4. Ten Steps to Discipline—Emphasis on stopping undesirable behavior, discouraging its reoccurrence, and working toward more responsible behavior with the ten-step disciplinary approach.

Title: Reality Therapy in High School
Author: William Glasser

Time: 29 minutes Color
Rental Fee: $45 per week Purchase Price: $395
Company: Media Five
3211 Cahuenga Boulevard, West
Los Angeles, California 90068
Synopsis: Authentic situations describing how to use Reality Therapy, and how it resulted in an over eighty percent drop in disciplinary problems the first year. Examines the effects of Reality Therapy on the total school climate.

Title: What Is Discipline, Anyway?
Author: William Glasser
Time: 30 minutes Color
(Leader's manual with 25 teacher packets—in-service workshop materials)
Rental Fee: $100
Company: Media Five
3211 Cahuenga Boulevard, West
Los Angeles, California 90068
Synopsis: A look at discipline, differentiating it from punishment. Demonstrates alternative methods of achieving discipline.

Title: A Success-Oriented Classroom
Time: 28 minutes Color
Rental Fee: $40 per week Purchase Price: $375
Company: Media Five
3211 Cahuenga Boulevard, West
Los Angeles, California 90068
Synopsis: A documentary film showing students working alone and with others on mini-contracts. Discussion of techniques and suggestions for guiding and checking student progress.

8

The Behavior Modification Model

It's early morning and the kindergarten children are entering the classroom. Almost all the children enter through the door next to the cloakroom, where they hang their coats and hats and then move into the classroom to begin working on coloring projects at their desks. However, there is one child, Jerry, who does not follow this pattern. Instead, he enters class through the outside hallway door and begins to wander about the room, still wearing his coat. Mr. Sills, the kindergarten teacher, surveys the scene and goes immediately to the first two children who have taken their seats. Standing near the children, Mr. Sills states in a clear, audible voice, "Judy and Robert, I'm so glad to see that you have remembered our classroom rules of coming in through the cloakroom, hanging up your coats, and then beginning to work at your seat. I have a special treat for the two of you. You may help me pass out our "snack" today *and* you may have the extra two cookies I have brought!"

The teacher then turns to the remainder of the students who have also followed the correct entrance pattern. He says, "Each of you who has remembered the classroom rules about 'coming in' will receive one paper punch on your 'play' cards, so that you may earn points to choose the toys you would like to play with during free play period." Jerry glances quickly at the other children, back to the teacher and, seeing what is transpiring, retreats out the hall classroom door and re-enters through the correct cloakroom door, hangs up his clothing, and goes quickly to his seat.

Mr. Sills resisted the tendency to single out Jerry to reprimand him for failing to obey "classroom rules." It would have been easy for him to command, "Go out and come inside like everyone else, Jerry! You know better than this!" Mr. Sills is a teacher who believes in the idea of controlling a child's behavior through the use of incentives and working within a behavior modification framework. A discussion of such techniques often elicits strong opinions. There seems to be little middleground. There are those who swear by behavior modification as the only realistic way of teaching children how to behave properly. There are others who feel that such practices are rigid, inhumane, and that they stifle the "spirit" or creativity of children. Although all of our other cited authors and models have their critics and proponents, none seem to have the "lightning rod" effect of attracting heated debate as the behaviorists have with their philosophy. In this chapter, we will explore the writings of those who advocate Behavior Modification being used in the positive sense of providing rewards and other positive reinforcements. In the next chapter, we will look at two well-known advocates of Behavior Modification who additionally emphasize the use of corporal punishment and other negative reinforcements as practices in shaping behavior. Their stance adds fuel to an already volatile argument.

The Behavioral Position

Behavior Modification techniques with humans came out of the experimental work of Pavlov with his famous (or infamous) salivating dogs. He found he could condition dogs to salivate by ringing a bell when they were about to be fed. During the process of repeated feedings, Pavlov eventually was able to substitute the bell for the food as the *stimulus* for the *response* of salivating. In other words, when the bell rang, even with the absence of food, the dogs got their digestive juices in gear. This admittedly is a somewhat fractured version of Pavlov's experiments, which the reader can pursue for greater accuracy and amplification in any introductory psychology text. The point Pavlov was making was that animal behavior could be explained in terms of stimulus and response. An animal's actions could be traced to an occurrence in the outer environment.

B. F. Skinner, the experimental psychologist, philosopher, and Utopian visionary, is the now recognized leader of the behaviorist movement. He, more than any other, has taken the stimulus-response theory of Pavlov, verified it with other animals (pigeons and mice), and has applied it to the human condition. In essence, a human is no different than any other animal. All human behavior can be explained as responses to environmental stimuli. There is no inner rational person. Any student who behaves rationally does so because of adults who have rewarded correct rational behavior and ignored (or punished) irrational action.

Using Skinner's work as a base, there is a host of writers, psychologists, and educators who have attempted to translate those behavioral principles for teachers to use in classrooms with children who misbehave. It is difficult to pick out one writer who is clearly identified as *the* behavior modification person for teachers. As a result we have drawn from the writings of some of the more popular ones—Axelrod,[1] Bandura,[2] Homme,[3] Madsen and Madsen,[4] Blackham and Silberman,[5] and Walker[6]—to show how these principles work. These writers share a common belief that a student's misbehavior can be changed and reshaped in a socially acceptable manner by directly changing the student's environment. The Behaviorist accepts the premise that students are motivated by the factor that all people will attempt to avoid experiences and stimuli that are not pleasing and will seek experiences that are pleasing and rewarding.

In discussing motivation and school discipline, Madsen and Madsen stated:

> Particular patterns of responses are learned from the external world (external stimuli). If a student is "motivated," it is because he has learned to associate certain behaviors with certain outcomes. Motivation does not exist in a vacuum; it is a way of behaving. If the teacher wants a student to behave in a certain way, the teacher must structure the student's external world (i.e., control his environment) to insure the desired outcome. The disciplined child is a child who (1) has learned to behave socially in appropriate ways, and (2) evidences proper patterns of responses to academic work. If either one of these two general categories of behavior is absent, we usually say the child "has a problem."[7]

Based on this position, Behaviorists would not engage in trying to do detective work to learn what might be the earlier origins of the child's problems. Their position is that the labeling of children as coming from a deprived family background, having a poor early academic background, having been an abused child, or the many other descriptors that suggest to us what has happened to the child gives little or no help to the classroom teacher who needs to deal, daily, with this same child's "acting out" behaviors. For the same reasons, it is useless to discuss a child's "inner feelings" or to expect the child to find his or her own solution. Rather, the teacher must ascertain what is happening in the classroom environment to perpetuate the child's behavior and in turn what can be changed in the environment "to reverse the tide."

Before we begin using the Teacher Behavior Continuum as our common construct in explaining particular teacher practices of the Behaviorists, the reader needs to reorient somewhat. *Because the concept of reinforcement is so powerful and influential, all the other categories (visually looking on, nondirective statements, questions, and so on) are advocated as practices only when they are a form of reinforcement.* In other words, the Behaviorists explain that all these practices emanate from the right-hand side of our continuum. This is illustrated as follows:

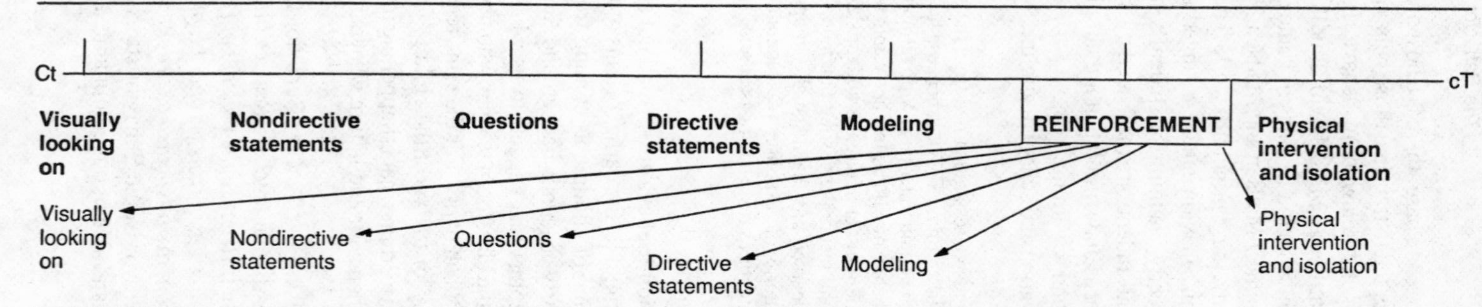

FIGURE 8–1. *Teacher Behavior Continuum (TBC)*

The Basics of Reinforcement

According to Blackham and Silberman,[8] there are three categories of positive reinforcement, as follows.

1. *Token Reinforcement*—A tangible item to be bestowed after desirable student behavior. The token has value in that it can be exchanged for materials or a reinforcing event.
2. *Social Reinforcement*—The use of teacher attention, approval, and praise after desirable student behavior.
3. *Primary Reinforcement*—A tangible item that satisfies a biologically based need. The use of sweets, popcorn, cereal, or something similar after appropriate behavior.

Reinforcers can be generally categorized as *positive* or *negative*. The rewarding of approved behavior with something desired by the student, such as extra recess, candy, praise, smiles, or special privileges, is an example of positive reinforcement. When the rewards are dispensed following a behavior, that particular behavior will increase its rate of occurrence. Negative reinforcers are those happenings or events that a student does not desire (extra homework, staying in at recess, being scolded, being frowned at, being isolated, and the like). The writers cited in this chapter are not strong advocates of the use of negative reinforcement as a practice of punishing a child for incorrect behavior. They believe that punishment is generally ineffective. If the teacher shouts at Judy (negative reinforcement) for talking and Judy stops for a short period of time, the teacher will, when Judy begins talking again, repeat this behavior thinking that the negative reinforcement worked before and will work again. Judy might become less sensitive to the teacher's reprimand, requiring the teacher to shout louder. The effect is one of the vicious cycle. The teacher yells, Judy gets noisier, teacher gets noisier, and the entire class is affected. This negative effect might also be seen when some speeding motorists have to pay fines. They, in turn, might not see the fine as a reason to stop their speeding. Instead, they simply become more skilled at evading the police by watching for them more closely, by purchasing a CB radio, or by buying a radar detector. In this case, the punishment resulted in an increased number of drivers who were in less jeopardy of being caught. A child must learn *how to* behave, rather than *how not* to behave. This learning takes place only when appropriate behavior is shown and is then positively reinforced.

Two interesting twists should be mentioned. First, a negative reinforcement can be used as a positive reinforcer. In other words, the lessening of an undesirable event or activity can be something that is desired. The student will tend to behave in ways to lessen discomfort. For example, the teacher might state, "Jimmy, you have 20 math problems to do for homework this evening. But, if you can remain in your seat and work without talking until the bell rings, I will drop off ten of the required problems.'' Again, just as with positive reinforcement, we get an increase in the desired behavior (seated and working) with the contingency that a negative reinforcer (homework) will be lessened. Secondly, reinforcers will vary in their degree of desirability from student to student. What we as adults assume to be a positive reward might be viewed quite differently by the child. Unbelievable as it may seem, there are some children who do not like ice cream, who do not enjoy the recess period, and who cannot stand listening to popular music or watching television! Not so unbelievable is the reverse observation. What we as adults assume will be unpleasant for students may not be at all. Some students do not mind staying after school, being sent to the principal's office, doing extra homework, and the like. The reader who wonders how the teacher will be able to identify valid reinforcers for individual children can refer to Chapter 6 on Reality Therapy and read Glasser's discussion of privileges.

Reinforcement is based on the premise that a teacher may observe and record behavior of students and the elements in their surrounding circumstances. It is presupposed that the specific behavior is heavily influenced by the events that follow the specific act. For example, if we want kindergarten children to enter the classroom in a certain way, to properly hang up their clothing, and to quietly begin to work at their seats, we follow those behaviors with such positive consequences as, ''You get one punch on your play card which will permit you to choose the play toys or activities you might prefer at 'free play' period.'' Thus, a ''contingency'' is created, which can be defined as those consequences that the student receives dependent on his or her earlier performance. When we order or arrange these ''contingencies'' (also called ''rewards'') and the desired behavior has increased, such as more children entering the classroom in a ''correct'' manner and more often, we can claim we have ''shaped'' or ''conditioned'' the students to behave in that way.

The behavioral technique, unlike our previous models, lends itself to being more exactly controlled and scientifically validated as to ''cause and effect.'' This is done by *recording observable behavior* of students through a process of (1) baseline measures, (2) reinforcement, (3) reversal, and (4) postcheck data.

Let's see how this procedure works. The teacher wants to use ''operant conditioning'' techniques to get his or her fourth-grade children to remain in their seats during ''work periods.'' There is a particular problem with three boys who are continually wandering around the room, and whose behavior has been most distracting. The teacher begins by simply counting the number of children out of their seats during three-minute intervals over a fifteen-minute period during normal work time for five days. The teacher counts fifteen to eighteen times per day and has a ''baseline'' score for ''out-of-seat behavior'' during a *Baseline Stage*. Having done this, the teacher prepares to enter the *Reinforcement Stage*. This stage begins when the teacher gives each student a score card with the numbers 1 to 25 enumerated on it. The students are told that periodically a number will be punched on their card when the teacher sees that they are staying in their seats during work time. Each completely punched card can be redeemed for a prize (ruler, pencil, eraser, candy bar). For the next five days the plan is carried out, with the teacher making a point to punch the cards of other students when the three troublesome youngsters are wandering around, or to punch troublesome children's cards whenever they do sit for a length of time. After a period of applying the reinforcement, the teacher takes a second score for "out-of-seat" behavior over the same three-minute interval for a fifteen-minute period. This score is plotted on a chart (see Figure 8–2) to permit a comparison to be made.

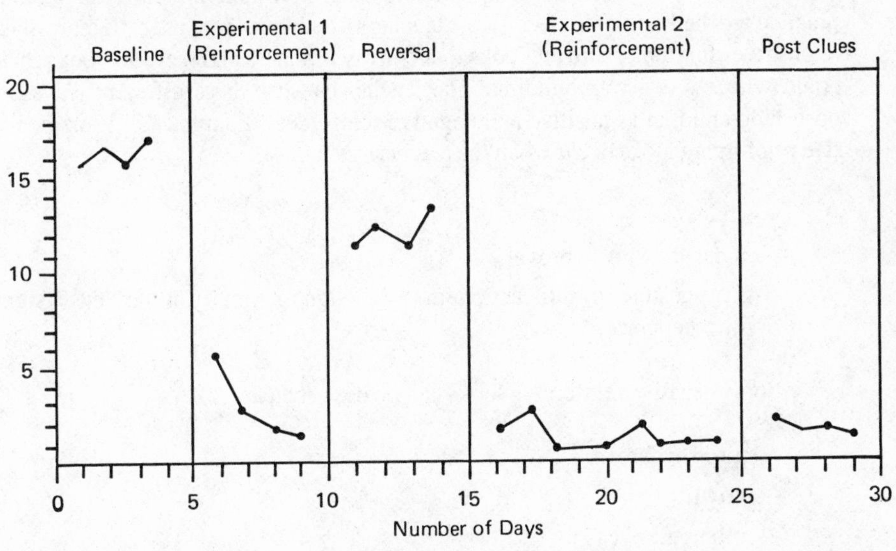

FIGURE 8–2. *Out-of-Seat Behavior*

Since the teacher is experimenting and does not know for certain that it is the reinforcement (punches on the play card) that is making the difference on the second score, the teacher now moves to a third stage called *Reversal*. During this period, the teacher withdraws the reinforcement (punch cards and prizes) and takes a new score of "out-of-seat" behavior. If the score during the *Stage of Reversal* rises dramatically, the teacher can be certain that his or her reinforcements are having an effect and, now, can reapply the reinforcement in the Second Experimental or Reinforcement Stage. If, again, the "out-of-seat" behavioral score drops, there is additional evidence that the contingency or reinforcement is effective. After a sufficient period of time, the reinforcement can gradually be dropped and a postcheck score taken to see if the behavior is lasting and having a long-term effect.

With this rudimentary understanding of reinforcement and the scientific stages of validating cause and effect, we will return to the categories of the Teacher Behavior Continuum as practices of reinforcement. We will move through each category and, when encountering the reinforcement category, we will extend the operability of schedules and different plans for shaping behavior.

Teacher Behavior Continuum and Behavior Modification

Visually Looking On

This generally unintrusive practice of the Non-Interventionists is a bold practice for the Interventionists. Most teachers know that there are different ways to observe children. There are looks that convey kindness and there are looks that could wither a concrete building. The teacher can use these different ways of observing children as positive and negative reinforcers. Examples of some positive reinforcing looks occur when the teacher:

—smiles

—nods, showing approval

—gives gestures of satisfaction (the "V" sign for victory or the "OK" sign for acceptance)

Some negative reinforcing looks can be described as:

—raised eyebrows

—scowl or frown

—rolling the eyes

—shaking the head

—staring menacingly

It might be of interest to a teacher who is experiencing difficulty with a particular child to privately judge (or have an outsider record a sample of time) how many times and types of *visually looking on* reinforcers he or she uses. The teacher might find that he or she is using negative looks at a ratio of ten to one over positive looks. With these data, the teacher may change the ratio to one of ten positive looks to one negative and use the four-stage experimental approach (baseline, reinforcement, reversal, and post check) to see what results may occur.

Once again, we must caution that reinforcers differ for individual students. A teacher working with a small group of children might suddenly stop writing an assignment on the chalkboard to look at Tommy who is crawling under his desk (looking for the pencil that he "accidentally" dropped). A few minutes later the same teacher again gives hostile attention to Tommy, who is now rummaging through his desk, followed by noisily sharpening his pencil, or "borrowing" a piece of paper from an unsuspecting neighbor. If the teacher were to take a baseline recording of the child's disruptive behavior and his or her reactive "visually looking on," the teacher might be surprised to discover that he or she was reinforcing these student behaviors with frowns, scowls, and stares. The teacher then might reverse the process and refuse to "look on" at the student's behavior, but instead only acknowledge Tommy by "visually looking" at him when he was working properly. Only when the teacher caught Tommy being good would his behavior be reinforced with the teacher's visual presence. For Tommy, any type of teacher attention was a positive reinforcement of his preceding behavior. By ignoring the incorrect behavior, the teacher was practicing what psychologists call *extinction*. By removing the reinforcement, Tommy will find his incorrect behavior useless, and therefore he will gradually decrease his practice of it.

The usual practice is for the teacher to ignore a student's misbehavior in conjunction with the awarding of approving looks for correct behavior. The beginning of this procedure is tough on teachers because the student's inappropriate behavior usually *rises* dramatically when it is first ignored. It is as though the child gets frantic, not believing that he or she can't get the teacher's attention as he or she has always been able to do in the past. As a result, the student "shoots the works" and goes through his or her entire previously successful repertoire. A teacher who can "grit out" this initial stage and continue to ignore the child will find his or her patience rewarded. Obviously, the exhibition of some extreme behaviors such as the student who attacks others physically, damages property, or inflicts self-mutilation will prevent a teacher from practicing extinction.

Nondirective Statements, Questions, and Directive Statements

The use of language is valuable both as an important reinforcer as well as a tool for setting up reinforcement plans. Upon detection of a student's misbehavior, the teacher might use quick, direct statements that tell the student to stop. One of our experiences with a student teacher made us more aware of the power of words. This student teacher was having difficulty trying to get Bubba in her fifth-grade class to listen to her. The school psychologist, who was working with the same youngster, sat in on her class. After the class the psychologist gave the teacher a simple analysis of the situation. The teacher had a quiet, soft voice. Whenever she told the offending student to do something, her voice would become high pitched and sound nonassertive. She would also follow up her pleas with a rhetorical question or explanation. She would ask her students to line up and direct a plea to her "problem" student by saying, "Bubba, it's time to get in line. OK? As soon as you do, we can all get going." The school psychologist advised her to go home and practice (using a tape recorder) giving assertive, direct commands in a low voice. Later, in a similar situation, she would be able to look directly at Bubba, make sure that eye contact was established, and then say in a low, clear voice, "Bubba, get in line!"

This change of voice and abbreviation of words worked more successfully than the teacher's earlier attempts with Bubba. Her whining voice, defensive questions, and explanations were a positive reinforcement for the student. He liked what his behavior was doing to her. When she took the offensive and showed control and authority, the language was no longer positively reinforcing to Bubba. Therefore we can see that *how words are said* and *what words are chosen* can be examined by a teacher as a practice to be considered for its reinforcing value.

Let us take a look at language as positive and negative reinforcement.

Questions—positive

—"Lucy, I'd like to help you. Do you need my help?"

—"Melinda, you're usually so happy. What's wrong?"

—"Melanie, did you start that fight? You're so honest that I know you'll tell me the truth. Did you?"

Questions—negative

—"Barbara, can't you do anything right?"

—"Stephanie, what is wrong now?"

—"Veronica, how many times do I need to tell you?"

Directive statements—positive

—"George, you're a smart boy. Use the tools properly."

—"Gus, show me how well you know how to listen."

—"Hector, let's keep cool. You're too good a kid to get into trouble fighting."

Directive statements—negative

—"Charles, you act like a baby. This is what you do."

—"Pete, I get so mad at you when you behave like that."

—"Fred, I'm so disappointed in you."

Most of the behavior modification advocates urge teachers to use language as a positive reinforcer of appropriate behavior and to avoid language as a negative reinforcer. We have already seen how negative reinforcers are often interpreted by students as being better than no reinforcement (or attention) at all. A teacher should be aware of the kind and amount of language that he or she uses with a particular student. It is clear that the ratio should favor the positive over the negative.

Language is also advocated as an information-gathering and explanatory device for setting up individual reinforcement programs with children. The teacher should state directly to the student, "If you do *X*, then you can do, or get, *Y*." (If you do your homework, then you can go out to recess.) It might be necessary to interview students to determine what they value so that you would know what to offer as a strong reward. One junior high school or middle school was having trouble getting students into the classroom immediately after changing classes. It was discovered after interviewing that the students really wanted most of all to be able to go across the street to a local fast-food restaurant during lunch period and to have a school dance on Fridays. The school, therefore, used "going across the street for lunch" and "Friday dances" as reinforcers or contingencies to get students to class on time.

In discussing language, we have deliberately neglected nondirective statements. We have shown how questions and directive statements are important for conditioning behavior. Nondirective statements have little reinforcing value. For a teacher to repeat a student's statement, "So you are mad at Sara for swearing at you," does nothing to correct the behavior. Therefore, behavior modification proponents have little use for such a teacher practice.

Modeling

The use of modeling is an important concept in the behavioral model, and it can be especially helpful for providing disruptive children with an example to imitate. There are three kinds of modeling: (1) modeling of peers (2) modeling of fictitious or idealized characters, and (3) modeling of an important adult. We will discuss each of them in turn.

To illustrate the modeling of peers, we see a kindergarten teacher seated before a semicircle of students. She wants to begin reading a story, but the children are shouting and inattentive. The teacher looks directly at Darlene, who is attentive and waiting patiently for the story to begin. The teacher states, "Darlene, I can tell by your behavior that you are ready for a story. You may be first in line for recess today. Now, I'm going to see who else is ready for the story and I will pick someone to be second." With statements like these repeated over following days, we will discover the students quickly becoming attentive. After a while, the teacher might simply need to say, "I see by Johnny's behavior that he is ready for a story." This teacher has put together modeling with the use of verbal statements as reinforcers to obtain the desired student behavior. Other examples of peer modeling can be seen in such school activities as appointing certain well-behaved students to be the class leader, or the use of school honor societies and award days. These students are held up as models to be emulated by others. When they get special rewards such as plaques, their names and pictures in the local newspaper, or recognition from teachers or administrators, other students may aspire to be like them. (There is always the danger that too much recognition of a particular few will cause envy and hostility. It is best to make such recognition attainable for all.)

The second form of modeling is that of fictitious or idealized characters. It comes as no surprise to teachers who have first-hand experience with students acting like Batman, Muhammed Ali, or Wonder Woman. Today, the characters in TV series, children's books, or films can have a powerful effect for reinforcing both positive and negative social behavior in students. The effectiveness of such modeling can be seen in recent studies (showing the relationship between how much time children view television and the increase in violence among school-age children).[9] In Chapter 6, which is devoted to Dreikurs, we have already mentioned how he uses storybooks and certain storybook characters as examples of behavior that students should follow. The same can be said for the use of television and film stories in the school.

The last form of modeling is that of an adult who is important to a child. In many cases a teacher fits this description (particularly with young children). According to Albert Bandura,[10] who has done the most extensive research in this area, a child will imitate those adults whom he or she would aspire to be like. Such an innocuous statement places a heavy burden on the teacher. *A teacher has to behave in the same manner as what he or she desires from a student.* Let us show how this works:

- A student who screams and is countered by a screaming teacher will continue to scream.
- A physically aggressive student who is disciplined by a physically aggressive teacher will continue to be physically aggressive.
- A perpetually tardy student corrected by a perpetually tardy teacher will continue to be perpetually tardy.

The Behaviorists' explanation for all forms of modeling is that the student observes and emulates behavior that is rewarded. It might be a storybook character who acquires many friends, a cultural folk hero who rises from poverty to fame, or a teacher who has status, authority, and wealth (if they only knew!). Observing this rewarded behavior stimulates a response to imitate. Such a theory makes it quite clear, for example, how a child's life in the ghetto can be turned around by having contact with a famous civil rights leader or a highly regarded teacher.

Reinforcement

Putting together the knowledge about the three kinds of reinforcement (token, social, and primary) and the scientific method of validation (baseline, reinforcement, reversal, and postcheck), with the use of language, the teacher can create a contingency management plan for individual children.

After the teacher determines the appropriate reinforcer, Homme[11] proposes the following steps:

1. Give immediate rewards for short, correct behavior (i.e., coming into the room and sitting attentively for the class to begin.)
2. Keep the rewards based on small steps of correct behavior (i.e., coming into the room quietly, sitting down, looking up).
3. Reward the correct behavior frequently (i.e., every five minutes that the student stays in his seat).
4. Reward the accomplishment, not the obedience (i.e., "If you stay in your seat quietly, you will be rewarded by . . . ," not, "If you do what I say, I will give you . . .").
5. Reward after the performance. Do not let the student determine the sequence (i.e., not the child saying, "I want to play ball another five minutes, then I'll get to work and be quiet." Rather the teacher saying, "You work and be quiet and then you'll have five extra minutes at recess to play.").

Homme refers to his system as contingency contracting, whereby the teacher lays out the bargain plan. "If you (the student) come into the room each day quietly, I'll give you a token. After you've earned ten tokens, you can redeem them for less homework (a magazine, time to play a game, and so on)." Homme goes on to explain that the contract must be fair, clearly understood, honest, positive (what the student will earn, not what he will be deprived of), and lastly systematic. The key to contracting is that the child gains a sense of accomplishment and satisfaction (rewards) for correct behavior.

The reader at this point might be thinking, "How, in my busy and full classroom, can I find the time to be constantly reinforcing one child?" The answer is that the teacher will need to spend a lot of time at first, but then can plan a schedule of reinforcement that is less frequent. There are two basic schedules, the *fixed interval* and the *ratio interval*. In the beginning of the contingency plan, the teacher might use the fixed interval plan, where the child receives a token every morning that he or she is on time and is sitting in his or her seat. After a period of time the teacher might go to a ratio interval, where the student will be given two tokens for behaving properly on "surprise days." The teacher needs to privately plan what days they will occur (Monday and Wednesday one week, Tuesday, Wednesday, and Friday the next). In this way, the child has the incentive to continue behaving each day, not knowing when the "surprise day" will be. The teacher is still dispensing the same ration of tokens, ten for ten days, but less often. There may be occasions when a teacher wishes to "shoot the works" and reinforce daily (or the same time each day), as well as use "surprise days." In this case we have a combination of fixed and ratio intervals. In all cases the point is the same, reward frequently at first and then once the proper behavior is occurring, taper off the frequency.

Another aid in saving time and frustration for teachers is the process of *shaping*. Basically, this is the breaking down of gross misbehavior into simple successive behaviors. The teacher then works on reinforcing behavior priority number one before thinking about number two, three, four, and so on. To be honest, as we all know, there are children who are considered general, all-around nuisances. Not only are they tardy, but they swear, bully, neglect homework, steal, lie, and defy their teachers. According to the tenets of shaping, one key behavior needs to be worked on at a time. Therefore, if the teacher feels that Dennis the Menace would be making some progress if he could get through the first five minutes of homeroom attendance-taking without fighting, then a contingency plan would begin there. (This doesn't help for the remaining six hours and twenty-five minutes, but it's a start.) After success is evident, then the teacher can move to Dennis' lack of attention during reading period, and so on.

Another example of shaping is the case of the teacher who believes that if Carol would work on, and complete, her math assignments that both her math abilities and her grades would improve. However, Carol only comes to school one or two days out of the week, and when she is there, she fights with other students, verbally offends the teachers, and will not remain in her seat, much less attempt to do the math assignments. Her teacher wishes to obtain the "terminal result" of getting Carol to do her math work. In Carol's case, therefore, the teacher initially needed her to simply come to school on a regular basis. Contingencies were set up and a reward was given for attendance. Once at school, the teacher then rewarded Carol for being simply near her desk even though she is still not seated. Finally, with Carol seated, the teacher began reinforcing the child when she picked up her pencil or had her materials at hand. The next step was to get her to finish one problem that the teacher knew she could do. This accomplishment was followed by the teacher gradually increasing the number and difficulty of tasks. Through this "shaping" process, Carol eventually performed the terminal behavior of doing her math assignments. Teachers who seem to have trouble with reinforcement techniques are those who move too fast and do not break the shaping tasks down into small, manageable behaviors that will lead to the final objective.

Physical Intervention and Isolation

As stated earlier, the Behaviorists suggest that there are times when children find misbehavior is more reinforcing (in terms of peer and teacher attention) than proper behavior. Also, it is obviously impossible to begin reinforcing appropriate behavior with desirable teacher rewards until a child exhibits some suitable activity. Mentioned before were the types of destructive behavior that a teacher cannot ignore. For all these reasons, there are times when a teacher is called upon to physically intervene by removing the student from the classroom setting and isolating him or her in a space lacking any reinforcing support. This is generally called a “*time out*” area. The “time out” area might be an isolated seat in the back of the classroom, the hallway, an isolated supply room, or even the principal's office where the child will be out of the view of his or her peers. In order for the “time out” intervention to be successful, the new environment must not be reinforcing for the child. If the student who is isolated doesn't want to be in the classroom with peers in the first place, the isolation becomes desirable and therefore reinforcing. He or she will continue to act out to get “timed out.” The next important consideration is that the area should be nearly void of all stimuli. If a student is sent to a room with toys or interesting magazines to read, or the school secretary chats with the student, then these objects or activities become reinforcing for the student and the “time out” area loses its effectiveness. Generally, the specified period that the student has to stay in the “time out” area should be established when the physical intervention occurs. Some kindergarten teachers might set a five-minute egg timer, while older children can be told the exact time period they will be isolated.

Another form of physical intervention within a behavioral modification framework is the use of *saturation*. There are certain behaviors that students first engage in, such as spitting or striking out, which are sporadic and appear difficult to eliminate with negative or positive reinforcers. The teacher can use saturation techniques to deal with these behaviors. Let's use the example of spitting. The teacher takes the saliva-expelling student to the bathroom and gives him or her several glasses of water. The child is required to spit until the supply of water is exhausted. Saturation can also be used by having an aggressive student repeatedly hit a pillow or inflated doll until he or she is tired. At first these actions are a delight to the child, but as they become tiresome, they become negatively reinforcing. By the time the student has finished, he or she has the feeling that, “I never want to spit (or strike) again.”

Isolation and saturation are not used as forms of punishment. Punishment is one person inflicting pain or discomfort on another. Isolation is used as a neutralizing action, while saturation is simply a forced repetition of the child's previous wrongful act. The repetition should become tiring, but the activity itself will not cause harm to the child. All the writers cited in this chapter resist the use of punitive physical intervention and isolation. They do not advocate corporal punishment or forcing a student to sit in a hostile environment. In the next chapter, we will see how some fellow Behaviorists depart from this position and advocate punishment as essential and effective in promoting good behavior.

Summary

The Behavior Modification writers cite the need for teachers to set easily understood standards of behavior. Their basic premise is that all children will learn

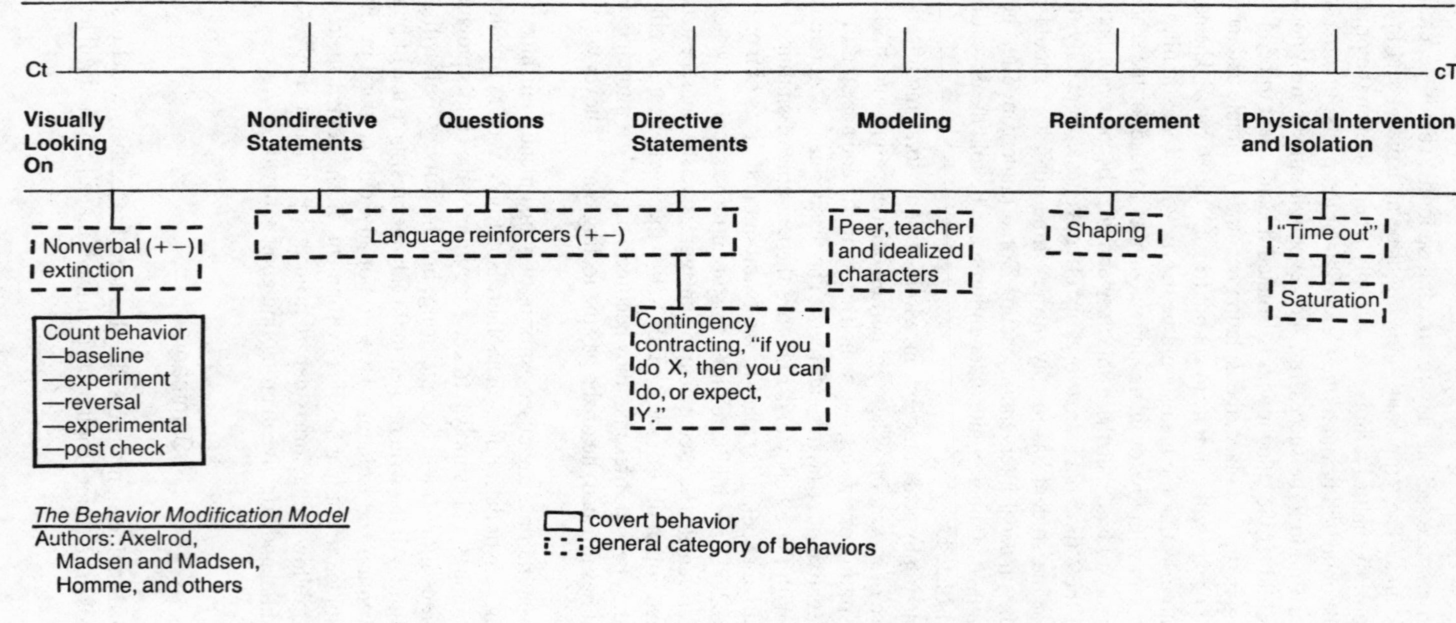
Ct
cT
Visually Looking On
Nondirective Statements
Questions
Directive Statements
Modeling
Reinforcement
Physical Intervention and Isolation
Nonverbal (+−) extinction
Count behavior
—baseline
—experiment
—reversal
—experimental
—post check
Language reinforcers (+−)
Contingency contracting, "if you do X, then you can do, or expect, Y."
Peer, teacher and idealized characters
Shaping
"Time out"
Saturation
The Behavior Modification Model
Authors: Axelrod, Madsen and Madsen, Homme, and others
covert behavior
general category of behaviors

FIGURE 8–3. *Teacher Behavior Continuum (TBC)*

to abide by these standards if they receive proper reinforcement. *Whenever possible, inappropriate behavior should be ignored and acceptable behavior rewarded.* If these means fail, then the teacher must resort to isolation and saturation but must stay away from punishment. The approach should be positive, and a teacher needs to check the quantity of positive (versus negative) reinforcement that is being dispensed.

Using the Teacher Behavior Continuum, we can identify the general categories of teacher behavior and covert behaviors offered in the Behavior Modification Model.

The teacher begins by covertly observing and counting the number of behaviors exhibited by the student(s) over an established time period to establish a *baseline.* Later, similar data are collected in *experimental* phases where reinforcement is applied, and then again when such reinforcements are withdrawn in *reversal* and *post check* phases.

The teacher may also use nonverbal behavior as positive and negative reinforcement, or withhold a "visually looking on" in the form of *extinction.* Depending how it is expressed, the use of language can clearly serve as a negative or positive reinforcement. Through directive statements we may establish *contingency contracts,* where a student agrees to work for some reward. Many behaviors can be learned or taught to students, directly or indirectly, through peers, teachers, and idealized characters, all of whom serve as models to imitate. Many behavioral changes can also be established through "*shaping,*" where the teacher reinforces a series of small behaviors that gradually moves the student towards the desired terminal behavior. The final tools in behavior modification are the use of "*time out,*" where the student is isolated from a reinforcing situation and then returns, usually with the establishment of a *contingency contract,* and the use of *saturation,* where we require the student to repeat an undesirable behavior until it becomes tiring and thus serves as a negative reinforcer.

Notes

1. Saul Axelrod, *Behavior Modification for the Classroom Teacher* (New York: McGraw-Hill, 1977).
2. Albert Bandura, *Principles of Behavior Modification* (New York: Holt Rhinehart & Winston, 1965).
3. Lloyd Homme, *How to Use Contingency Contracting in the Classroom* (Champaign, Illinois: Research Press, 1970).
4. Charles H. Madsen and Clifford K. Madsen, *Teaching Discipline: Behavioral Principles Towards a Positive Approach* (Boston: Allyn and Bacon, 1970).
5. Garth Blackham and Adolph Silberman, *Modification of Child and Adolescent Behavior* (Belmont, California: Wadsworth Pub. Co., 1975).
6. James E. Walker and Thomas M. Shea, *Behavior Modification: A Practical Approach for Educators* (St. Louis: C.V. Mosby, 1976).

7. Madsen and Madsen, *Teaching Discipline: Behavioral Principles Towards a Positive Approach*, p. 7.
8. Blackham and Silberman, *Modification of Child and Adolescent Behavior*, pp. 144–51.
9. Charles Wolfgang, "It's O.K. I'm Biomic!" *Phi Delta Kappan*, 59 (1978):10.
10. Albert Bandura, *Social Learning Theory* (Englewood Cliffs: Prentice-Hall, 1977), pp. 39–48.
11. Homme, *How to Use Contingency Contracting in the Classroom*, pp. 18–19.

References

Axelrod, Saul. *Behavior Modification for the Classroom Teacher*. New York: McGraw-Hill, 1977.

Blackham, Garth, and Silberman, Adolph. *Modification of Child and Adolescent Behavior*. Belmont, California: Wadsworth Publishing, 1975.

Bandura, Albert. *Principles of Behavior Modification*. New York: Holt Rinehart & Winston, 1969.

Bandura, Albert. *Social Learning Theory*. Englewood Cliffs: Prentice-Hall, 1977.

Hessman, Therese. *Creating Learning Environments—The Behavioral Approach to Education*. Boston: Allyn and Bacon, 1977.

Madsen, Charles H., and Madsen, Clifford K. *Teaching Discipline: Behavioral Principles Towards a Positive Approach*. Boston: Allyn and Bacon, 1970.

Homme, Lloyd. *How to Use Contingency Contracting in the Classroom*. Champaign, Illinois: Research Press, 1970.

Instructional Media

Films

Title:	Behavior Modification in the Classroom		
Time:	24 minutes	Color	
Rental Fee:	$22	Purchase Price:	$300
Company:	University of California, Extension Media Center 2223 Fulton Street Berkeley, California 94720		
Synopsis:	Demonstrates teachers using positive reinforcement techniques to modify the behavior of students whose performances suffer because of their distracting behavior or daydreaming.		

Title:	Behavior Modification—Teaching Language to Psychotic Children		
Time:	43 minutes	Color	
Rental Fee:	$55 per day	Purchase Price:	$600

Company: Prentice-Hall, Inc.
Sylvan Avenue
Englewood Cliffs, New Jersey 07632

Synopsis: Examines the steps involved in teaching psychotic children the functional use of speech and discusses the need for correction of self-stimulation and destructive behavior before learning can begin. Describes how instruction may proceed through reward and punishment techniques in the imitation of sounds, labeling of objects, discrimination among alternatives, recall of experiences, and the development of a degree of spontaneity.

9

The Behaviorism/ Punishment Model of Engelmann and Dobson

Ms. Sieckle was writing the spelling words for the day on the chalkboard with her back turned to her class of third-graders. Sitting near the front of the class, Mary Jane Fischer began to make circles with her fingers. She circled her head and then pointed her finger at the teacher's back. The class began to giggle. Ms. Sieckle turned around and faced the class. She spoke sternly, "Let's stop this talking this minute. I have two more words to write down and then we'll begin our spelling lesson."

Mary Jane, who had quickly put her hand down when the teacher turned toward the class, was just as quick to resume her gesturing now that Ms. Sieckle was back at work at the board. Her circular hand motions concluding with the pointed finger was an "in" symbol meaning that the person pointed at was crazy, "cuckoo," or "off his or her rocker." The students could no longer contain their giggles, and unrestrained laughter erupted.

Ms. Sieckle quickly turned, and this time caught Mary Jane in the midst of her antics. She said, "Mary Jane, you stop that this very minute. Do you understand me?" Mary Jane bowed her head and with a sheepish grin mumbled, "Yes, Ma'am." The class was quiet again, but with their attention riveted on Mary Jane. They knew there would be more. Mary Jane would surely have the last word. Sure enough, as soon as Ms. Sieckle turned her back to the class again, Mary Jane's hand went into motion. This time she augmented her circular motions by sticking her tongue out and making faces.

"Actually, it's a rather old form of behavior modification therapy."

Raymond E. Vogler, from *Phi Delta Kappan*

Ms. Sieckle, knowing that Mary Jane was a child who constantly challenged authority, was expecting more defiant behavior. Midway through writing the last spelling word, she spun around and caught Mary Jane with tongue distended, face grimacing, and finger waving. She spoke, "Mary Jane, I told you to stop and you continue to misbehave. I've warned you and now you'll have to be punished." As the teacher spoke, she walked over, grabbed Mary Jane firmly by the arm, and pulled her out into the hall. Closing the classroom door behind them, the teacher spanked Mary Jane hard on the buttocks. Mary Jane felt the pain and began to cry.

After the crying subsided, Ms. Sieckle put her arm around the girl. Quietly, she spoke to the child. "Mary Jane, you can be a very good girl when you want to be. I do not like to punish you, but if you do not do as you're told, you will be punished again. I will not put up with you trying to be the boss. I am in charge in this classroom, not you. Let's see if you can do better." With that last statement, Ms. Sieckle hugged Mary Jane and they both returned to the classroom.

The use of corporal punishment in school is one of the most controversial issues debated between and among educators, psychologists, and parents. In some school districts, as well as in some states, it is absolutely impermissible; in others it is an accepted means of discipline. Any book that purports to contain the major popular approaches dealing with children and the issue of discipline would be remiss if it did not discuss the rationale and practices of those authors who espouse physical punishment as an effective and essential method of controlling children's classroom behavior.

We realize there are some readers who object to this method so strongly that they are about to close this book. There are other readers who are saying, "Well, it's about time we got into the real way of dealing with disruptive behavior." To both kinds of readers we say, "Let's read and think about this chapter carefully." We must not take such a prejudicial stand that our minds are closed to the arguments and evidence pertaining to both sides of this issue. The reader who firmly believes in such an approach has already read through six previous chapters devoted to those authors who believe that physical intervention is morally wrong and/or ineffective. Therefore, it would appear only fair that the reader who is firmly against physical intervention should give at least equal attention to this chapter.

Both Siegfried Engelmann (in his books, *Teaching Disadvantaged Children in the Preschool* and *Preventing Failure in the Primary Grades*) and James Dobson (in his books, *Dare to Discipline* and *Hide or Seek*) have positioned themselves firmly as advocates of corporal punishment. They reserve such punishment primarily for young children. (Dobson approves of its use until the ages of 8 to 10; Engelmann, through the primary grades.) Engelmann admits such a position is not popular. He and Carl Bereiter wrote:

> The writers are quite aware that their suggestions about behavior and especially about punishment, represent an unpopular viewpoint. They were tempted, in fact, to do what some others probably do when offering suggestions about handling behavior problems; say what is more popular, even if it is not what they think . . . the test of whether an adult means what he says is to ignore him and see whether punishment follows.[1]

James Dobson has evidence to indicate that such a position is not so unpopular. His book, *Dare to Discipline,* a clear challenge to teachers and parents to use firm punishment, has sold over 500,000 copies. He sees the reasoned use of physical punishment as essential to rearing children effectively. He wrote:

> How can we teach constructive attitudes to a generation of young people which is no longer listening to our advice? We can't. We must direct our attention toward the next generation of Americans—the children who are still pliable to guidance and training. Not only must we reinstate discipline at home (the first obligation) but the authority of the school must also be reconstructed. Parents have the primary responsibility in both objectives, since the school is largely responsive to their wishes. They should let the teachers and administrators know that they favor reasonable control in the classroom, even if it requires an occasional application of corporal punishment.[2]

The Rationale for Physical Intervention

Engelmann and Dobson justify the use of physical punishment according to the need for children to learn standards of behavior. Engelmann is concerned with those "disadvantaged" students whom he feels have been deprived of the early learning experiences that are common to middle-class youngsters. This deprivation of early home preparation for school results in children from low economic and minority cultures being behind at the beginning of school and falling further behind throughout their school experiences. The focus of his books is not on a child's social-emotional welfare but on ways to accelerate learning. He wants to prevent failure of disadvantaged youngsters by having them undergo direct, repetitive, and sequential instruction in basic skills. He sees such structured instruction as their only hope of "making it" in later society. Many educators take issue with Engelmann's stance, particularly in regard to his definition of "disadvantaged." Such a debate, although important and of interest to many, is not germane to this book. What we are concerned with is, "Why does Engelmann believe in physical punishment?" The answer is that his instructional system is predicated on efficiency. The teacher needs the disadvantaged children to cram in as much instruction in the shortest time possible in order for them to catch up with their middle-class counterparts. A student's misbehavior impinges upon his or her own time as well as the class' instructional time. To use the methods of the Non-Interventionists or the Interactionalists consumes more of that precious time in dialogue, conferences, and the like. The student(s) and teacher could be using that time for academic learning; therefore, dealing with disruptive behavior should be quick and to the point. If a child is doing something wrong, he or she is not learning; thus, the teacher needs to stop the misbehavior and get back to instruction. The quickest way to stop severe misbehavior is to physically punish the child.

Dobson has a different rationale for the use of corporal punishment. Unlike Engelmann, he is concerned primarily with the child's overall social and moral development. Where he is in disagreement with most other writers is that he sees the child as "going to hell" without firmly imposed boundaries. The words "going to hell" are not used in jest. Dobson is a firmly religious person who believes that Christian principles, as he interprets them, should be the guiding rules for working with children. He does not have an optimistic faith in the child's own capacities for solving problems. The varying degrees of reason that the Non-Interventionists and Interactionalists credit the growing child with is absent in Dobson's writings. Dobson takes clear issue with those who do give such credit. In regard to child rearing, he wrote:

> This mother had read that a child will eventually respond to patience and tolerance, ruling out the need for discipline. She had been told to encourage the child's rebellion because it offered a valuable release of hostility. She attempted to implement the recommendation of the experts who suggested that she verbalize the child's feelings in a moment of conflict: "You want the water but you're angry because I brought it too late"; . . . "You wish you could flush Mommie down the toilet." She has been taught that conflicts between parent and child were to be perceived as inevitable misunderstandings or differences in viewpoint. Unfortunately, Mrs. Nichols and her advisors were wrong![3]

Instead, Dobson sees the need for adults to make very clear moral, ethical, and behavioral rules for children, and when those boundaries are violated, the offending youngsters are to be disciplined. In writing how children should be raised according to God's values, Dobson stated:

> Fortunately, the Bible provides the Key to God's value system for mankind, and in my judgment, it is composed of six all-important principles. They are: (1) devotion to God; (2) love for mankind; (3) respect for authority; (4) obedience to divine commandments; (5) self-discipline and self-control and (6) humbleness of spirit . . . when applied, they encourage a child to *seek* out the opportunities in this world rather than forcing him to *hide* in lonely isolation.[4]

Dobson, a former educator who is now a psychologist, does not separate his psychological views from his religious ones. They are integral to each other. Many of us do the same. Although we know that public schools are legally bound to avoid religious teaching, we as individuals cannot make that kind of separation. The ways that we believe and act in our professional lives have to be influenced by our personal, philosophical, and religious beliefs. In Dobson's writings we see a clear rationale for intervening and shaping a child's behavior in order to adhere to his (Dobson's) established religious standards.

Engelmann and Dobson both use the need to attain standards as the justification for teaching the practice of bold intervention. Yet each man's standards differ from the other's quite markedly. Engelmann's is a standard of efficiency and academic attainment; Dobson's is a standard of religious values.

Before we explore their concrete teacher applications through our Teacher Behavior Continuum, a few more words about these two corporal advocates are necessary. *Neither Engelmann nor Dobson advocates the unrestrained, unplanned use of corporal punishment*. They are not advocating physical violence or abuse. *They are not "mean" people who want to see children beat upon*. Whenever they speak of physical punishment it is only in regard to specific situations and to using it with restraint.

Dobson in particular makes a plea that his advocacy not be taken as an excuse for excess. In an interesting aside, he notes how the use of controlled physical punishment by adults might actually protect the child from extremes in this area. His argument goes like this: A teacher (or parent) is having a hectic day and has developed a splitting headache. One child is being particularly bothersome, and the teacher tells the child, "Look, I am tired, have a headache, and want you to keep quiet. Take out a book and read silently." If the child refuses and continues to be obnoxiously loud, the teacher can act in one of two ways: The teacher who does not believe in corporal punishment can, with mounting frustration, continue to tell or ask the child to be quiet. Eventually faced with repeated refusals by the child to calm down, the teacher might explode and irrationally shake or slam the child and inflict real harm. After such an explosion, not only will the teacher feel remorse and shame, but he or she might be vulnerable to legal action. On the other hand, if the teacher believes in corporal punishment, then, after the first instance of refusal, the child's backside gets smacked and the child quiets down. Thus, with the consistent administration of expected and restrained physical punishment, the matter is over. So Dobson's rationale makes for an interesting twist. According to him, reasonable corporal punishment will prevent possible physical harm of an excessive nature.[5]

Regardless of the reader's attitude to this controversial topic, let us all agree with a few points as we begin the Teacher Behavior Continuum. Engelmann and Dobson are respected, educated persons. They, as the other writers cited in this book, want the best for children. With the goal of optimizing every child's development, they have techniques that they believe will work and will be in the best interest of children. Although they realize their techniques may be outside the "popular arena," they have the courage of their convictions and speak out to advocate them.

The Teacher Behavior Continuum with Punishment

Visually Looking On

Engelmann and Dobson use visually looking on as an information-gathering device. They want the teacher to record the circumstances surrounding a child's misbehavior. What is it about the environment that is affecting the student's actions? In most instances, it will be found that the child is receiving a higher payoff in receiving the class' or teacher's attention than if he or she were acting appropriately. This information will serve as the basis for later reversing the payoff for the child.

The teacher does not simply stand back and observe a child when misbehavior is noted. Rather, he or she should step in immediately with directive statements to the child.

(*Note:* Neither Engelmann nor Dobson makes any mention of *nondirective statements,* and neither author is concerned with *questions* as a teacher practice.)

Directive Statements

This is the beginning of Engelmann and Dobson's Interventionist program. Both feel that the teacher should "lay the law down" at the outset of the school year. The teacher should make perfectly clear how students will be expected to behave. At the beginning of the year, the teacher should go over the rules every day and have the students repeat them. For example, some rules might be:

- There is to be quiet during work time.
- Raise your hand and stay in your seat when you want to speak.
- Line up and stay in line when we walk into and out of the classroom.

The teacher, when presenting the rules, should be businesslike, serious, and firm. The rules are not to be changed or discussed; they simply are the laws to be followed. At the same time, the teacher should make clear that those who follow the rules will be better off than those who do not. In fact, children should be told that those who do not follow the rules can expect to be dealt with severely. Dobson cited an appropriate teacher discourse as follows:

> This is going to be a good year and I'm glad you are my students. I want you to know that each one of you is important to me. I hope you will feel free to ask your questions, and enjoy learning in this class; . . . But there's one thing you should know: if you choose to challenge me I have one thousand ways to make you miserable. If you don't believe me, you just let me know and we'll start with number one.[6]

Obviously the teacher should be prepared to back up a statement of this nature. The first time a child misbehaves, he or she should sternly be told to cease. Both Engelmann and Dobson believe firmly in the power of positive reinforcement, but they acknowledge it contains an inherent deficiency. The child who chronically misbehaves provides little opportunity to be positively reinforced for appropriate behavior. It follows that the teacher must coerce the student into making an appropriate response in order to dispense the reward. Only then does a child have an opportunity to see what behaviors have the greatest payoff. Engelmann wrote that the teacher needs to take "the bull by the horns":

> For the serious behavior problem, begin with commands that can be enforced. . . . Start with a set of simple commands, such as "stand up" and "sit down." If the child does not stand up on command, forcefully stand him up. From time to time remind him, "When I say 'stand up,' you stand up." If he manages to make the other members of the group laugh, ignore their responses. If he turns his head away or tries to communicate with other members of the group, forcefully turn his head back. Do not repeat commands. Say, "stand up," count to three to yourself, and forcefully stand the child up.[7]

Modeling

The manner in which a teacher behaves has a powerful effect on his or her students. Teachers who remain businesslike and serious will convey an attitude that they mean what they say. There are more informal times (at recess, lunch, or on the playground) when teachers might loosen up and be more relaxed with students. However, when it comes to teaching and learning, there is work to be done, and the adults in charge need to set that tone.

Dobson takes issue with those who claim that a teacher who uses corporal punishment is serving as a model of physical violence whom students will emulate. He says such an argument is fallacious. A restrained use of corporal punishment does the opposite. The child who goes around smashing things or hitting people must learn that uncontrolled violence is unacceptable. The teacher who uses the paddle or hand on the child's derriere is showing the child that if one goes about being destructive then one can expect to be hurt. Dobson uses the example of a child yanking the dog's tail. The child has every right to be bitten and to learn something about dogs' tails from that moment on. There are ". . . painful consequences of acting selfishly, rebelliously, and aggressively."[8]

The teacher, then, is a model of one who is wiser and more experienced than the student. It is his or her job to circumscribe boundaries of acceptable behavior. When a student transgresses, the teacher is to enforce the consequences, even those that are painful. This does not mean that the teacher is not loving or affectionate. He or she is. The teacher shows genuine love, respect, and understanding for students. Part of this caring attitude is displayed when a teacher takes the time and responsibility to enforce boundaries of behavior.

Reinforcement

Dobson and Engelmann are advocates of behavior modification. They write about the use of all the various types and conditions under which behavior modi fication can be used, with reinforcement, as outlined in the previous chapter. Where they depart from the Behaviorists of the preceding chapter is in their stress on punishment as an equally vital and perhaps more effective tool than any others possessed by the teacher. We must caution the reader again to understand that to only stress the use of punishment as a conditioner, without equal stress on positive reinforcement, tokens, schedules, extinction, and so on, would be doing the models formulated by Dobson and Engelmann a disservice. It would be wrong to think they are negativists rather than positivists in their approach to behavior. Yet, their uniqueness lies in their willingness and commitment to explain how a negative use of reinforcement will work. It is in this realm that we will focus our discussion.

Punishment occurs, showing that the consequences of misbehavior are more costly than the consequences of behaving appropriately. Engelmann believes that punishment is very effective as a negative reinforcement and that a teacher should use it only to turn around a child's misbehavior; then the teacher can resort to positive reinforcement. He suggests that the teacher use negative reinforcement as a last resort, when all other means fail, and then quickly move away from it. Dobson, interestingly enough, disagrees with Engelmann. In our previously mentioned example of his rationale for using immediate physical punishment to save the child from later excessive harm, he urges the teacher to use such punishment of defiant behavior as an initial step.

As the reader may recall, all Non-Interventionists and Interactionalists disagree with the use of punishment. Rudolf Dreikurs and William Glasser in particular point out the difference between punishment and logical consequences. As for an adult using coercive force to inflict psychological or physical discomfort on a child, Dreikurs and Glasser believe it is not only wrong but totally ineffective. Dobson tries to link his interpretation of punishment with that of a logical consequence. He says that when an adult temporarily inflicts pain on a child who is defiant, then that action can be viewed as a logical consequence. He attempts to describe his argument as being compatible with Glasser's view, but we're afraid that one simply cannot link the two. Glasser and others make it clear that infliction of physical pain is not a logical consequence.[9]

What are examples of punishment? Punishment would include some of the following:

- Depriving a student of something of value (recess time, taking away pleasure books, or not allowing a child to see a movie or engage in a prized activity).
- Intimidating the child in a loud, clear, authoritarian voice.
- Isolating a child in a bare enclosure, where the student is forced to stay until the teacher decides when he or she may come out.
- Keeping a student after school.
- Giving the student repetitive and/or undesired work (write fifty times, "I will not do . . .").
- Inflicting physical pain (paddling, spanking, shaking, or using pressure points).

Engelmann and Bereiter see such punishment as only the beginning of treatment. It is used only to stop the student's inappropriate behavior and should be followed by more positive methods of conditioning.

Physical Intervention and Isolation

Isolation: Engelmann, writing with Carl Bereiter, suggests that isolation should be another form of punishment. A child who is acting up should be told to cease. If it's necessary to speak to a child a second time, he or she should be warned that failure to comply will result in being put into the isolation room. The third time is "strike three" and out the child goes. They make it clear that isolation is not to be a pleasant or neutral experience:

> The "isolation room," if it is to be effective, should be an unpleasant place, providing an atmosphere that is far less enjoyable than that of the study room. A small, poorly lighted closet with a single chair will serve quite well.[10]

Dobson also sees the use of isolation from the teacher's point of view. A student who is constantly showing off and being a general nuisance should be put into an isolated area. This area should be away from all activity. However, the offending child should be able to see the activities that he or she is missing. Every time the child acts up, the teacher should increase the child's time in the area. When the teacher re-admits the child, the teacher should attempt to use positive reinforcement (or what Dobson calls the "miracle tools of bribery") to give attention to correct behavior.

The teacher regulates the amount of time in isolation. Unlike models described by other writers, students in this model do not decide when they are ready to return. The child who fails to return to the classroom with acceptable behavior can expect to be kept in isolation for increasingly longer periods of time. Even though certain children might dislike school, most dislike being alone even more. Eventually, the disruptive child will decide to learn how to act in school in order not to be banished.

Physical Intervention: As previously explained, Dobson and Engelmann advocate the use of physical intervention, not only in the sense of isolating a child or preventing a child from hurting himself or herself and others, but also for the purpose of causing physical pain and thus "teaching the child a lesson." They agree that it is a particularly effective measure and that it works well with young children. Once a child has reached adolescence, physical punishment is no longer advocated. It causes older students who think of themselves as adults uncalled-for humiliation. A teacher who uses paddling or spanking with an adolescent is not only compounding the student's problem but is also setting up himself or herself for severe reprisals We know of students who have lashed back physically, have slashed tires, and have used knives and firearms in retaliation. The teacher who uses physical punishment on a potentially violent adolescent is simply "asking for it."

Dealing with a younger child (up to fourth grade or about age ten) is a different matter. This child, according to Dobson and Engelmann, needs to be startled by pain as part and parcel of child rearing. Only when they are hurt as youngsters do they learn the boundaries of acceptable behavior to be remembered for adult life. This is why students who have had teachers who physically drew the line with them in the early and intermediate grades will theoretically not need to be physically "hurt" in adolescence. Reinforcement and reasoning at that age should do the job. Of course, as reasonable as this sounds, it does not help the middle-school teacher who is dealing with students who failed to learn the original lessons. For help, these teachers must return to the teacher behaviors and principles of behavior modification as described in direct commands, reinforcement, and isolation, in this and in the previous chapter.

How does the teacher of young children use corporal punishment? Let's begin with Dobson. He believes that the teacher must distinguish between intentional and unintentional behavior. The student who knowingly breaks a rule should not be "hit." It is only when the student is told *(direct statements)* to cease and the child openly defies the command that he or she deserves a little pain. Let us look at the example in the beginning of this chapter. If Mary Jane had stopped her finger waving and funny faces after the first (or even the second) time, then the matter would have been settled. Ms. Sieckle only spanked Mary Jane after the child was fully aware of what the teacher wanted her to stop doing and yet persisted in her behavior. Inflicting "pain" should only result when a child challenges the teacher's authority. It is the Interventionist's position that the teacher has to have power and control over the child's behavior. When the child challenges that power, the teacher needs to exert the necessary authority to show that he or she is indeed the boss. Following are examples of situations that *would* merit physical punishment:

- The child talks back to the teacher after being told not to.
- The child refuses to pick up or clean up after being told to.
- The child taunts the teacher by telling the class that the teacher is wrong and that the students should listen to him or her instead.
- The child knowingly lies to the teacher, and when confronted, refuses to confess.

Following are examples of situations that *would not* merit physical punishment:

- The child gets into an argument or fight with other students.
- The child does not finish his or her classwork (or homework) on time.

- The child breaks an object by mistake.
- The child spontaneously yells out of turn.

Once a teacher has clear evidence that the student is testing *(openly and defiantly)* his or her authority, the teacher should proceed in a three-step, restrained, calm manner. The first step is that the child should be taken away from the eyes of others. Second, the teacher should tell the child why the punishment is occurring and then spank or paddle the student once on the padded part of the buttocks. Dobson cites an alternative to spanking. It involves squeezing the shoulder muscle. He wrote that:

> The shoulder muscle is a surprisingly useful source of minor pain; actually it was created expressly for school teachers.[11]
> . . . when firmly squeezed, it sends little messengers to the brain saying, "This hurts; avoid recurrence at all costs."[12]

The third step is that, after the punishment has been meted out, it is time to comfort, console, and give affection. The child will usually cry and feel badly; he or she is ready to be loved and told how to avoid such a recurrence in the future. *Dobson is adamant about giving love and warmth to the offending child.* The teacher should not remain angry, aloof, and unapproachable. The matter is over with and the teacher should welcome the child back.

Engelmann supports the use of physical intervention when a student is not attending to the lesson at hand. His concern is with children "catching up" academically. When a student is being disruptive, precious moments are being wasted. He also adds that one cannot begin to use behavior modification approaches with a student who displays no appropriate behavior to reinforce. Therefore, initially the child must be forced to behave properly. The student who is constantly out of his or her seat should be grabbed and forcefully put down.

Engelmann believes that the teacher should use physical punishment with a student who is engaging in habitual, unthinking behavior. This is a different criterion than Dobson's view of using such punishment for a student who is engaged in openly defiant behavior. Engelmann's opinion is that it is the unthinkingly loud, active, aggressive, or destructive student who needs immediate punishment. This child has no alternative behavior; he or she has always acted in this manner, and the teacher must forcefully stop it. Only then can new behaviors be learned. The use of verbal commands (directive statements) alone is not effective with this child. Bereiter and Engelmann wrote:

> In such a situation, the meaning of the teacher's words should be made clear by demonstrating the consequences that result when they are ignored. Sometimes the best definition comes in the form of anger—a slap or a good shaking.[13]

Comparing Engelmann and Dobson with Others

The one issue that clearly separates Engelmann and Dobson from the other authors of child management books is their belief in corporal punishment. The Behaviorists cited in the preceding chapter urge the use of positive conditioning but resist the use of negative reinforcement or physical pain. The Non-Interventionists and Interactionalists are even more adamant in this view. They believe that the teacher does not have the ethical or moral right to use such force, and furthermore, it's use merely adds to a student's problem. Glasser and Dreikurs take issue with Engelmann and Dobson over the effectiveness of punishment. They state that inflicting physical pain is totally *ineffectual* in changing a child's behavior. Engelmann and Dobson state that inflicting physical pain is the *most effective practice* a teacher has at his or her disposal.

Four "experts" have been presented with two diametrically opposed positions. Who is right? The reader will need to make his or her own determination.

Summarizing Engelmann and Dobson

Although Engelmann and Dobson have some differences, we can extract some common procedures for dealing with disruptive children along the Teacher Behavior Continuum (see Figure 9–1). Covert teacher behaviors are as follows: (a) The teacher observes the circumstances surrounding a child's misbehavior. He or she judges what is reinforcing the behavior. (b) The teacher models behavior that is serious and businesslike, particularly during class work time.

The overt teacher behaviors are as follows: The teacher gives (1) *directive statements*. He or she tells the class repeatedly what the class rules are. The student who misbehaves is immediately told to stop and behave appropriately. If the child conforms, the teacher uses (2) *reinforcement*. If the child does not behave correctly, the teacher uses (3) *isolation* in an uncomfortable setting with the teacher deciding when the student can return. However, if the student's inappropriate behavior is an open challenge to the teacher's authority (Dobson), then the teacher needs to use (4) *physical intervention* by paddling, spanking, or squeezing. If the inappropriate behavior is habitual (Engelmann), the teacher needs to shake, slap, or spank. Once correct behavior is forthcoming, the teacher returns to (5) *reinforcement*.

Notes

1. Carl Bereiter and Siegfried Engelmann, *Teaching Disadvantaged Children in the Preschool*, (Englewood Cliffs, N.J.: Prentice-Hall, 1966), pp. 90–91.
2. James Dobson, *Dare to Discipline* (Wheaton, Illinois: Tyndale House Publishers, 1970), p. 107.

Ct —— cT

Visually Looking On	Nondirective Statements	Questions	Directive Statements	Modeling	Reinforcement	Physical Intervention and Isolation
(a) Observe, gather information on circumstances. (What is the payoff?)			(1) Tell students the rules; repeat many times. — Tell student to stop misbehaving. —Tell student what to do.	(b) Teacher behaves businesslike.	(2) Reinforce appropriate behavior. (5)Reinforce appropriate behavior.	(3) Isolate for inappropriate behavior in uncomfortable place on teacher's terms. or (4) If student is defiant (Dobson) or unthinking (Engelmann), inflict physical pain.

The Behaviorism/Punishment Model

Authors:
James Dobson
Siegfried Engelmann

FIGURE 9–1. *Teacher Behavior Continuum (TBC)*

3. Dobson, *Dare to Discipline*, Introduction.
4. James Dobson, *Hide or Seek* (Old Tappan, N.J.: Fleming H. Revell Company, 1974), p. 158.
5. Dobson, *Dare to Discipline*, pp. 24–25.
6. Dobson, *Dare to Discipline*, pp. 98–99.
7. Siegfried Engelmann, *Preventing Failure in the Primary Grades* (New York: Simon and Schuster, 1969), p. 77.
8. Dobson, *Dare to Discipline*, p. 41.
9. William Glasser, "Disorders in Our Schools: Causes and Remedies," *Phi Delta Kappan*, January 1978, p. 331.
10. Bereiter and Engelmann, *Teaching Disadvantaged Children*, p. 83.
11. Dobson, *Dare to Discipline*, p. 26.
12. Dobson, *Dare to Discipline*, p. 24.
13. Bereiter and Engelmann, *Teaching Disadvantaged Children*, p. 87.

References

Bereiter, Carl, and Engelmann, Siegfried. *Teaching Disadvantaged Children in the Preschool*, pp. 90–91. Englewood Cliffs: Prentice-Hall, 1966.

Dobson, James. *Dare to Discipline*, p. 107. Wheaton, Illinois: Tyndale House Publishers, 1970.

Dobson, James. *Hide or Seek*. Old Tappan, New Jersey: Fleming H. Revell Company, 1974.

Engelmann, Siegfried. *Preventing Failure in the Primary Grades*. New York: Simon and Schuster, 1969.

Instructional Media

Films

Title: New Approaches to Big Problems

Time: 29 minutes — Color

Rental Fee: $45 per week — Purchase Price: $395

Company: Media Five
3211 Cahuenga Boulevard, West
Los Angeles, California 90068

Synopsis: Ideas on a variety of problem areas including discipline, human relations, authority, self-concept, truancy, and violence are presented in this film. Illustrated documentary segments.

Filmstrips

Title:	Dare to Discipline
Author:	James C. Dobson Two filmstrips with two cassettes with Teacher's Guide
Purchase Price:	$45 Color
Company:	Media Five 3211 Cahuenga Boulevard, West Los Angeles, California 90068
Synopsis:	Demonstrates the "take charge" approach to achieving discipline in the classroom. The approach enables teachers to set firm, consistent limits while recognizing students' needs for warmth and positive support.

10

Decision Making: "The Teacher's Point of View"

Having gained an understanding of the various Teacher-Student Interaction models and techniques and how they are positioned on a "power" continuum, we now look at ways a teacher might use these methods. How these methods are employed will be based on a decision-making process that uses as its foundation, the teacher and his or her values. There may be many teachers who feel, "I simply do not like the verbally controlling and powerful techniques used by the Interventionists." These teachers may feel that those models dehumanize students, training them "as if they were animals" lacking in rational thought. Such teachers would, based on their values, be most likely to use behaviors with students similar to those held by the Non-Interventionist models. There might be other teachers who also reject the Interventionist techniques, but who may feel that the Non-Interventionists live in an idealized world, using techniques that might be appropriate in a theoretical situation but would not work in a dynamic classroom. These teachers might feel quite at home with the use of the Interactionalist techniques and models. Finally, there will be teachers who state, "Students must show me first that they can be trusted! Until that occurs I will decide on appropriate behavior and then go about getting that behavior from students." Of course, this group of teachers has the powerful Interventionist techniques available to them. For the reader who needs help to clarify his or her beliefs, a survey of "Beliefs About Discipline" is included in Appendix A.

The teachers just described would seem to be comfortable employing only those models and methods associated with one school of thought. This might be well and good, if each of these techniques were to *always* work with *all* children. In our experience, however, this is generally not the case. The danger, we believe, in defining oneself too narrowly with one school of thought or one model lies in the possibility that one might be limiting his or her choices. If teachers were to eclectically broaden their decision-making bases, they might well find they were able to utilize the valuable elements possessed in all models. Our position is that teachers today need *all* of the techniques available in working with diverse populations of students, and that by combining and using the elements of each approach, a teacher can truly become more effective. How can this be done? We suggest a series of three pathways, based on the teacher's decision-making processes.

Before taking a journey down these pathways, it is imperative to determine where the journey will end. What is our final goal when it comes to the issues of desirable behavior for students?

It is our contention that the aim of education in today's society, a time of intense change, is to promote free-thinking, rational, sensitive, and internally motivated, cooperative workers. In talking with psychologists and educators of various orientations (Non-Interventionists, Interactionalists, or Interventionists), there seems to be a surprisingly high degree of consensus on such matters as the aims of education, as well as the ultimate goal of all disciplinary approaches. These individuals generally agree that the ideal outcome would be for students to achieve self-control over their own behavior. Their disagreements and what is central to the issues that divide them into separate schools of thought and action are the procedures to be followed to achieve the ultimate outcome, and the assumptions each accepts on what it is that motivates human behavior.

The Non-Interventionists believe that a self-monitoring individual is developed by means of minimal adult control. The Interactionalists believe that such a student is developed by a mutually active exchange between teacher and student. The Interventionists believe that a student's self-control is promoted by systematic external teacher reinforcement that becomes habitualized by the student. Therefore, although the goal of self-control is the same, the three schools of thought are quite different, especially in regard to the use of power by the teacher and the amount of autonomy given to the student.

We are asking the teacher to share with us a belief in this ultimate goal: the realization of students who have achieved self-control and who can use self-discipline. With acceptance of this goal, the teacher may understand the rationale and direction of the three eclectic pathways we will now describe.

Three Pathways and Their Directions

If the teacher were to take a broad view of all the overt teacher behaviors described in the many models placed along the power continuum, three pathways might be suggested.

Pathway I, "From Student Power to Teacher Control," can begin with the methods suggested by such Non-Interventionists as Gordon and his *T.E.T.* techniques. These techniques give students a lot of power to control their own behavior and make decisions. However, if such methods did not work for the teacher, then he or she would have the option of moving gradually up the continuum of models, attempting first the Interactionalists' techniques and finally, if need be, using the powerful Interventionists' techniques to obtain the desired student behavior. To repeat, Pathway I, "From Student Power to Teacher Control," asserts that students should be and can be given the power and autonomy to maintain control over their own behavior. Should this method fail with a particular child or the class, however, the teacher then is not locked into the less powerful model. Instead, the teacher is free to gradually change his or her techniques to travel across the continuum to more powerful models until the desired success is obtained. (See Figure 10–1.)

Ct		cT
Non-Interventionist	**Interactionalist**	**Interventionist**
Pathway I: Begin - - - - - - - - - →	(lack of success)	- - - - - - - - - - - → End
Pathway II: End ← - - - - - - - - - - -	(with success)	← - - - - - - - - - - Begin
Pathway III: End ← (with success) ← - - - -	Begin	- - - - → (lack of success) → Go to (Pathway II Begin)

FIGURE 10–1. *Directional Pathways for Teacher Movement*

Pathway II, "From Teacher Power to Student Autonomy," suggests a directional movement opposite from that taken by Pathway I. The teacher begins with powerful Interventionist techniques; when these methods are *successful,* the student is gradually given more power as the teacher changes his or her techniques to fit the Interactionalist mode; with continued success, the teacher is able to retreat to minimal power techniques found in the Non-Interventionist model. The movement of Pathway I implies that a *failure* of the teacher techniques might occur, and a gradual movement to more teacher control would be necessary. Then, once control is obtained, the teacher might return to Pathway II. This move suggests that the techniques have succeeded and that students can be given more power, autonomy, and choice, and this success finally leads the teacher to move to a

Non-Interventionist position. One can see that, for each pathway, the ultimate goal is to finally move to the Non-Interventionist techniques with a parallel movement whereby students become autonomous and self-disciplined. (See Figure 10–1.)

Pathway III, "From Shared Power to Student Autonomy *or* Teacher Control," presents a fork in the road at which the teacher can branch off into one of two directions. The teacher can begin with the shared power techniques of the Interactionalists and, having found success with these techniques, take the branch of the fork that leads along the continuum to the Non-Interventionist techniques, much like Pathway II. If these shared power techniques do not succeed, the teacher can take the other branch and progress to the powerful Interventionist techniques, similar to Pathway I. (See Figure 10–1.)

Operationalizing the Pathways

In all three pathways the procedure is to move along the pathways, using the necessary power not only to find techniques that work but also to gradually move to the Non-Interventionists' position giving students freedom to make choices and to control themselves. The teacher, of course, could follow this progress with one student or work with an entire class. Such a directional movement might sound logical, but how does one teacher integrate such eclectic models?

All of the specific overt (and some covert) teacher behaviors of each model have been extracted onto a single chart entitled The Teacher Behavior Continuum for All Models. (See Chart 10–1.)

This "smorgasbord" of teacher behaviors can now be used in an eclectic manner based on the pathway that a teacher believes in. A teacher who chooses to use Pathway I should begin on the left-hand side of the chart, using those overt behaviors found in Visually Looking On and Nondirective Statements (critical listening, acknowledgments, adult responses, "I" messages, active listening). A teacher who chooses to use Pathway II should begin on the right-hand side of the chart, using those overt behaviors found in Isolation, Physical Intervention and Reinforcement (Isolation in uncomfortable area, time out, negative punishment, saturation, positive reinforcement, shaping). A teacher who uses Pathway III should begin in the middle of the chart, using those overt behaviors found in Questions, Directive Statements, and Modeling (verifying questions of social goal, confronting, mutual plan, plan with logical consequences, and classroom meetings).

This book is for *professional* teachers, people who can make decisions based on the knowledge of available alternative techniques. To tell the reader to actually begin at a certain block of overt behaviors and then to follow an exact step-by-step progression would be insulting to a professional. Instead, *parameters* for deciding upon where to begin and a general *direction* of movement are what we advocate.

	Non-Interventionists			Interactionalists		Interventionists		TBC
Overt Behaviors				as a part of logical consequences	(4)institution (3) out of school (2) school off to (1) class	time out nonreinforcing area	isolation in uncomfortable area	Isolation
				as a part of logical consequences		saturation	punishment (physical)	Physical Intervention
		affirm student OK feelings		reap natural or logical consequences encouragement	reap consequences of plan	positive shaping	negative positive	Reinforcement
	6 steps to problem solving Method III	class discussion and exercises with PAC	group exercises	class discussion	classroom meetings	positive model with (+) reinforcement	businesslike attitude by teacher	Modeling
	Influencing	adult responses		make a plan corresponding to goal tell logical consequences confronting	make a mutual plan	contingency contracting	tell rules tell to stop tell what to do	Directive Statements
	door openers	adult responses	confronting, probe for value	verify questions 1, 2, 3, 4	confronting "stop" confronting "what?"			Questions
	"I" messages active listening		active listening					Nondirective Statements
	acknowledgments critical listening	adult responses				extinction reinforcing (−)(+)		Visually Looking On
Models	Gordon's Supportive	Communication (T.A.)	Valuing	Dreikurs's Social	Glasser's Reality	Behavior Modification	Behavior Modification with Punishment	TBC
Covert Behaviors	determine problem of ownership	diagnosis teacher and student PAC	look for value indicators	observe the student ask oneself questions 1, 2, 3, 4	observe the student		observe (what is the payoff)	

CHART 10–1

Following is a guide for making teacher choices according to the three pathways. We leave it to the teacher to make the actual decision of what techniques to employ. The reader might wish to refer to Appendix B, where three samples of actual case studies, written by teachers, are included.

Due to the technical explanations to follow, the reader might wish to simply look at Figures 10–2 through 10–10 and then move on to the next chapter. At the end of the book, the teacher might return to these explanations in developing his or her own plans.

Pathway I: "From Student Power to Teacher Control"

The beginning point in "choice A" for the teacher (see Figure 10–2) who wishes to start from a position of awarding students maximum power is an evaluation of the problem in relationship to Gordon's "problem ownership." The question is, as a teacher, does this problem have a *concrete* effect upon me? If not, the student "owns" the problem, and our response is simply to use *active listening* and attempt to maintain an emotionally supportive relationship with the student but not to accept the responsibility to solve this child's problem. Or, the teacher may wish to help the student explore his or her problems, and thus use *values clarification* to help the student to reflect more critically on the dilemma facing him or her.

The problem a student presents to us might not have a direct concrete effect on us. However, one can assume that, because of the "areas or sphere of freedom" a teacher has working in a school structure, it is possible for teachers to get into difficulty with those in authority, such as the principal, superintendent of schools, or school board because of the problem. (Or, the problem might even have legal implications for the teacher.) For example, you, as a high school teacher, have been given the responsibility to supervise an outdoor area during the lunch period, during which time you are to also enforce a "no smoking" rule. You are aware that a small group of students frequently hide behind the corner of the school building to smoke cigarettes during the lunch break. What are you to do? You are placed in a real moral dilemma, particularly since many of the students realize that you also smoke. Teachers often find themselves in such situations, whereby on one hand the student's actions do not have a "concrete effect" on them, but on the other they are supposed to enforce an arbitrary unilateral rule. One way of solving such a dilemma is to decide whether such bureaucratic rules, much like early attempts at prohibition in this country, are really enforceable. You therefore might dare to simply "ignore" the behavior and risk censure by the principal. A high school teacher taking this position would simply walk near to the smokers' corner of the school building and stop for a few minutes to talk loudly to nearby students, before turning the corner to find there was not a smoker in sight!

You may also choose to "do your duty" and enforce the unilateral school

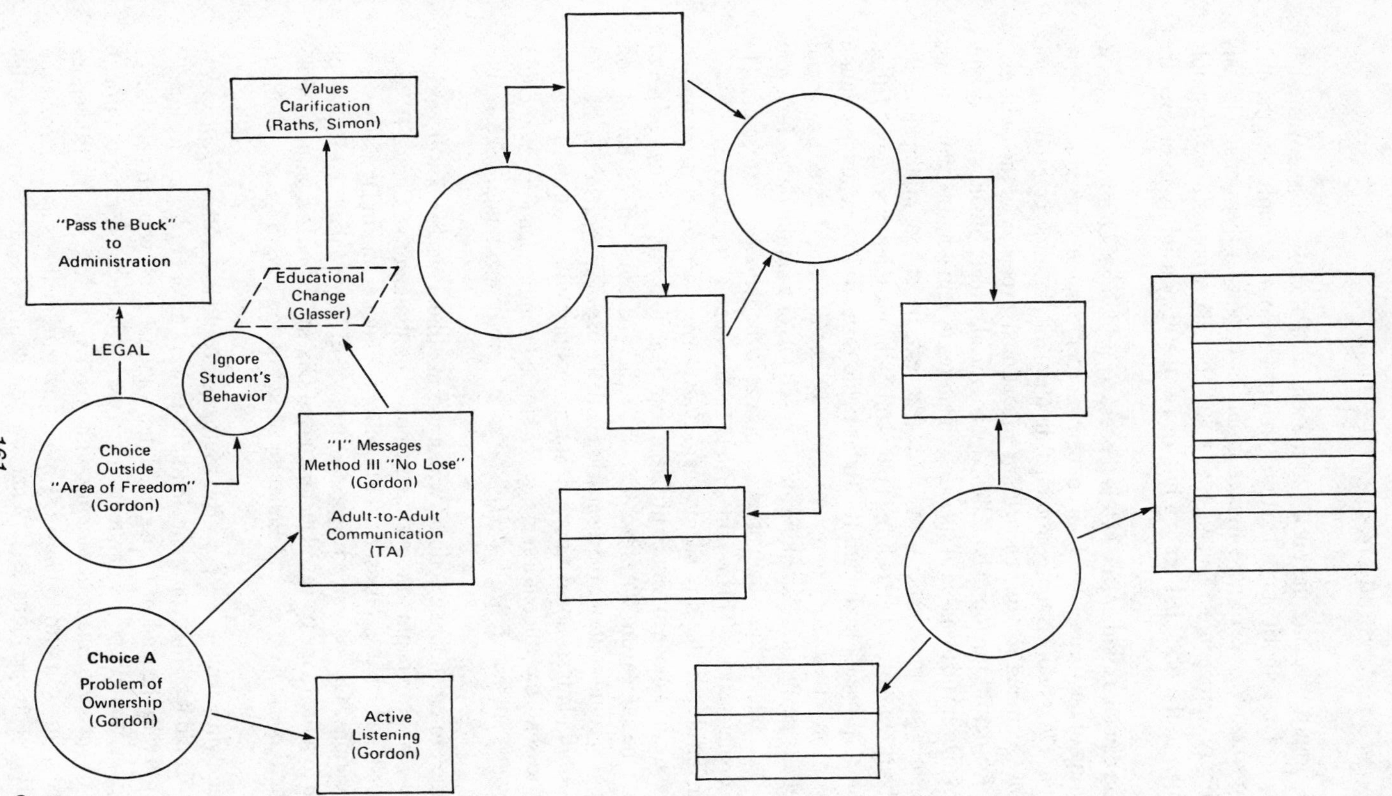

FIGURE 10–2. *Pathway I, "From Student Power to Teacher Control," Choice A*

rules by simply "passing the buck" to the administrator. If the rule was established by higher authority outside your "area of freedom," simply turn the misbehaving student over to those figures in authority and let them deal with any "disciplinary" procedures. Students can be taken to the school office and simply turned over to the principal, giving him or her the responsibility to enforce the rule.

You can take another step in this process by bringing such arbitrary rules to the attention of the faculty or school council in order to make some educational or rule changes that address these problems. In terms of the smoking problem, you may want to embed in your curriculum educational experiences that will give students factual information about the psychological effects of smoking, or you may want to bring up the issue of sneaking cigarettes in value-clarification sessions with your classes. In working with fellow teachers, the school principal, or the student-body council, you may bring up this problem and attempt to use a Method III "no lose" process (see Figure 10–2) that could result in an acceptable solution for everyone involved. For example, it might be decided that the students would want a legally designated "smoking area" in school, or a similar desire for a rule change. The students could then bring a proposal to the school board to attempt to get these changes made. This would seem to be democracy in practice.

Conversely, if the original problem *does* have a concrete effect on the teacher, you could move to a much different path of action. First, you would begin by sending the student an *"I" message* to show the "behavior-effect-feeling" on yourself. You could continue the discussion with the use of *active listening* or with *Adult-to-Adult* (Transactional Analysis) statements that will be carefully worded so as not to send the student a message of crossed communication. You could also enlist the student in *Method III "no lose"* problem solving. (See Figure 10–2.)

If the aforementioned actions, which use minimum teacher power, are not successful, you can begin to move up the power continuum to "Choice B" (see Figure 10–3), which uses Glasser's *confronting* techniques and/or Dreikurs's *verifying* questions. Or you can advance to "Choice C" (see Figure 10–3), which moves on to more of the powerful techniques of Glasser's "*make a plan,*" Dreikurs's *logical consequences,* and Behavior Modification's *contingency contracting.*

When you take the less powerful route, you could ask such *verifying questions* as "Could it be that you want attention? power? revenge? to be left alone?" After identifying the student's misguided motivational goal, you can help him or her to begin to achieve power or attention in a socially acceptable manner through your use of *encouragement* or *shaping* with positive reinforcement. If this does not succeed, you can turn to Glasser's more powerful methods and *confront* the student with such questions as, "What are you doing?" and "How does this help?" Then, when you are faced with "Choice C," you can press the student to "*make a plan*" while using *contingency contracting* or *logical consequences.*

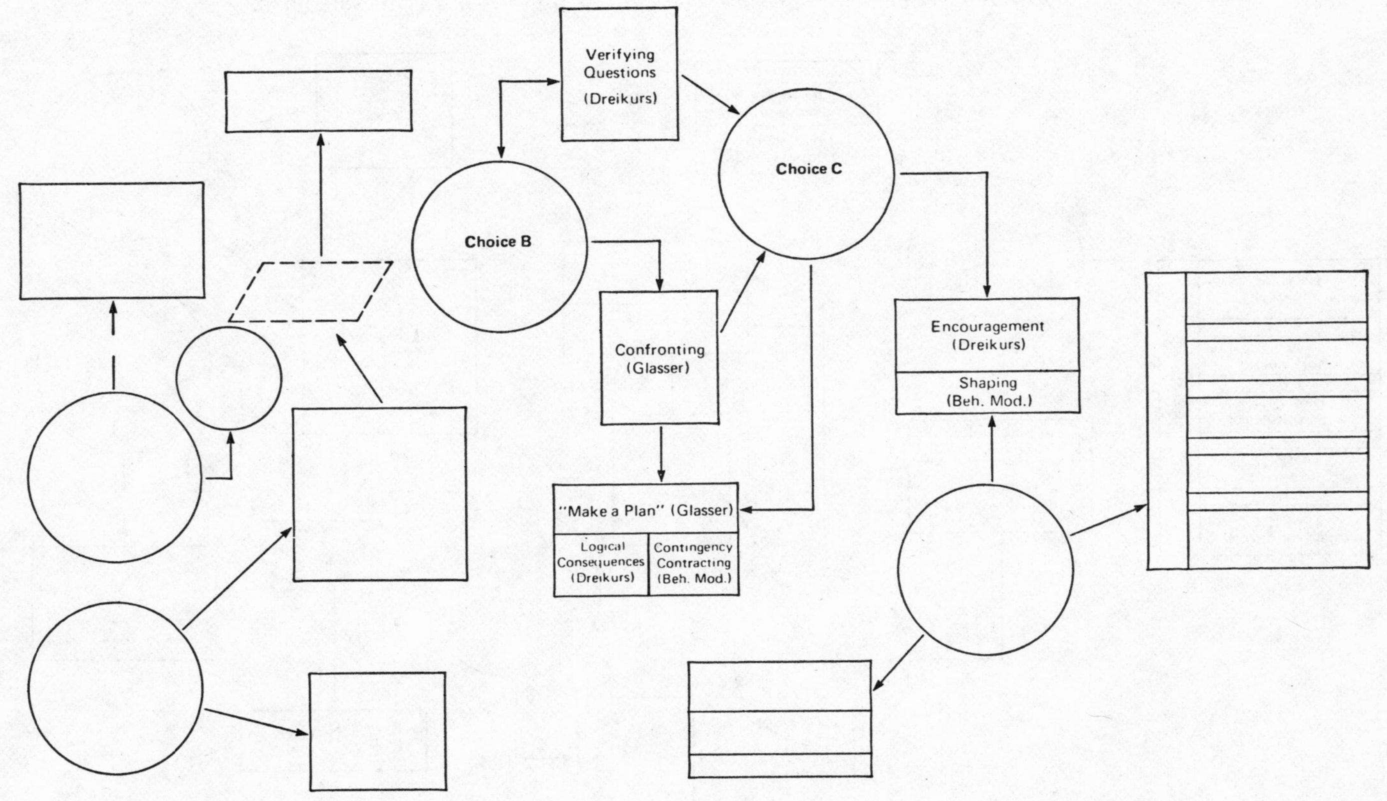

FIGURE 10–3. *Pathway I, "From Student Power to Teacher Control," Choices B and C*

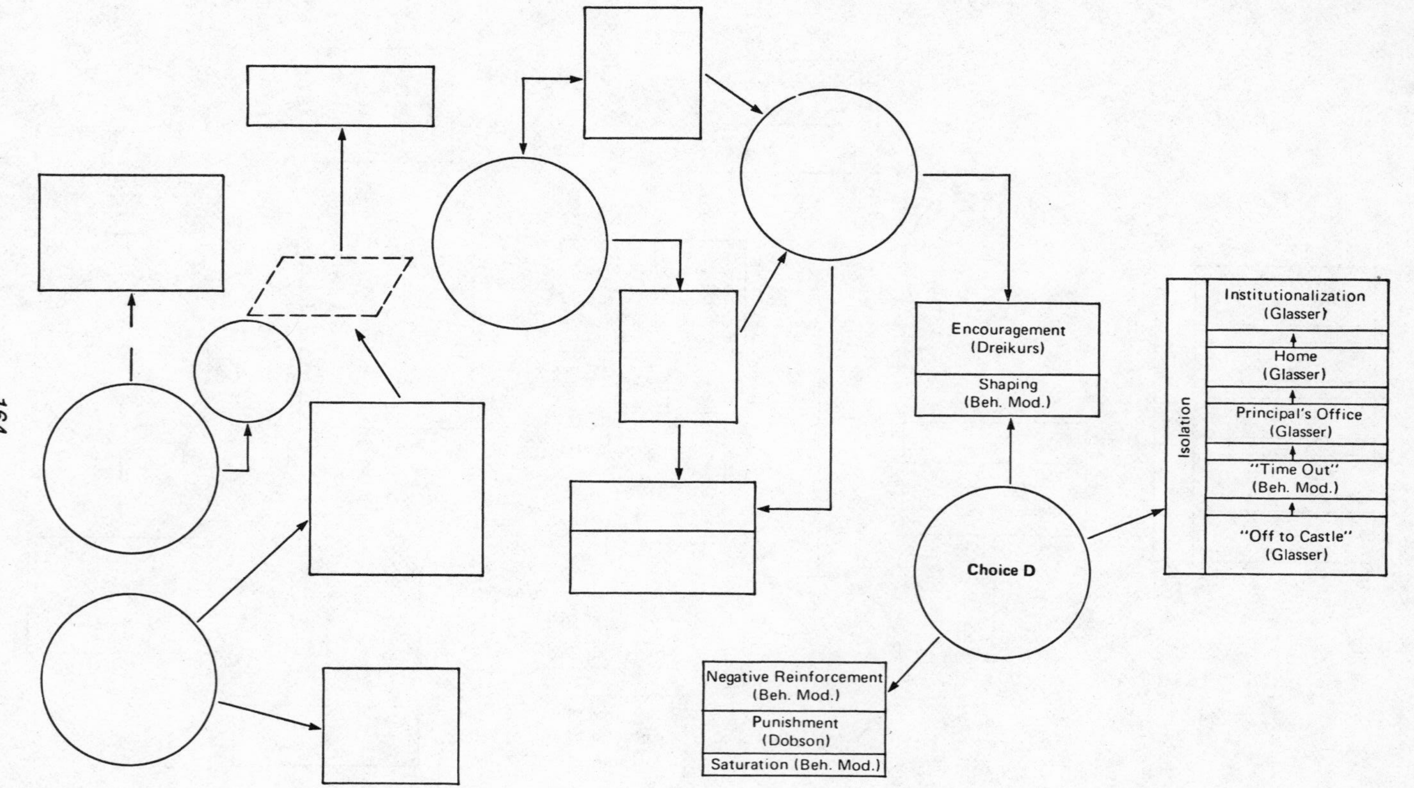

FIGURE 10–4. *Pathway I, "From Student Power to Teacher Control," Choice D*

(See Figure 10–3.) This choice can lead you to the more positive techniques of *encouragement* and *shaping*.

If you continue to be unsuccessful, the next step found in "Choice D" (see Figure 10–4) would be to turn to *negative reinforcement, punishment* (Dobson), or *saturation*. If none of these works, or if you wish to substitute for these strong techniques, you may use isolation in terms of "*off to the castle*" or "*time out*" in the classroom. After a period of isolation, you can return to "make a plan," "contingency contracting, " or "logical consequences," depending on which method you find to be the most acceptable.

If you need to continue to more powerful techniques, you can move to *school isolation,** with the principal or some other school authority using "make a plan," contingency contracting, or logical consequences to determine when the student is to return. The next step in the process of power escalation is to move the student to *out-of-school* isolation, wherein the parents are brought into the process. Before the student can re-enter school, the parent, principal, or teacher (or all three) can press the student to "make a plan," establish a contingency contract, or suffer the logical consequences. Finally, failure at the end of this pathway would lead to "institutionalization." If all actions have failed to influence or modify the student's behavior, school authorities can, if the behavior is serious enough, have the parent enlist the help of a child development clinic or that of juvenile authorities.

The line of movement in Pathway I is generally a process of escalating teacher-power techniques with students whose actions are a continual threat to the learning environment, to the teacher or students, or even to themselves. You would, of course, begin to retreat on this power continuum should you begin to detect success evidenced by a change in the student's outward behavior.

Pathway II: "From Teacher Power to Student Autonomy"

The gradual retreat on the power continuum from maximum teacher power in the first use of the Interventionists' techniques to the Interactionalists' and finally the Non-Interventionists' position, is based on the premise that your techniques have worked and you are gradually granting the student or students more autonomy or power over their behavior and decision making.

To begin this process, you can start to gather baseline data as suggested by the Behaviorists. Take a *baseline reading* of the behavior of the student. With these data, you may branch in one of two directions. If the student's actions would endanger the student or others or possibly destroy property, or if the attention the student receives from others would reinforce the "misbehavior," you can choose "Choice A," moving up or down the negative branch with the use of classroom "*time out,*" *saturation,* or *negative reinforcement* as described by Dobson. (See Figure 10–5.) After using these physical intervention techniques, you may decide

*It might be advisable for a school staff meeting to be held at this time. (See Chapter 13, "Mainstreaming" the Difficult Student: The School Staff as a Team.)

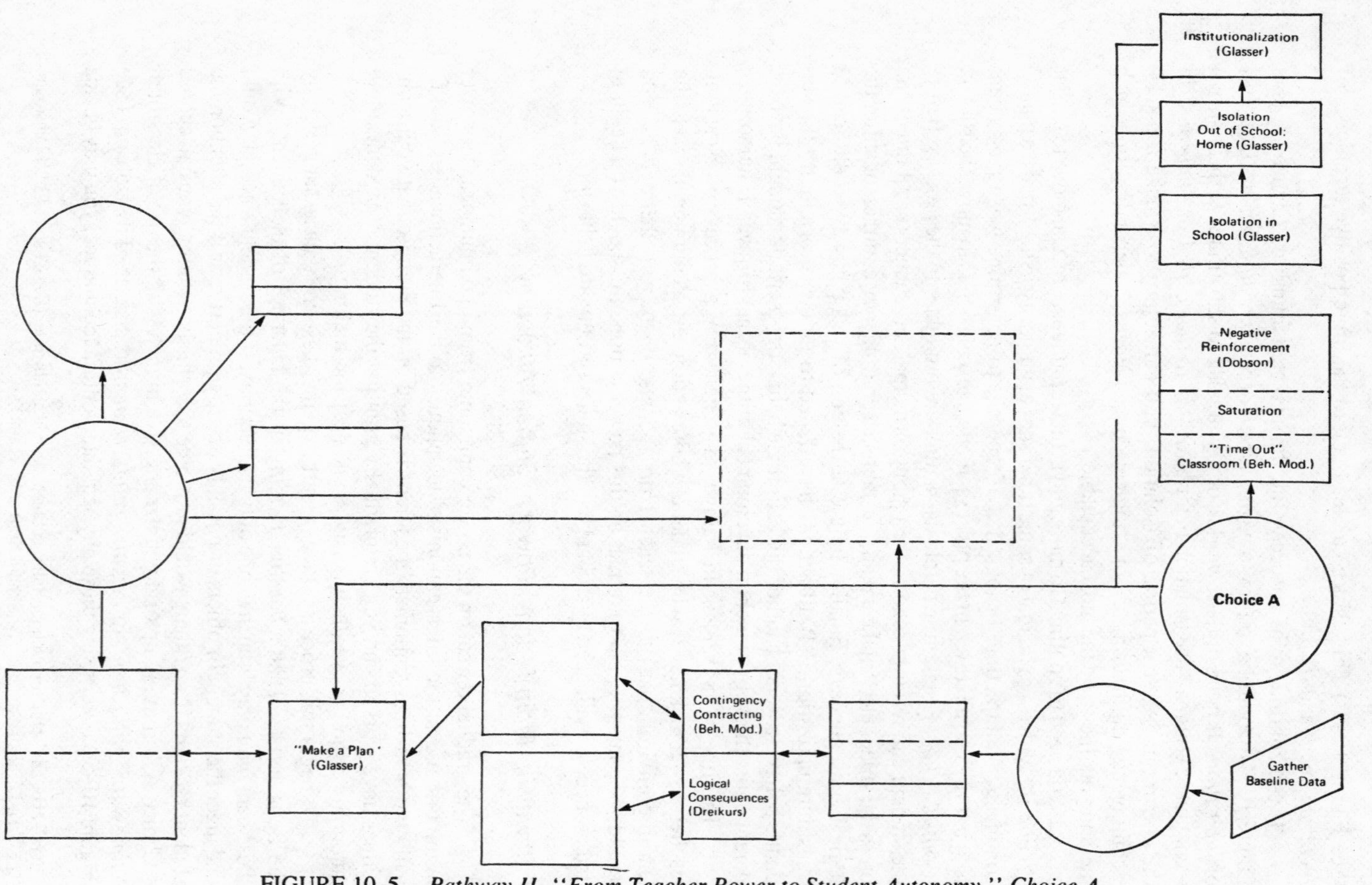

FIGURE 10–5. *Pathway II, "From Teacher Power to Student Autonomy," Choice A*

to follow up with *contingency contracts, logical consequences,* or "*make a plan.*" If a plan is made and not kept, you may again have the child feel the logical consequences or, if the student fails to receive the planned-for reinforcement because he or she did not exhibit appropriate behavior for contingency contracting, steps may be taken involving *isolation* in the school office.*

The principal or other school authorities can repeat this cycle to establish a new framework for contingency contracts, logical consequences or "make a plan." If these techniques still do not work, isolation can be escalated to "out-of-school," and when the child returns you can repeat "*make a plan,*" and if this does not work, you can turn to contingency contracting or logical consequences for the third time. Should these efforts fail, the final step on this negative branch would be to have the child turned over to outside authorities. This would mean the school made every effort to socialize the student's behavior, but the techniques needed lie outside the school's sphere of competency. Therefore, the parents are advised to seek a developmental clinic, mental health center, or psychiatric help for the student. Some very serious situations might require the involvement of a juvenile agency. Eventually, if the student is returned to the classroom, the teacher can repeat the cycle of "make a plan" and contingency contracts or logical consequences.

A more hopeful and optimistic line of movement is to anticipate that these powerful Interventionist techniques *will* work and that, after gathering baseline data, it will be easy to elect "Choice B." This choice will require you to withdraw such reinforcements as visual attention and, through the process of *extinction,* eliminate the misbehavior. Another approach would be to determine the terminal behavior that you wish to obtain, break this larger goal into a smaller sequence of tasks, and begin the process of *shaping*. If you find the use of reinforcements is unacceptable, the process of *encouragement* can be used. (See Figure 10–6.)

While beginning these attempts to shape the student's behavior, you can also review your educational practices to see whether *educational change* can be made that begins to give the student successes, possibly by making substantial changes in educational practices or by making physical changes in the classroom setting.

With some initial success with shaping, you may now retreat to the use of contingency contracts or logical consequences, which draw on the more rational abilities of the child.

If you continue on this pathway with increased success, you can advance to the use of confronting questions such as, "What are you doing?" "How does this behavior help?" "What are you going to do to change?" and then press for a plan. If this is not successful, you can reverse this progression and, again, use more powerful techniques: first, with logical consequences and/or contingencies, and finally, shaping or isolation. The general idea is to use as few of the power techniques as possible to achieve the positive change in behavior that you want, and

*Again, a staff meeting is advisable.

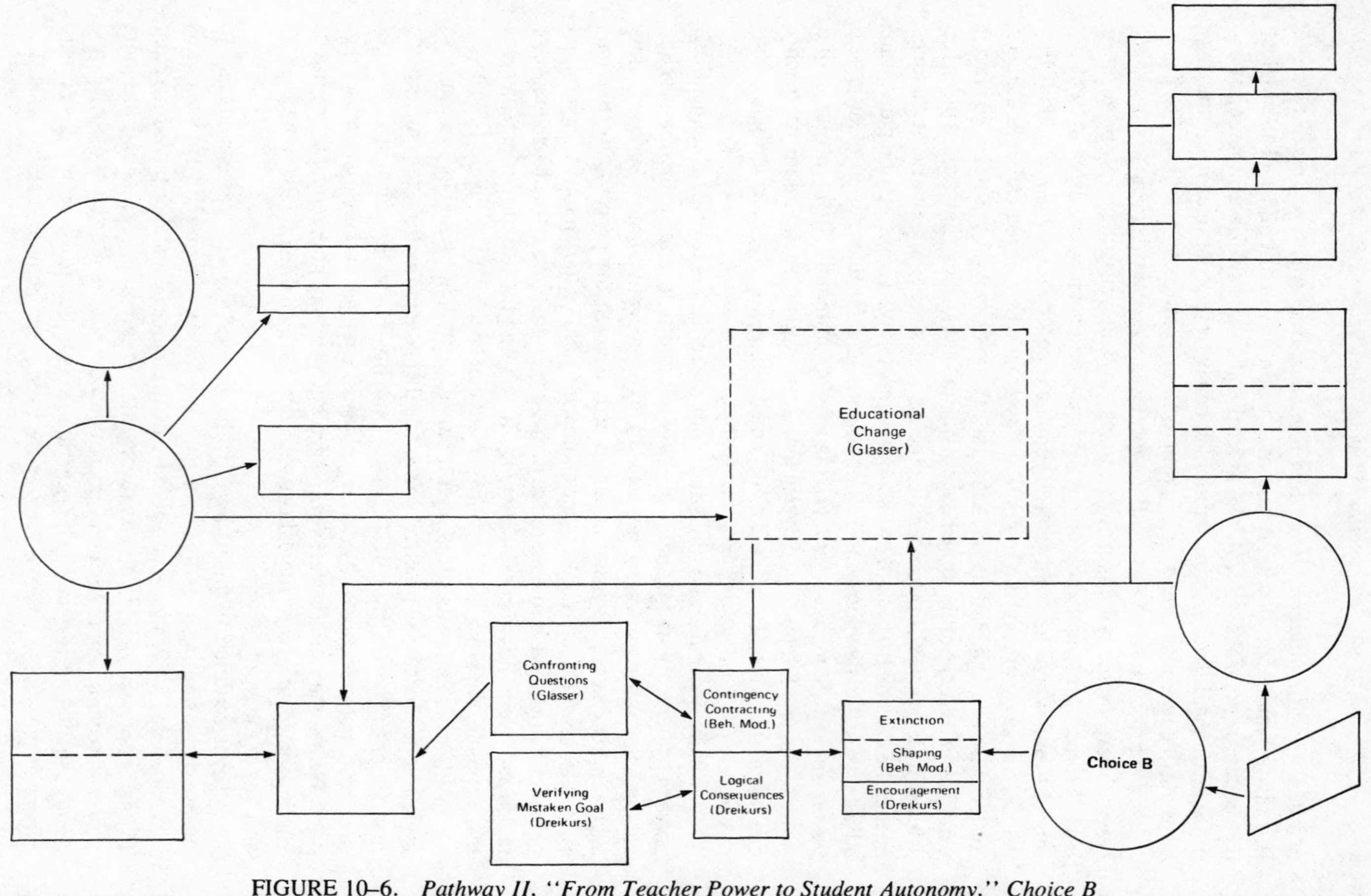

FIGURE 10–6. *Pathway II, ''From Teacher Power to Student Autonomy,'' Choice B*

then to gradually move down this pathway, giving the student increased power or autonomy as you retreat to minimum teacher control.

At this point, you can attempt to *verify* the student's mistaken goal by asking the student such questions as, "Could it be that you want attention? power? revenge? to be left alone?" You would then assist the student in obtaining social acceptance by making some *educational change* that attempts to give the child power or attention in acceptable ways.

Still continuing down this "yellow brick road" of successes, you can now retreat to the use of minimum power techniques such as *"I" messages* and Method III *"no lose"* problem-solving techniques. These movements into Gordon's Teacher Effectiveness Training techniques suggest that you must begin to use "Choice C" by defining *problem ownership.* If the problem *does* have a concrete effect on the teacher, use "I" messages and Method III "no lose" problem solving. If the behavior of the student is a problem because his or her actions are outside your *"area or sphere of freedom,"* you may fail to enforce the school rules, thus allowing yourself to *ignore* the behavior and hope for *extinction,* or you may choose to "pass the buck" to the higher administrator who is responsible for enforcing arbitrary school rules. You may, of course, work to make educational changes that would eliminate these arbitrary rules.

Finally, if the student "owns" the problem, you can maintain a position of *active listening,* and, if so desired, you can also elect to use *values-clarification* techniques.

Pathway II: "From Teacher Power to Student Autonomy" should be viewed as a guide to demonstrate to teachers how they can use power as a tool in terms of how it relates to the teacher techniques found in the various models. The general goal of this pathway, we may repeat, is to use maximum power and then, with success, gradually move to less powerful techniques. This will allow the student more autonomy and will call upon the increased use of the student's rational abilities until, finally, he or she can become self-disciplined.

Pathway III: "From Shared Power to Student Autonomy or Teacher Control"

The use of Pathway III: "From Shared Power to Student Autonomy or Teacher Control" is for those teachers who now are, or who may wish in the future, to become practitioners of the Interactionalist theory, using the techniques of Glasser or Dreikurs. From this beginning, you can move to the use of Non-Interventionist techniques that permit the student to demonstrate maximum autonomy and to achieve self-discipline. Or you can begin as an Interactionalist and find that under certain conditions, with very difficult students, these methods do not seem to work; the use of Pathway III would then permit you to begin to use more powerful Interventionist techniques until control finally is established.

To describe the movement on Pathway III (see Figure 10–8), the teacher has "Choice A" to begin to use the Dreikurs techniques of *verifying* the mistaken

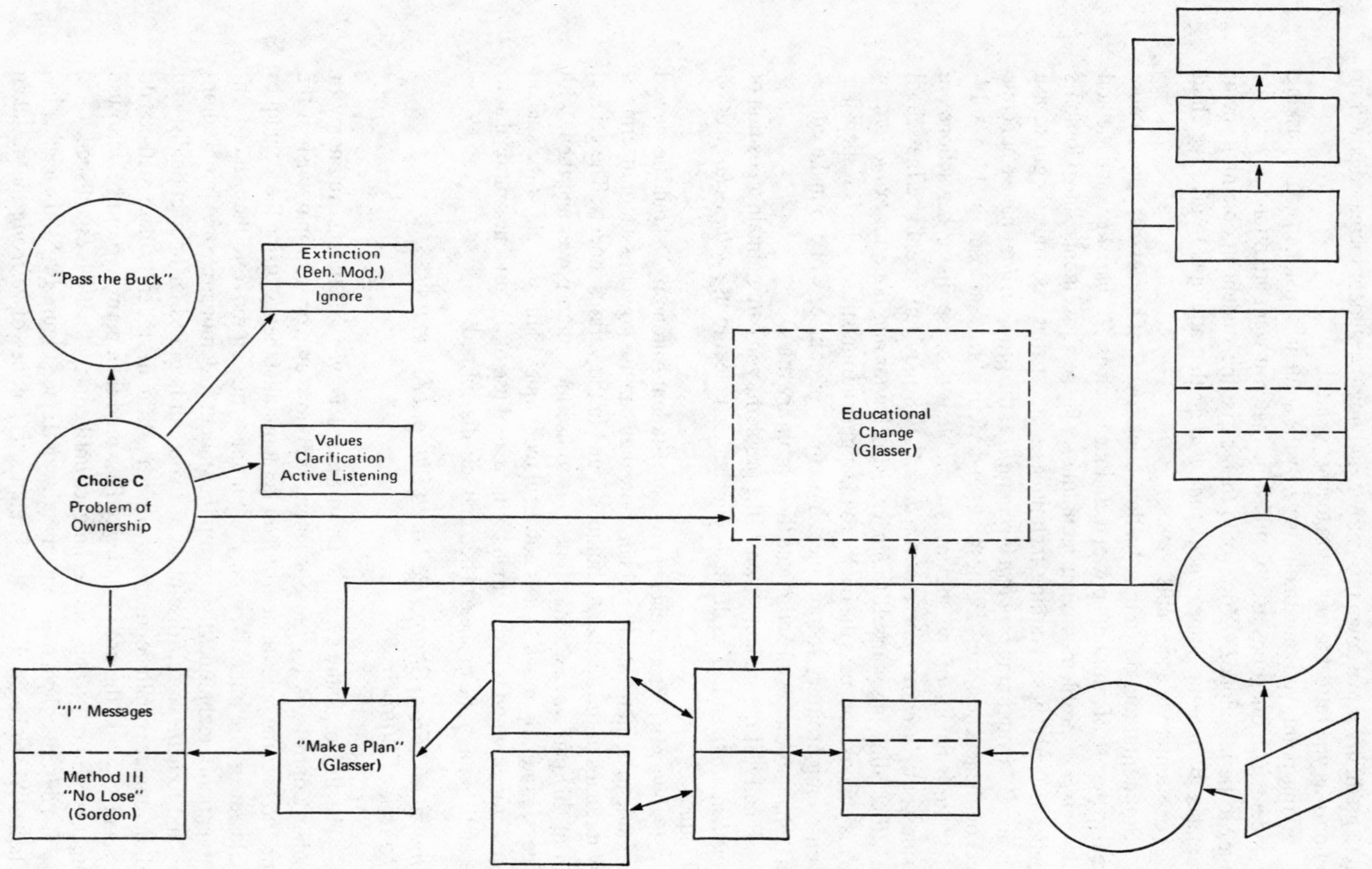

FIGURE 10–7. *Pathway II, "From Teacher Power to Student Autonomy," Choice C*

motivational goal by asking, "Could it be that you want attention? power? revenge? to be left alone?" or Glasser's *confronting questions* of, "What are you doing?" and "How is this helping?" Both models suggest that you make *educational changes*. If these techniques are successful, you can retreat on the power continuum to the use of Gordon's Teacher Effectiveness Training techniques, whereby you have "Choice B" (see Figure 10–9) of determining *problem ownership*. If the problem brought by a student does *not* have a concrete effect on you, use the nondirective techniques of *active listening,* and if you wish to help the student to explore some of the value-laden problems, you can use *value-clarification* techniques.

If the problem does not have a concrete effect on you but lies outside your *"area of freedom,"* you are again faced with a moral dilemma. You can choose to take a "law-and-order" approach and forward the student and the student's problem to those administrators who have established the unilateral rule, while you work within the system to make *educational changes* in school policy and rules. Or, you might dare, where you believe certain unilateral school rules to be unenforceable and unrealistic, to simply ignore the problem, knowing that to do so you are placing yourself in conflict with school policy.

On the other hand, if the problem does have a concrete effect on you, you can express this to the student with the use of *"I" messages* and attempt to solve the problem through Method III "no lose" problem solving. The Method III approach might lead to a compromised solution and bring about some *educational change*. If these limited teacher power techniques do not work, you can, of course, begin to apply more powerful techniques, moving back into the Interactionalist methods as needed. The preceding path moves from Interventionist techniques to those of the Non-Interventionist, giving students added power as they demonstrate that they are becoming more autonomous. The opposite movement will occur if a student's behavior fails to improve.

You can begin again at "Choice A" with the Interactionalist (see Figure 10–8) techniques of Dreikurs or Glasser. In one approach, you can make *educational changes* or help the student find social acceptance, and then, either by the use of *verifying questions* or *confronting questions,* you can respond to misbehavior with *"make a plan," contingency contracting,* or *logical consequences*. If these techniques are unsuccessful, you would be faced with three decisions involving "Choice C." (See Figure 10–10.) One decision is that you can move to the positive use of reinforcement or *encouragement* and begin a process of *shaping*. The second decision is to choose the strong techniques of *saturation, punishment* (Dobson), or *negative reinforcement*. The third decision is to use isolation, which first begins in the classroom as *"time out"* or *"off to the castle,"* and continues, if necessary, to *school isolation,* home isolation,* and, as a last resort, to an *outside institution*.

*Again, with this step a staff meeting is advised.

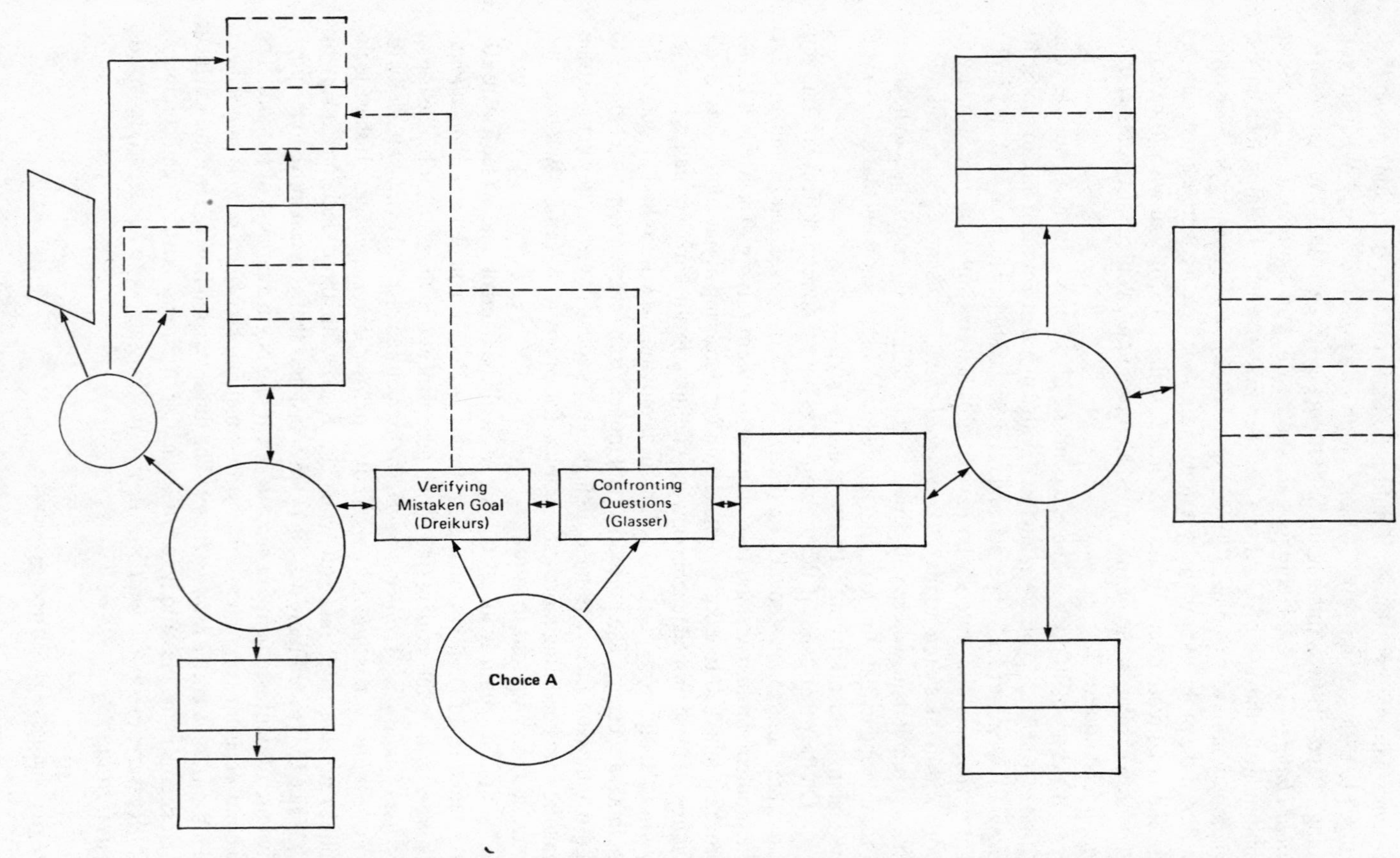

FIGURE 10–8. *Pathway III, "From Shared Power to Student Autonomy* or *Teacher Control," Choice A*

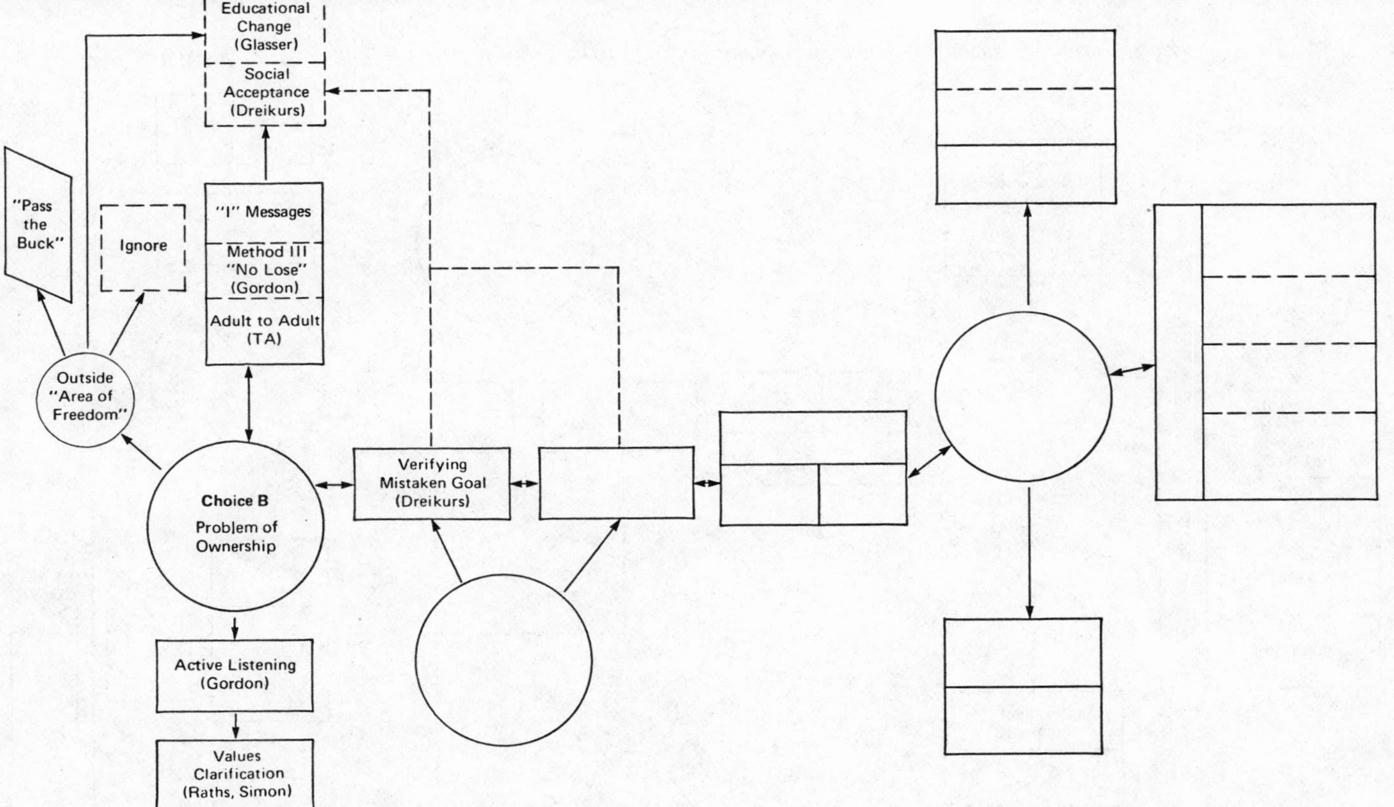

FIGURE 10–9. *Pathway III, "From Shared Power to Student Autonomy* or *Teacher Control," Choice B*

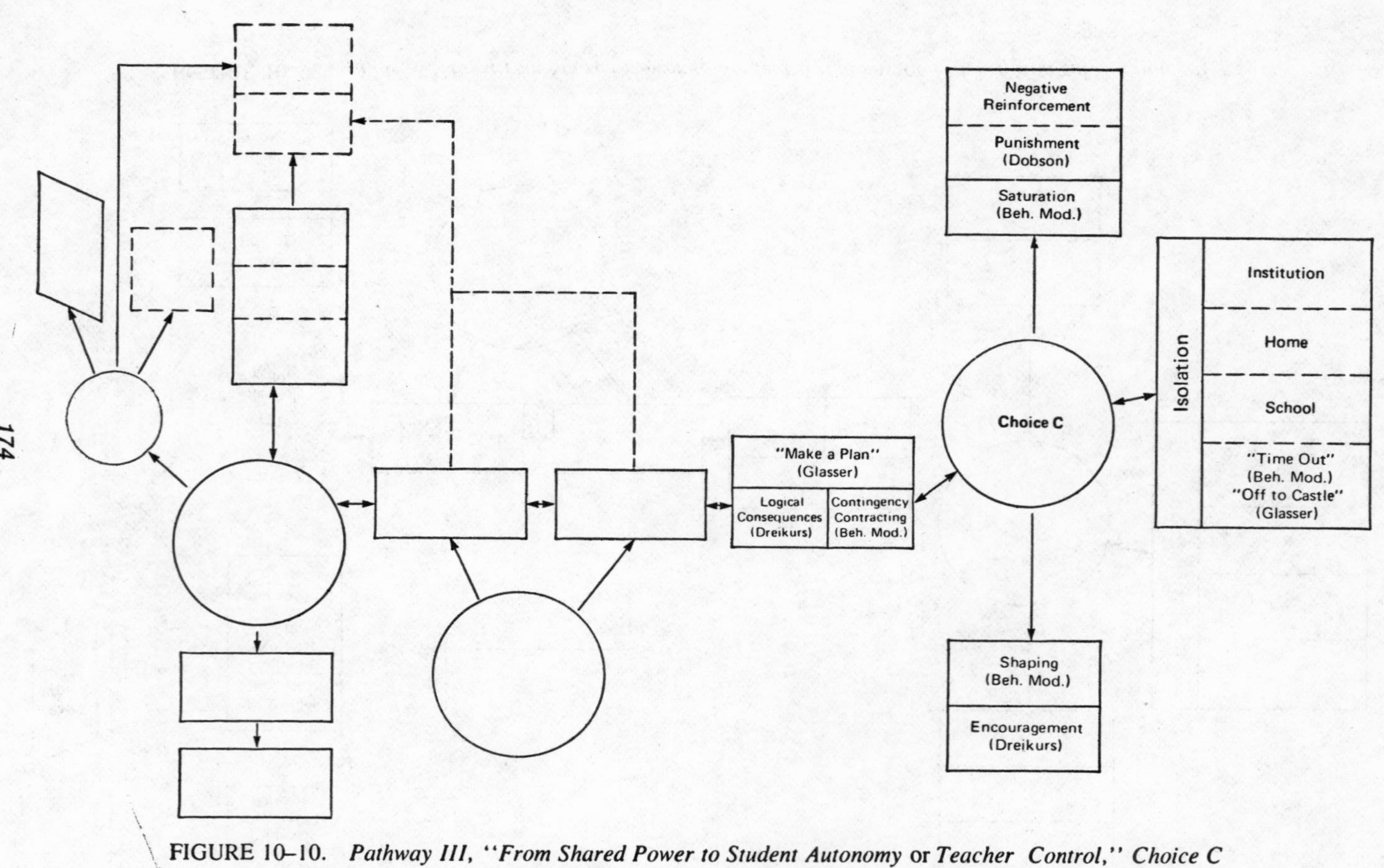

FIGURE 10–10. *Pathway III, "From Shared Power to Student Autonomy* or *Teacher Control," Choice C*

When any or all of these techniques work, you can plan to retreat across the power continuum. For example, after isolation you would try "make a plan," logical consequences, or contingency contracting. With success, the strategies gradually move to those suggested by the Non-Interventionists' techniques.

Summary

In summary, all the pathways described suggest that the teacher advance and retreat across the power continuum using techniques based on whether they succeed or fail to change student behavior. We have used the three directional pathways as constructs to demonstrate how we can carry out such a progression and regression of teacher power. The teacher should not employ these constructs as rigid recipes and should not move mechanically through the techniques without real rational thought or sensitivity. It becomes both the teacher's responsibility and challenge to use the constructs and techniques in a sensitive manner. The creative teacher will, at times, devise his or her unique pathways based on personal values, professional skill, the realities of the situation, and uniqueness of the student.

11

Socialization: A Developmental Perspective

After looking at the choices available from the three directional pathways described in the last chapter, there may be some teachers who reject the decision-making process based on these described teacher values. Such teachers resist aligning themselves with Non-Interventionists, Interactionalists, or Interventionists. Instead, they say, "I do not accept any singular model or school of thought. I see value in all models and would like to choose techniques based upon what I know about the individual student." Through their years of experience and professional training, such teachers believe that students (even those of the same age) grow, behave, and respond differently according to varying stages of growth and maturity. As suggested by Dreikurs, development of all behavior is an orderly process. This process is somewhat akin to the acquisition of motor skills: children learn to wiggle before they crawl, to walk before they run. If human behavior is orderly in its development, then generalizations can be made about what can be expected from a student at a certain time in his or her development. With knowledge of this developmental order, specific teacher interventions, based on models or pieces of models, can be judged to be the most compatible with certain times, conditions, and developmental stages of student behavior. With an understanding of these developmental patterns of socialized growth in their students, teachers can work in tune with these growth patterns. Conversely, there exists the possibility that, unknowingly, teachers might be using methods that are beyond a student's ability to comprehend, and thus the techniques being employed will fail or, worse, their use will retard the student's growth toward maturity.

The material that follows on moral and social development might not seem, at first, meaningful to the upper elementary and secondary teachers who may question the relevance of focusing on the early development of their older students. Such questions are understandable because the study of social development stresses the early years of a youngster's life; however, it is only with an understanding of this period in a child's life and the *sequence* of the child's social and moral development (the sense of right and wrong), that the teacher can assess what stages a student has undergone and what stages are to follow.

Only then can the teacher be on target with disciplinary or intervention techniques *appropriate to the development stage and not the chronological age*. A quick example should suffice. It will soon be explained that, at the beginning stage of moral reasoning, a child (usually four to seven years old) will behave according to his or her egocentric view of the consequences of his or her behavior. Behavior is judged to be right or wrong by the child only in terms of whether he or she will be rewarded or punished. If the behavior is not punished, then it is all right to do. The effects of such reasoning can also be seen among teenagers and adults. During the New York City blackout, when many adults went on a rampage of looting, the nation was provided with ample evidence of such first-stage moral reasoning. A television interviewer asked a looter carrying off a stereo set, "Why are you doing this?" The answer was, "Because it's dark, and I won't get caught." To try to reason with a person using adult ethical principles would be for naught. Teachers who deal with students *of any age* can make a diagnosis and determine appropriate teacher action based on knowledge of the student's moral stage acquisition. The description that follows of social and moral stage acquisition will set a foundation for the making of decisions on appropriate teacher intervention.

Socialized Behavior: A Developmental Process

The acquisition of socialized behaviors by students, like all other forms of development, goes through stages. This development begins in early childhood (infancy through preschool), when the child is considered to be *prerational* and *egocentric* (self-centered). The child is highly demanding, shows little restraint in his or her interaction with others, and displays an attitude of, "I want it when I want it." This self-centeredness dissipates dramatically during the early elementary grades, when the school-age child generally becomes a cooperative, well-socialized worker. This school-age student learns to control his or her body impulses and refrains from using materials destructively, and he or she can carry out agreed upon tasks with others to achieve a common goal (i.e., team games or group projects).[1] Although the elementary student has become a stable, cooperative rule-player and worker, it will not be until he or she has reached middle school, junior high school, or adolescence that the student will acquire sufficient intellectual abilities to be able to *fully* discuss and analyze his or her values and moral behaviors as they might relate to such issues as stealing, violence, drugs, sex, and prejudice.

What, then, is misbehavior from a developmental perspective? At the beginning, there is an infant living between two large islands of pleasure and discomfort. When the infant needs to be cared for (fed, diapered, or held), he or she expresses the need by crying and screaming. Obviously, for an infant, these forceful bodily demands cannot be labeled as "misbehavior," but as appropriate behavior for that stage. It would be unrealistic to expect an infant not to cry. The term "misbehavior" can only be applied when the behavior related to a stage is used at an age beyond the appropriate time. For example, parents would not become concerned about a baby who cries frequently at the age of two, but they would become increasingly concerned with episodes of frequent crying when the child is eight years of age. Parents and teachers usually can expect a student to be a socialized worker by the age of seven. This age serves as a general reference point for judging good behavior and misbehavior. We then ask, "How does this development proceed through the first seven years?"

The First Seven Years of Social Development

Passive Body-Centered Behavior

We have already mentioned the first year of life, when the child can be viewed as a relatively passive organism who reacts through bodily impulses. The infant's energy is directed to having bodily needs met. The infant, without mobility or coordination, is almost totally dependent on his or her caretakers.

Physically Aggressive Behavior

In the second year of life, the child learns to walk, and, as a result of his or her new-found mobility, can put distance between self and parents. As a result, the child often has to be supervised when he or she walks beyond the adult's immediate grasp. Parents, attempting to protect the innocent child from potential danger, inundate the two- or three-year-old with prohibitions in the form of such "no's" as, "*No* you cannot play with mother's sewing kit," "*No,* give me the dangerous scissors," "*No,* don't ever run near the street," "*No,* stay away from the electric outlet!"[2]

These "no" commands continually interrupt the child's natural curiosity to see, touch, taste, and feel everything in sight. Remember, during the first year of life, the infant needed only to whimper or cry before the adult world would run to provide care. Suddenly, the tables are turned. Instead of parents accommodating the child, the child is being asked to accommodate the wider world. This is not an easy change to make. Imagine what it must be like for a child to be told, "Wait until after supper before you eat that piece of candy," or, "Use your spoon instead of your hands to eat your mashed potatoes." These commands, which delay immediate gratification and help in the socialization process, are necessary, but so are the child's early predictable responses to prohibitions.

Initially, the child reacts to those repeated "no's" and demands for delayed gratification with the first stage of *passivity.*[3] A child who is caught pulling the leaves off a house plant and is told "no" will often become immobile, possibly with thumb sucking, and will look at the adult with a glassy-eyed stare. However, this passive retreat does not last for long. With repeated prohibitions or "no's," the child lashes back with physical aggression.

In another example, when a child's father stops the toddler from exploring his shaving cream can, the child screams, cries, and strikes at the father by kicking, biting, or hitting. When the child previously responded with passivity, his or her energy was directed inward. With continued adult interference and socializing "no's," that energy is now directed outward in the form of physical aggression. For the immature toddler, as with the infant, it is accepted that such *aggressive behavior cannot be labeled as "misbehavior," but simply as a reflection of the toddler's immature abilities to understand and perform "correct" behavior*. This aggression is seen simply as energy turned outward, however misdirected it may be.

Verbally Aggressive Behavior

In late toddlerhood, this development of impulse control and physical aggression reaches a third phase called "verbal aggression." As an example, three-year-old Tommy discovers a five-pound box of Christmas chocolates. He rummages through the box, pushing large handfuls of candy into his mouth while scattering the excess across the living room rug. His mother suddenly appears from the kitchen and finds him in his full, chocolate-spattered glory. Upon seeing his mother, her expression, and the sudden movement towards him, Tommy begins to shout, "No, no, no!" at her.

How does one interpret his words? Children are not born with an understanding of how they are to behave and what they may and may not do. They must learn these prohibitions primarily from adults, either directly or by example, and the process is one of *setting limits.*[4] When we see Tommy saying "no" to his mother in this incident, we see that he is beginning to internalize or learn the prohibitions. Although, at this immature stage, they are easily forgotten, Tommy *at least* remembered the prohibition when his mother appeared. This is only one step away from remembering "no, no" beforehand, or for Tommy to intellectually say "no" to himself and thus inhibit his own behavior. The child verbalized what the adult would say. This internalization of "no's" or prohibitions is not fully complete until about the age of seven, when a rigid conscience is acquired (a reflection of early moral reasoning to be described later).

Children have a need to use language in an aggressive way to attempt to learn how language can be used to control their world, have their needs met, and to precipitate action. Children's use of verbal aggression such as "no" or the use of profanities toward adults may not be pleasurable by the adult's standards, but the child is learning an important lesson.[5] He or she is learning that language can be the vehicle for expressing actions, and that in turn it will inhibit the need for physical aggression. This use of language as verbal aggression is in direct contrast to the previous phases of physical aggression, when children attempted to "be the cause" through direct physical aggression toward others or when they experienced the initial phase of retreating into helpless passivity (i.e., immobility, staring blankly). Now that a child can use language outwardly to attack, it will not be long before he or she can use it inwardly to think about his or her behavior before taking action and in turn to censor his or her own behavior.

From a developmental perspective, one would prefer to have the preschooler or kindergarten child who has lost his toy to a classmate show such verbal aggression as, "No! No, you poopie-pants boy" rather than to show physical aggression by striking the classmate with a large building block. This can also hold true for the much older student who, when experiencing frustration, shows greater socialized stage development by swearing rather than physically striking out. Although it may be difficult to accept that verbal aggression is more mature than physical aggression and that physical aggression is more mature than passivity, this structure provides the teacher with the "building blocks" for matching intervention techniques with the socialization scale and its accompanying behavior. In other words, a teacher needs to facilitate verbal aggression when a student continually displays physical aggression, and, to facilitate controlled forms of physical aggression when a student displays passivity, even though the actions being facilitated are not viewed as "correct" adult behaviors.

Effecting Social Interaction Through Language—The Socialized Cooperative Worker

With the internalization of limits in the form of "no's" and the development of socialized language, the child can use this language to encode his or her strong feelings and to satisfy his or her needs.[6]

Internal language, as thought, is used to prohibit or censor certain actions before their enactment, and external language is used to ask for or to discuss with others ways of achieving desired ends. At the beginning of the elementary grades, the student has acquired these skills and has generally matured to the cooperative worker stage.

Reaching the acquired worker stage does not mean, however, that the socialization process is at an end. The student can work with others, but only within a framework of rigid adult rules that have been imposed and internalized. First-grade teachers can attest to this fact with their steady stream of students earnestly tattling on others who "broke the rules." It is not until much later that students become social persons or "adults" in the sense of having true consideration for others as well as a sense of moral principles.

Conceptualization Through Language—The Attainment of Adult Maturity

At the approximate age of adolescence, most students acquire well-developed language and cognitive skills that enable them to think in terms of abstract concepts.[7] With this increased conceptual ability they can reflect on their behavior in relation to others and establish some guiding and individual principles. When they can understand why and how others act as they do and when they can clarify their own behavior in the context of long-range goals, they will emerge as truly "social persons" in their adult forms.

The Developmental Socialization Continuum (DSC) shown in Figure 11–1 illustrates the developmental progression from the stage of passivity to that of physical aggression, to the stage of verbal aggression, to the facilitation of social interaction through language. The span of time from passivity to social interaction through language generally covers the first seven years of life and is described as the prerational period. It is the period comparable to that of Dreikurs's "misdirected goals"[8] or one's immature attempts to have one's needs met. The stages evolve as the passive child withdraws from prohibition, growing into a physically aggressive child who attacks the prohibitions through vengeful action. The child then becomes verbally aggressive, using language as a powerful tool to overwhelm the prohibition, and finally develops into the beginning social child who uses language as a means of expressing to others his or her needs. Through these prerational stages, the child behaves in descending degrees of conflict with others, as indicated by Harris's[9] "I'm Not OK" feeling of the *Child*.

The period from social interaction to conceptualization through language, from age seven to and through adulthood, can be called the rational period. It is the period of expanding moral reasoning and when such reasoning is no longer based on conflict but on mutual understanding. The student now acquires an "I'm OK" feeling of the *Adult* and the sense of Dreikurs's *Belongingness* or *Social Acceptance*. The key to this rational evolution is higher cognition, language abilities, and emotional security. For a more detailed explanation of the substages of moral reasoning, the reader may wish to refer to Appendix C.

Summarizing Developmental Theory

For the first seven years of life, the child behaves without the use of rational language. All developing children go through the phases of *prerational* behavior (passive, physically aggressive, and verbally aggressive) that eventually fade away and are replaced by the *rational* levels. (See Figure 11–1, Developmental Socialization Continuum.)

From approximately the age of seven onward, the normal child will begin to use language and thought to understand his or her current behavior and to direct future behavior. As he or she moves from concrete to abstract thinking, reasoning as to the correctness of one's behavior similarly moves from self-centered standards ("What is going to happen to me?") to other-centered standards ("What would my teacher or friend say?") to societal standards ("What is the law?") and finally to individual standards based on self, others, and society ("What is morally right?").

Although these stages are described as distinct, it would be incorrect to view them as totally separate. In each case, the maturing child will show "carryover" examples of behaviors from previous stages. With the attainment of new stages, behaviors of previous stages will become less frequent; yet, such behaviors will still appear. These appearances might at times be appropriate. For example, when we are under great danger, such as being held at gunpoint, it might be prudent to be passive. We may even need to be physically aggressive to remove the traveling salesman from our door. Verbal aggression may also be needed before this salesman will finally leave. Fortunately, though, most mature adults can hold their impulses and strong feelings in check and deal with each other in a conflict by using socialized language. In our churches, courts of law, gatherings of friends, and in classrooms, adults can exchange opinions with each other in order to conceptualize ideas about today's social or moral problems and thus manifest a higher level of moral behavior towards others.

In many cases, the dilemma of working with misbehaving students could be that they are behaving at a level of development that is inappropriate. For example, a physically aggressive fifteen-year-old is of much greater concern than a physically aggressive five-year-old. The teacher who has a knowledge of development could more readily tolerate the five-year-old, but must act quickly to move the fifteen-year-old to the next, less harmful stage of verbal aggression.

Teacher-Student Interaction Models and Developmental Theory

With the Developmental Socialization Continuum (Figure 11–1) as a construct for viewing how children grow socially, two questions need to be asked.

1. What models will be the most effective at what ages of a child's development?
2. What models will permit the child to move to higher levels of moral understanding?

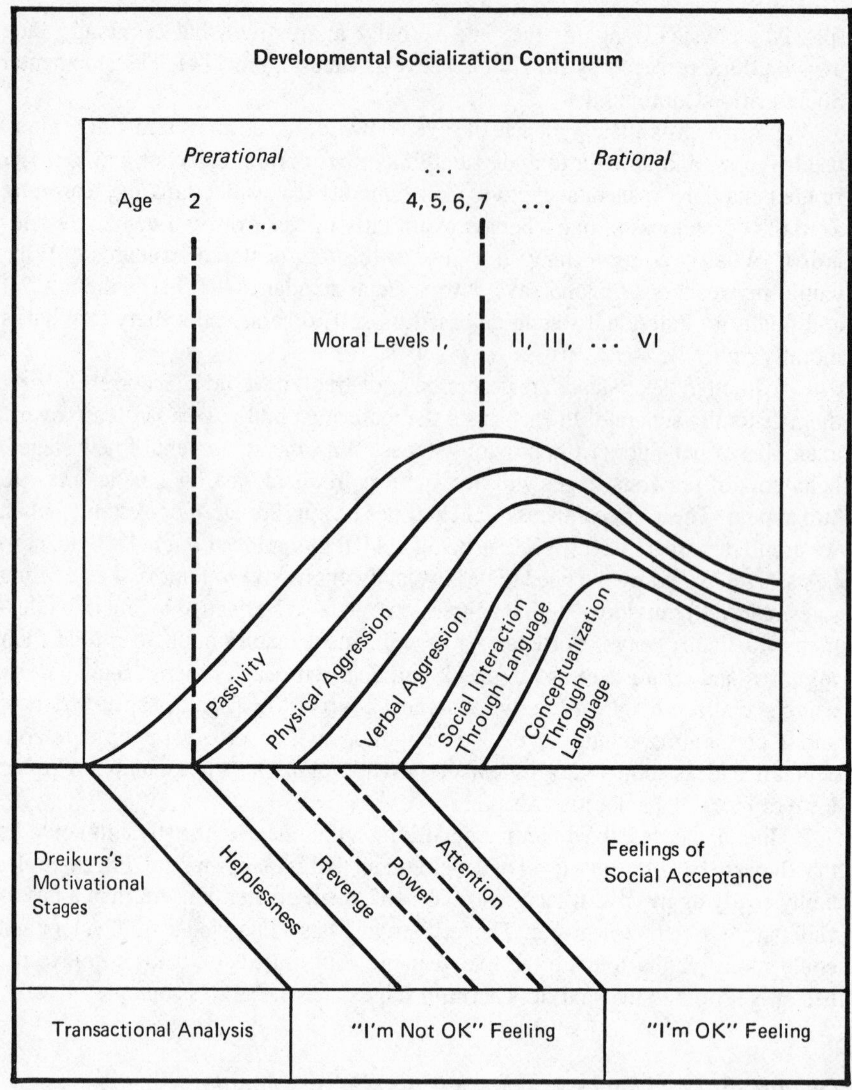

FIGURE 11–1. *Developmental Socialization Continuum (DSC)*

With some general brush strokes (Figure 11–2, Moral Centeredness and Intervention Models), the following suggestions can be made.

1. Interventionist Models that are not based on the rational capacities of students might be highly effective with young children (prerational period) who have limited cognitive and language abilities.

2. The Interactionalist Models that are predicated on negotiation and peer collaboration might be ideally suitable for students in middle childhood (approximately ages seven to eleven). At this age, the student's reasoning is moving from Levels I and II or "What's in it for me?" to that of Level IV, "What are the rules of our society?" The student is becoming increasingly concerned with others and the larger social order.
3. The Non-Interventionist Models, which assume rational and independent thought on the part of the student, might be most suitable for those in the age group of adolescence to adulthood. During this period, the student can think abstractly about his or her behavior and its present and future consequences.

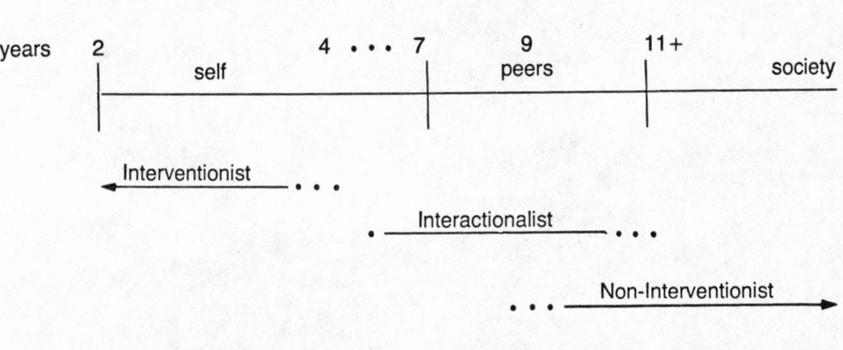

FIGURE 11–2. *Moral Centeredness and Intervention Models*

Placing the schools of thought (Non-Interventionist, Interactionalist, and Interventionist) over our age continuum related to rational and prerational thought would create an overlap onto various stages of moral centeredness. With these developmental concepts and constructs in mind, we may now turn to specific techniques and various models to apply with stages of social development.

Notes

1. Anna Freud, *Normality and Pathology in Childhood: Assessments of Development* (New York: International University Press, 1968).
2. Rene Spitz, *No and Yes* (New York: International University Press, 1957).
3. Anna Freud, *The Ego and the Mechanisms of Defense* (New York: International University Press, 1971).
4. Selma Fraiberg, *Magic Years* (New York: International University Press, 1959).

5. Susan Isaacs, *Social Development of Young Children* (New York: Schocken Books, 1972).
6. Charles H. Wolfgang, *Helping Aggressive and Passive Preschoolers Through Play* (Columbus: Charles E. Merrill Publishing, 1977), p. 6.
7. Jean Piaget, *The Construction of Reality in the Child* (New York: Ballantine Books, 1971).
8. Rudolf Dreikurs and Pearl Cassel, *Discipline Without Tears*, rev. ed. (New York: Hawthorn Books, 1972), p. 32.
9. Thomas A. Harris, *I'm OK—You're OK: A Practical Guide to Transactional Analysis* (New York: Harper and Row, Publishers, 1969), pp. 37–53.

12

From Development Theory to Teacher Behavior

Rational and Moral Progression and Regression

The developmental socialization processes and continuum (DSC) described earlier chart the ideal development path and are based on the normative or "average" behavior of children as they progress and mature through age levels and stages of development. But it is not our "average," well-socialized student who gives the classroom teacher the conflict or behavioral problem. It is the one or two nonsocialized children in every classroom who "keep the teacher awake at night."

We hypothesize that these children have had their socialization retarded and have not progressed from passive or aggressive defensive behavior to that of employing rational abilities with their accompanying socialized behavior. This implies that elementary and secondary students, or even adults, demonstrate acting-out, destructive behavior that is prerational, much like the young toddler or preschool child.

We also suggest that these children or students have progressed or developed to the more rational forms of social behavior, but, because of some immediate emotional frustration or pressure, they have temporarily been emotionally "flooded" by their inner feelings. Thus, they have regressed to a more immature prerational behavior that erupts in the form of passive resistance, physical aggression, or verbal hostility to those whom they must deal with in a classroom environment.

We accept the position of the Interventionists, who say that simply labeling a student (poor academic background, deprived home, low socioeconomic status, or even mentally retarded) does not change the situation; the teacher still needs to deal with the student's acting-out behaviors in the classroom. It is therefore our intention to select those overt and covert behaviors suggested by the many models presented to intervene with our ''misbehaving'' student whose actions place him or her somewhere from prerational behavior (passive, physically aggressive, and verbally aggressive) to rational behavior on the developmental continuum. This intervention, it is hoped, will help the child to attain the growth necessary to achieve a conceptual understanding of his or her own values and moral behaviors.

The Passive Student (Helplessness)

The passive student, if viewed on our Developmental Socialization Continuum (DSC), has either not been able to find social acceptance or has retreated from the social world of peers, family, or school and appears to maintain himself or herself as if ''hidden inside a shell.'' Dreikurs, we will remember in Chapter 6, suggested that such students could have retreated into a state of helplessness, where they want to be ''left alone'' and wish for the world to make no demands on them. We further suggest that Berne and Harris, in the Transactional Analysis model, characterize such passive students as having an ''I'm Not O.K.'' view of themselves. (See Figure 12–1.)

Characteristics: Generally such passive students or children are described as:

- Being in a dream world, as if in a fog, and appearing flat and expressionless in facial expressions and body behavior.
- Rejecting comfort, both in physical and verbal forms, from teachers and peers.
- Being social recluses and not joining peers in activities or games appropriate to their age group.
- Being difficult to arouse, stimulate, or motivate and being afraid to tackle new tasks.
- Usually drifting from activity to activity, never completing anything.
- Doing the opposite of what is asked.
- Saying, ''I can't,'' rather than trying to do what is requested, with the request often having to be repeated.
- Being ''lazy'' and listless in class.

Often these passive children are described by parents and by some busy teachers as ''well behaved,'' which suggests that they are not generally causing

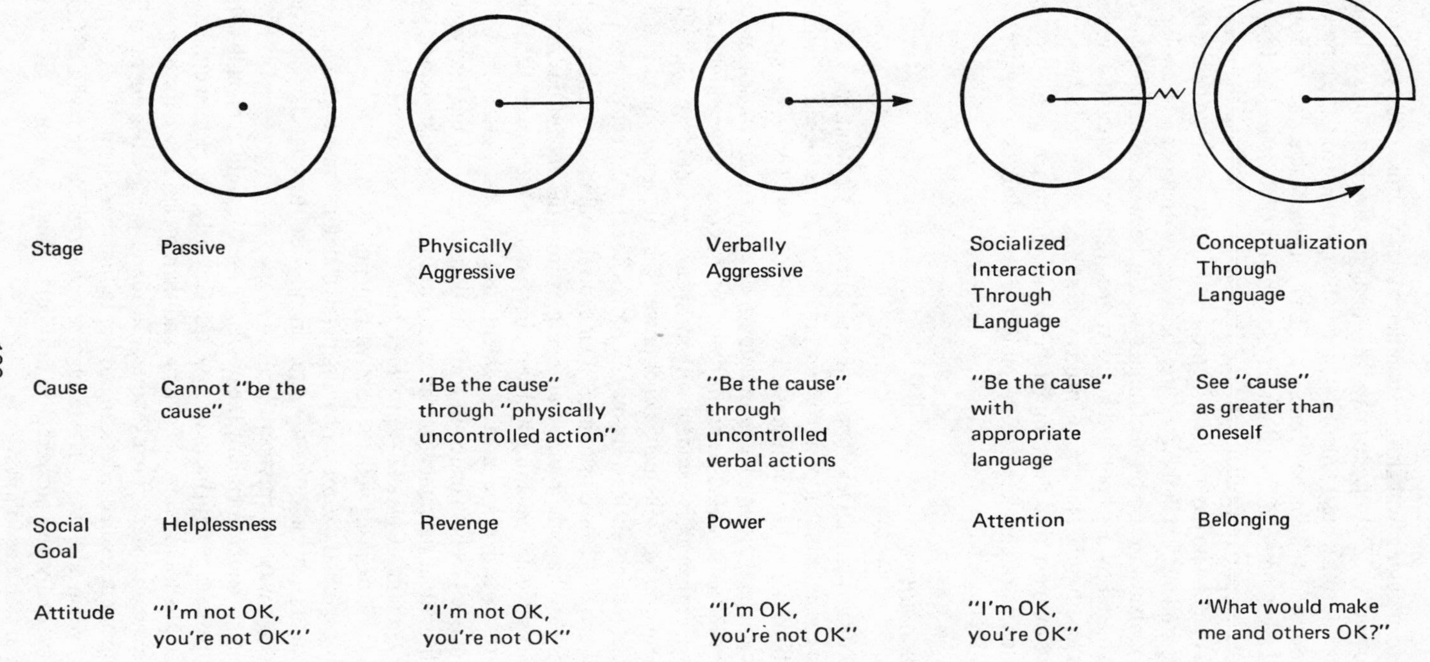

Stage
Passive
Physically Aggressive
Verbally Aggressive
Socialized Interaction Through Language
Conceptualization Through Language
Cause
Cannot "be the cause"
"Be the cause" through "physically uncontrolled action"
"Be the cause" through uncontrolled verbal actions
"Be the cause" with appropriate language
See "cause" as greater than oneself
Social Goal
Helplessness
Revenge
Power
Attention
Belonging
Attitude
"I'm not OK, you're not OK"'
"I'm not OK, you're not OK"
"I'm OK, you're not OK"
"I'm OK, you're OK"
"What would make me and others OK?"

FIGURE 12–1. *Social Unfolding*

disruptions or engaging in aggressive conflict, and, therefore, they seem to "fade into the woodwork." Because the passive, nonaggressive behaviors exhibited by these students during a busy school day generally go unnoticed, the more aggressive acting-out student is in the "limelight" and gets the teacher's attention. If we accept our Developmental Socialization Continuum (DSC), we might suggest, along with the support of Dreikurs and the Transactional Analysis theory, that it is the passive student who has the greater emotional difficulty. It can be inferred that such passive students are in the grey area between normality and pathology. The teacher who wishes to use the techniques would be wise to initially have such students evaluated by a school psychologist or neighborhood child development clinic to see whether the child might need more skilled psychiatric intervention or therapy. We suggest that there might be some students who are outside the teacher's "sphere of competency," a subject we will discuss in greater detail at the end of this chapter.

Teacher Techniques

Based again on the Developmental Socialization Continuum, we hypothesize that the passive student of any age seems either to be locked into immature prerational behavior or to have regressed to that position. The teacher techniques or models that would provide the most help for this student are those that we have labeled Interventionist, as these are *not* based on the cooperative rational abilities of the student. If the passive student will not speak, we would have little success with such nonintrusive (minimal teacher power) techniques as found in the Non-Interventionist models such as Thomas Gordon's Teacher Effectiveness Training and its approach of "active listening." Our central goal in intervening with passive students is to have them turn their energies from the *inward* destructive behavior of excessive daydreaming and self-absorption to the *outward* energies directed toward an active social involvement. We suggest the covert and overt teacher techniques recommended in the behavioral model of the Interventionist school, with gradual movement to those of the Interactionalist school, such as Glasser and Dreikurs. Chart 12–1 provides a list of teacher behaviors that would be appropriate for working with the passive student.

Keeping in mind the goal of having passive children turn their energies outward, we can experiment or more systematically use these teacher behaviors in our own creative way and approach.

The *Interventionists* employ the powerful use of reinforcement to help passive students to engage with the outside world. Covertly, the teacher collects baseline data, establishes terminal behaviors, and then breaks down the terminal behavior into sequential steps. For example, Caroline's passive behavior is reflected by her resting her head on the desk and by her failure to respond, either verbally or nonverbally, when addressed. The teacher sets the terminal behavior of Caroline responding (verbally and nonverbally) to others. This behavior is broken down into sequential steps, as follows.

COVERT BEHAVIORS	OVERT BEHAVIORS
Interventionists	
a. Count student behavior (baseline experiment) b. Establish terminal behavior desired c. Break down terminal behavior into sequential steps for shaping	1. Shaping—Reinforcement 2. Modeling —peer —adult 3. Commands 4. Avoid negative reinforcement or physical punishment
Interactionalists	
Glasser	
a. Observe —the student —the situation b. Assess —what the teacher is currently doing	1. Make classroom reorganization
Dreikurs	
a. Observe and collect information about the student —with peers —with family —with other teachers b. Ask oneself "Do I feel . . . 1) annoyed—attention getting 2) beaten—power 3) hurt—revenge 4) incapable—helplessness c. Watch for recognition reflex d. Plan to incorporate student with others	1. Questions of social goals: "Do you want to know why you are behaving like this?" "Could it be that you want to be left alone?" 2. Encouragement —recognize student's attempt to improve

CHART 12–1. *Passive Student and Teacher Techniques*

1. Caroline will hold her head up and keep it off her desk for periods of five minutes.
2. She will look at the teacher when she is asked a question.
3. She will verbally respond when her name is called.
4. She will answer the teacher's questions with more than one-word responses.
5. She will initiate conversation by raising her hand and asking questions.

After identifying the sequence for shaping, the teacher will now use overt behaviors. Beginning with Caroline's first behavior (holding her head up for five minutes), the teacher will reinforce the desired behavior with a *continuously fixed schedule*. Once that behavior is conditioned, a random schedule can be used and the next behavior can be reinforced. The teacher can also use forms of modeling, through adult and peer examples, those behaviors that should be imitated. The most intrusive form of teacher behavior would be commands. "Caroline, get your head off the desk and hold it up" could be combined with physical modeling, such as, "Hold it up like this." The teacher physically holds Caroline's head up along with his or her own. Once Caroline imitates correctly, the teacher returns to reinforcement. Negative reinforcement or physical punishment should be avoided, as the passive child already feels worthless, and punishment may drive such a student into further despair.

The *Interactionalists*' techniques applicable to the passive stage can be found in both Glasser's and Dreikurs's work. Glasser's contributions are largely covert teacher behaviors, as his overt use of confronting questions and classroom meetings is predicated on a student actively responding. However, having the teacher observe the passive student and the situations where passivity is most or least evident can be very helpful. The teacher can assess what he or she is currently doing with the student in terms of instructional activities, materials, grouping, and physical placement. A determination can then be made as to whether certain materials, groupings, and so on, might be changed. Overtly, changes in the classroom can be then made that would be of greater interest and comfort for the student.

The Dreikurs model appears to provide some further understanding of the motivation behind passivity and how a teacher can help to redirect that motivation. Dreikurs's point of view is that the passive child has the mistaken goal of "helplessness," reflected in a desire to belong, but has given up. The teacher can help that student to learn to belong. The behaviors used would be directed toward affirming the student's goal of helplessness before determining a plan. The teacher would collect information about the student's interaction with peers, family, and other teachers. The teacher would ask, "How do *I* feel toward that student?" If the answer is "incapable," then helplessness can be suspected as the student's goal. The student would then be asked the verifying questions, and the teacher would look for the *recognition reflex* rather than for a verbal response. With the goal established, the teacher would then develop a plan for the passive student that would include a lot of encouragement from the teacher for the slightest attempt by the student to improve. The plan would also provide the student with tasks that he or she could handle successfully and that would help the class, and it would show other students that the student can be a contributing member.

Transition from Passivity to Physical Aggression

Fortunately or unfortunately, when the teacher is successful in turning the inner energies of the passive student outward, the student's behavior becomes physically aggressive. The student has a new awareness that he or she can have an impact on those outside persons from whom he or she previously had withdrawn. This new-found euphoria of control manifests itself in a testing of the limits and of finding out how much of a controller one can be. When the previously passive student comes out into the world and is then frustrated or denied by an object or person, it would be common for the student to lash out by kicking, spitting, or hitting. The student would try "to ram his or her will" against others.

The Physically Aggressive Student

Description: It might be a difficult premise for some teachers to accept, but the expression of physical aggression by a previously passive student is a desired collection of behaviors that indicate the student is moving up the stages of socialization. The goal for a physically aggressive student is to help the student channel those physical acts into expressions of language. In the process of channeling those acts, the teacher must carefully guard against driving the student back into passivity.

The physically aggressive student finds the world a prohibitive place. Persons are always trying to stop the student from gratifying his or her desires, and the student feels that the way to get something is to attack. According to Transactional Analysis, the student has an "I'm OK, you're not OK" attitude, and, according to Dreikurs, the student is operating with the misguided goal of *revenge*, to get back at those who prohibit.

This student needs little introduction to the experienced classroom teacher. He or she stands out and causes the teacher to always be wary. The teacher likens the student's presence to sitting near a keg of dynamite. Unlike dynamite, the student does not explode once and disintegrate; instead, he or she continually explodes with irrational, physical outbursts of behavior. As a result, this student often endangers others, personal and school property, and, at times, himself or herself.

Characteristics: Physically aggressive students usually display the following behaviors:

- When asked to move, look at their work, or any other similar request, they will physically refuse to do so.
- When frustrated because they do not get their way, they will throw a temper tantrum.
- If physically restrained by the teacher, they will fight back.
- They will constantly punch, kick, or trip other students.
- They will hurt themselves by taking unreasonable risks; e.g., jumping across a large hole, running into a wall, scaling and balancing from dangerous heights, or driving a vehicle to the edge of disaster.

- They will misbehave during classwork sessions, throwing spitballs and airplanes, grabbing books and papers, and throwing chairs to get the teacher's constant physical attention.

Teacher Techniques

Keep in mind that the teacher's task is twofold: first, to restrain the student's actions from hurting others or destroying property; second, to transfer physical action to verbal action. This brings back memories of a primary school teacher who had the following two classroom rules:

1. No hitting or swearing.
2. If you are going to hit, then swear instead.

Intuitively, this teacher knew that verbal aggression was to be valued over acts of violence.

The *Behaviorists*' approach of covertly collecting baseline data and deciding on a reinforcement plan would use the specific teacher behaviors of shaping, modeling with language, "time out," saturation, and extinction. *Shaping* would be targeting one desirable behavior at a time and reinforcing it. *Modeling with language* is a technique where the teacher stops a student from attacking and shows the student how to verbalize his or her feelings. For example, a student who begins to fight after being shoved by another student is stopped by the teacher and told (to state with Gordon's "I" message), "When I am shoved, I'm afraid I will fall and injure myself; that makes me frightened and then angry" (behavior effect-feeling). "*Time out*" is a technique that can often be used by removing the student from classroom activities to an area void of any stimulation. A time period should be established. If the student returns to the class and behaves in the same manner, the student should be removed again and the time period increased. The teacher can also use the process of *saturation*, where the student is made to repeat his or her aggressive act until it becomes tiring and negatively reinforcing. Such a case is the student who destroys the papers and work of others. This student could be required to take a large stack of old newspapers and tear page after page into little pieces. Obviously such techniques involve a great deal of teacher power, and they may come close to becoming negative reinforcement. On the other hand, if a student's aggressive behavior is not causing human or property damage, a less intrusive approach such as *extinction* can be used. The teacher simply withdraws any attention from the misbehavior. Such withdrawal usually causes an initial increase in the misbehavior before it begins to decline.

Interactionalists' approaches attempt to help the student to verbalize concerning his or her actions. Glasser tells the teacher to covertly observe the classroom situation to decide first whether any reorganization of the student's environment should be attempted. The teacher then proceeds to force the issue. This is

COVERT BEHAVIORS	OVERT BEHAVIORS
Interventionists	
Behaviorists	
a. Collect Baseline Data b. Decide on reinforcement program	1. Shaping 2. Modeling with language 3. "Time out" 4. Saturation 5. Extinction
Interactionalists	
Glasser	
a. Observe —the student —the situation b. Assess —what the teacher is doing —what success the student is having	1. Make classroom reorganization 2. Confront the student with commands. "Stop that." "The rule is . . ." 3. Confront the student with "what" questions in private or *classroom meeting:* "What are you doing?" "What are the rules?" "In what ways is your behavior helping you?" 4. Press for a Plan 5. Reap the Consequences 6. Levels of Isolation —repeat steps 2, 3, 4, and 5
Dreikurs	
a. Observe and collect information about student —with peers —with family —with other teachers b. Ask oneself "Do I feel . . . hurt? revenge?" c. Recognition reflex after verifying question	1. Questions of social goals: "Do you want to know . . . ?" "Could it be that you want to hurt others?" 2. Make a plan, protect the student from being hurt. 3. Use the whole class for support 4. Natural/logical consequences 5. Encouragement
Non-Interventionists	
Gordon	
	1. Verbalizing student actions
Harris	
	1. Teach T.A., emphasizing the *Child* Construct

CHART 12–2. *Physically Aggressive Student and Teacher Behaviors*

done by confronting the student with commands and repeating the rules. The student is asked to describe his or her behavior, explain the rules, determine the effectiveness of aggression, and detail a collaborative plan. This is followed by being held accountable for the agreed-upon consequences of the plan. Failure to comply results in being placed in a level of isolation (in class, in school, at home, or in an institution), with the student having the opportunity to remake a plan at every level. It is important to note Glasser's advocacy of *classroom meetings* and how they apply to the physically aggressive pupil. The student who is ruled by his or her bodily impulses thinks of no one else but self (egocentric, prerational thought). The classroom meeting, as a forum for an all-class plan, might facilitate a student's thinking about others. All students have the opportunity to tell the physically aggressive student point-blank the effect that his or her behavior is having on them. Such a group encounter, wherein the offending student is put on the spot, might seem overly harsh, but it could be just what the student needs to hear.

Dreikurs's use of collecting information and then using social-goal questions is another way of introducing language as a substitute for physical aggression. Once the teacher has verified revenge as the misdirected student goal, he or she can develop a plan that will incorporate a lot of care, attention, and protection for the student. The teacher will not play into the student's game by showing hurt, but instead will try to remain calm and friendly. The teacher could privately ask the class for help by having them be responsive to the student, by including the student in their activities, and by walking away from any conflict with the offending student. Any aggressive behavior by the student should be met with natural or logical consequences rather than with punishment, such as having the student repair the broken chair (and standing at his or her desk until the glue sets) instead of being required to stay after school or being scolded. The process of encouragement, including recognition of the student's attempts to improve and having faith in that improvement, should be an ongoing one.

A few of the *Non-Interventionists*' techniques are also suitable to this stage of development. Gordon's use of nondirective statements, wherein the teacher gives verbal meaning to a student's action, facilitates social growth. For example, the teacher who says, "Tina, you must be mad at Charles to tear his sweater," enables the student to see the relationship between thought and action. Likewise, Harris's *Child* construct is similar to the actions of the physically aggressive student, and the terms *Parent, Adult,* and *Child* can be taught to the student to permit the child to reflect on his or her actions.

Transition from Physical Aggression to Verbal Aggression

One form of "adult misbehavior" replaces another as a student moves up the ladder of social development. The physically aggressive student who learns to use verbal aggression is making progress. The teacher should support (within realistic limits) students who fight with their mouths instead of their hands.

The Verbally Aggressive Student

Description: The consolidation of this stage is evident by the student who "leads" with his or her mouth. He or she is the boss, commanding, scolding, yelling, and demanding. The student is using words to get his or her way. The louder and more violent the language, the student reasons, the greater will be his or her success. This posture, according to Transactional Analysis, is still an "I'm OK, you're not OK" view. According to Dreikurs, the misguided social goal is now control, to manipulate others through language. The student is still prerational and egocentric, thinking only of his or her needs rather than the needs of others. Students of this stage are perhaps seen as the most common "problems" in elementary and secondary schools. Be of good cheer, as this is only one stage from rational, socialized thought.

Characteristics: The verbally aggressive student displays some of the following behaviors:

- Makes fun, teases, and ridicules other students.
- Swears at other students.
- Jokes and laughs when asked to be serious.
- "Sasses" or is sarcastic toward the teacher.
- Yells out with inappropriate comments during class instruction.
- Gets into frequent shouting matches.
- Laughs and is openly amused when other students are being reprimanded.

Applying Techniques

Unlike the physically aggressive student, these pupils generally do not cause physical harm or destruction. Instead, they are a constant nuisance and annoyance to the teacher and class. As a result, the teacher no longer needs the powerful controlling techniques of the Interventionists; instead, he or she may now want to employ techniques of the Non-Interventionists, who support the use of language, and then move to the Interactionalists, who put language to use in a purposeful and constrained manner. Please refer to Chart 12–3.

Verbal aggression is the student's attempt to verbally *encode* his or her feelings and ideas. Statements like "I hate you" or "You're a turkey" are beginning efforts (however poor) by a student to tell someone what he or she really means and feels. In detailing techniques, teachers should believe that verbal aggression is a stage that must be temporarily accepted so he or she will respond (as Dreikurs

COVERT BEHAVIORS	OVERT BEHAVIORS
Non-Interventionists	
Gordon	
a. Reorganizing the space b. Reorganizing the time	1. Critical listening 2. Acknowledgment responses 3. Door reopeners 4. Active listening 5. "I" messages 6. Method III "no lose" problem-solving
Harris	
a. Diagnose interaction state—verbal aggression as a "child/or parent" state	1a. Ask the student questions, adult to adult b. Reply to student's verbal aggression with adult statements c. Use adult responses to clarify student's verbal aggression 2. Affirm the student as "OK" with complementary transactions
Interactionalists	
Dreikurs	
a. Observe and collect information about the student —with peers —with family —with other teachers b. Ask oneself, "Do I feel . . . beaten"—control c. Recognition reflex after verifying question	1. Confronting: "Do you want to know why you are behaving like this?" 2. Verifying: "Could it be that you want . . . to be boss"—power 3. Make a plan according to verified goal—let the student have power 4. Use the class group 5. Natural/logical consequences 6. Encouragement
Glasser	
a. Observe —the student —the situation b. Assess —what the teacher is currently doing —what success the student is having	1. Confront the transgression: "Stop that, the rule is . . ." 2. Ask "what" questions: "What are you doing?" "What are the rules?" "In what ways is your behavior helping you?" "What is your plan?"

CHART 12–3. *Verbally Aggressive Student and Teacher Behaviors*

	3. Press for plan
	4. Have student reap the consequences of plan Use levels of isolation—repeat steps 2, 3, 4, 5
	5. Classroom meetings
Interventionists	
Behaviorists	
a. Collect baseline data	1. Nonverbal extinction
b. Decide on reinforcement	2. Contingency contracting

CHART 12–3. *Verbally Aggressive Student and Teacher Behaviors (cont'd)*

suggests) in a way that is disengaged from the emotion, without feeling beaten and without verbally lashing back. If the teacher responds harshly, then the student's poor attempt to communicate is cut off and the child may be driven back to committing physical aggression as the only way to communicate his or her feelings and desires.

The techniques of Teacher Effectiveness training are a good starting point. Covertly, the possibility of classroom reorganization needs to be considered if circumstances exist that would trigger the child's verbal barrage. The overt techniques would be to listen to the student's emotional responses, remain detached, and wait for the student to calm down and think about what is being said. This can be accomplished through critical listening, acknowledgment responses, door openers and reopeners, active listening, and, if the behavior has a concrete effect on the teacher, the use of "I" messages. After the student has been supported in expressing his or her true feelings, socialized language can then be attempted by using Method III "no-lose" problem-solving techniques.

The other Non-Interventionist model that speaks to verbal aggression is *Transactional Analysis*. Such language is conveyed through either the impulse-ridden *Child* or the overbearing *Parent*. The teacher should ask questions from the *Adult* state directed to the student's *Adult*. Affirming the student as "OK" with a complementary transaction is important, for if there is cross-communication (i.e., Parent to Child), then the student would retreat into an "I'm Not OK" view, give up using language, and resort to violence.

Once a student has become calm, then almost all the overt and covert behaviors of the Interactionalists could be used. Dreikurs's concept of the "power" hungry child intertwines with the verbally aggressive stage. After verifying the goal, the teacher could then establish a plan that would give the student power in a socially acceptable manner. The teacher needs to avoid becoming involved in an escalating power struggle with the student, where one of them will win big and the other will be humiliated.

Only sections of *Glasser's* model would apply to this stage. His covert observations and assessments and overt classroom changes used as preventive measures are valuable; yet, the reader will notice how the uses of confrontation and isolation have been omitted in Chart 12–3. The student needs the opportunity to defuse his or her emotions through verbal communication; confrontation and isolation stop the student from doing so. On the other hand, after the student has gained some control over his or her strong feelings, then "What" questions pressing for a plan, reaping the consequences, classroom meetings, and possibly isolation would be in order. In the same manner, the Behaviorists' use of nonverbal extinction, wherein they ignore the child's behavior but still allow the student to express himself or herself and then reward social or appropriate language through a contingency contract, could also be justified.

Transition from Verbal Aggression to Social Interaction Through Language

The student begins to think not only of his or her wants but also of the consequences of his or her actions. The student's verbal aggressions become less frequent, and he or she settles down and is able to talk about why they occurred. The student's moral reasoning begins to emerge in its most elementary form at Level I—The Punishment and Obedience Orientation—and Level II—Instrumental-Relativist Orientation. Previous prerational explanations for verbal aggressions such as, "He's a jerk! I hate him!" change to concrete statements such as, "Because I wanted that pen, I thought it was mine!" or "I don't like to be pushed around," or "It's not *fair* for them to do it when I can't!"

The Social-Interaction-Through-Language Student

Description: At this stage of development, it is difficult to classify behaviors as disruptive. Students will fight, they will verbally attack, and they will not always respond to the teacher's commands; yet, these students are seen as "normal" because the teacher can reason on a basic level with them. Dreikurs would classify their goal as attention, and to achieve it they will annoy the teacher from time to time; yet, they have enough language ability, self-control, and reasoning to know how far they can go before the teacher will become excessively angry. In other words, they think through their actions. Harris would say that they have an "I'm OK, You're OK" attitude. The only missing aspect of true social behavior is logical adult reasoning that takes the standards and concerns of others into consideration.

Characteristics: Students possess some of these divergent characteristics:

- Being teacher's pet: they are over eager to please, and will volunteer for anything.
- Being the class humorist: they interject laughter or jokes that break up the class and amuse the teacher.
- Being the cause of occasional "accidents": someone gets tripped, or a chair falls backwards and disrupts the classroom decorum.
- Pretending to need help with their classwork, from the teacher or from other students, when none is really needed.
- Being quick to point out others who are breaking the rules.
- Conforming to peer standards of dress and manners.

Application of Techniques

The central goal of working with a student at this stage is to consolidate the student's awareness of his or her behavior and then expand the student's awareness of consequences to include a concern for others. The models that most closely represent this stage are the Interactionalists and the comprehensive treatment of the Non-Interventionists.

Glasser's step of asking the student "what" questions enables the student to focus on the outcome of his or her behavior (Level I—Moral Reasoning: The Punishment and Obedience Orientation). "What" questions, followed by *Dreikurs's* verified goal of attention, help to formulate a plan that gives the student the attention he or she craves. A plan that incorporates logical consequences provides the student with further consideration of what he or she gains by acceptable behavior (Level II—Moral Reasoning: The Instrumental-Relativist Orientation).

Aside from a disruptive incident, *Gordon's* use of active listening combined with certain *values-clarification* exercises enlarges the student's awareness of other criteria for behavior (Level III—Moral Reasoning: The Interpersonal Concordance, and Level IV—Law and Order Orientation). To help the student to further organize his or her thinking about present and future behaviors, the teacher can use values-clarification questions and formal exercises such as ranking, sorting, role playing, assigned reading, and composition.

Transition from Social Interaction Through Language to Conceptualization Through Language

A student who is moving across stages will no longer be disruptive. He or she might break a class rule, but it will be because of a rational decision to do so. One of the signs that the student's use of language is becoming more abstract and

COVERT BEHAVIORS	OVERT BEHAVIORS
Interactionalists	
Glasser	
	1. Confront the student with "what" questions: "What are you doing?" "What are the rules?" "In what ways is your behavior helping you?"
Dreikurs	
a. Verify the goal—attention	1. Make a plan—give attention 2. Logical consequences
Non-Interventionists	
Raths, Harmin, and Simon	
a. Avoid judging, influencing, or imposing teacher values b. Look for values indicators —clues with teacher —clues with others	1. Look for values indicators 2. Informal values questions: seven criteria 3. Formal exercises: —ranking —sorting —role playing —literature —composition
Gordon	
	1. Active listening

CHART 12–4. *The Social Interaction Through Language and Teacher Behaviors*

indicative of higher levels of moral reasoning (Levels III and IV) is when he or she shows obvious interest in listening to another student's ideas of how to resolve real-life dilemmas. Although the student's reasoning is still based on a "What's in it for me?" outlook, eventually the student will begin to reason according to considerations of others (i.e., "What would others think?" and "What are the laws of society?").

The Conceptualization-Through-Language Student

Description: This is the stage where most of us would like to see all our students. The student reasons as a mature adult and wishes to grapple such value issues as war, sex, drugs, and crime. He or she is interested in knowing how these issues relate to society at large. The student might challenge the teacher's authority or label the rules of a particular class or society as being "unjust," but the student will be open to debating the issue. The teacher may need to be sufficiently flexible to change a classroom rule if the student has a valid point. A teacher who fails to use higher moral reasoning at this juncture and stands behind the "cloak of authority" could make a student retreat to previous stages.

Characteristics: Following are some behaviors of conceptualization-through-language students.

- They question the teacher and students about their own beliefs and behaviors.
- They actively listen and respond to group discussions about classroom and societal issues.
- They bring such considerations as "the good of all of us" into discussions.
- They attempt to reason with others who are practicing behaviors (stealing or drugs, for example) that they feel are detrimental.

Application of Techniques

The goal of the techniques involved is to facilitate a student's moral development from Level III (Interpersonal Concordance) and Level IV (Law and Order Orientation) to Level V (Social–Contract) and Level VI (Universal–Ethical). It would be unrealistic for us to attempt to describe or even profess the ability to know how to do this in a systematic way. These students are not disruptive and are therefore largely beyond the scope of this book; however, we would suggest the use of the Interactionalists' classroom meetings, educational change for a democratic classroom and the Non-Interventionists' group discussions of values, moral dilemmas, and "no lose" problem solving as particularly applicable.

Dreikurs's notion of reassessing for educational change is applicable when the teacher allows the individual student to choose many of his or her own activities and schedules, thus facilitating individual responsibility independent of imposed rules and regulations (Level V—Moral Reasoning–Social Contract). The same independence can be promoted by allowing students to engage in Glasser's classroom meeting, where real classroom problems are discussed and group rules are made. Group exercises of Raths, Harmin, and Simon that stimulate alternative actions through role-playing or discussion of moral dilemmas can facilitate all levels of moral reasoning. *Gordon's* use of individual problem solving through Method III is an excellent means for a student to plan behavior according to personal codes of right and wrong.

COVERT BEHAVIORS		OVERT BEHAVIORS
	Interactionalists	
	Dreikurs	
a. Reassessing for educational change for democratic living		1. Individual student choice of activities and schedules
	Glasser	
		1. Classroom meetings
		2. Group rules
	Non-Interventionists	
	Raths, Harmin, and Simon	
		1. Group exercises —role-playing —moral dilemma discussion
	Gordon	
		1. Method III "no lose" problem solving

CHART 12–5. *The Conceptualization Through Language and Teacher Behaviors*

The Class as a Social Unit

After outlining stages of progression of individual social development, matched with applicable techniques, it can be hypothesized that groups show the same development.

We have previously described the assistance teachers can provide to individual students along the Developmental Socialization Continuum to help the students achieve more mature social behavior. Many readers probably have memories of certain classes in which the students created a collective personality. Often these classes would match their collective will against the teacher. This can be a natural tendency when a group of students who know each other first meets a new teacher and little trust exists. The teacher might see the same behavioral progression or regression in the class as a whole, as is seen through the stages of socialization. If trust is not quickly established, verbal aggression could be directed at the teacher in comments that might begin in a relatively mild way, such as, "Why do we always have these lousy assignments?" These aggressions could continue with harsher outbursts, such as, "Teacher, you're crazy!" or "We all hate this class!" If the teacher does not meet these verbal aggressions by "listening" to what the students are really trying to say, and instead uses either inappropriately harsh or permissive techniques, the class might regress into physical aggression by throwing objects at the teacher or each other, destroying property, or even making direct assaults on the teacher. If the teacher were to react with severe punishment that evokes fear, the class might further retreat into passivity, where little work is done, students do not talk, and the class becomes bored and expressionless. The teacher may have won the battle, but he or she has lost the war.

If a teacher finds this regression occurring, he or she can respond to the entire class as though he or she were dealing with one student. The goals would be to encourage activity at the passive stage, verbal aggression at the physically aggressive stage, and rational dialogue at the verbally aggressive stage.

Spheres of Competency

Previously it was mentioned that there might be pupils who are outside the teacher's *sphere of competency*. As Gordon, in *T.E.T. Teacher Effectiveness Training,* delineated "spheres of freedom" with concentric circles, so may "spheres of competency" be drawn. (See Figure 12–2.)

Teachers have many skills for organizing educational experiences for students. With a further knowledge of management models, pathways of teacher choice, and the application of techniques to social development, the reader will have gained insights in how to help students acquire higher levels of socialized behavior. Hopefully this book will widen one's sphere of competency; yet, there may be a student who is outside a teacher's capability to help. Throughout one's teaching career, it is rare not to have a few such experiences. After having attempted many eclectic approaches, a teacher should not feel inadequate by seeking outside help. Chapter 13 offers a staff approach for gathering outside assistance for a student whose misbehavior is creating difficulties beyond the classroom. If such a team approach is not available, or if the student needs more specialized help, then referrals should be made to those with more specialized experience. Referrals would proceed to school counselors and, if necessary, would continue to further levels of competency, such as a psychologist, psychiatric out-patient clinics, and, ultimately, psychiatric institutionalization.

It would be self-deceiving for a teacher to think he or she can help every student. A teacher may have twenty-five to thirty students a day in an elementary school class or more than one hundred students a day in secondary school classes. The models and approaches of this book are based on what a teacher can do with an individual student within the constraints of regular teaching time. A teacher who has an eclectic knowledge of various models can find ways to help most students; he or she can help students who show an *orderly* unfolding of human behavior. Students who need psychiatric help are those whose behavior is *not orderly* and *not predictable*. Whether such a student is deeply passive or violently aggressive, the teacher would be doing the student and himself or herself a disservice by not asking for the needed help. A classroom teacher who must attend to many students and a multitude of tasks could become terribly frustrated from

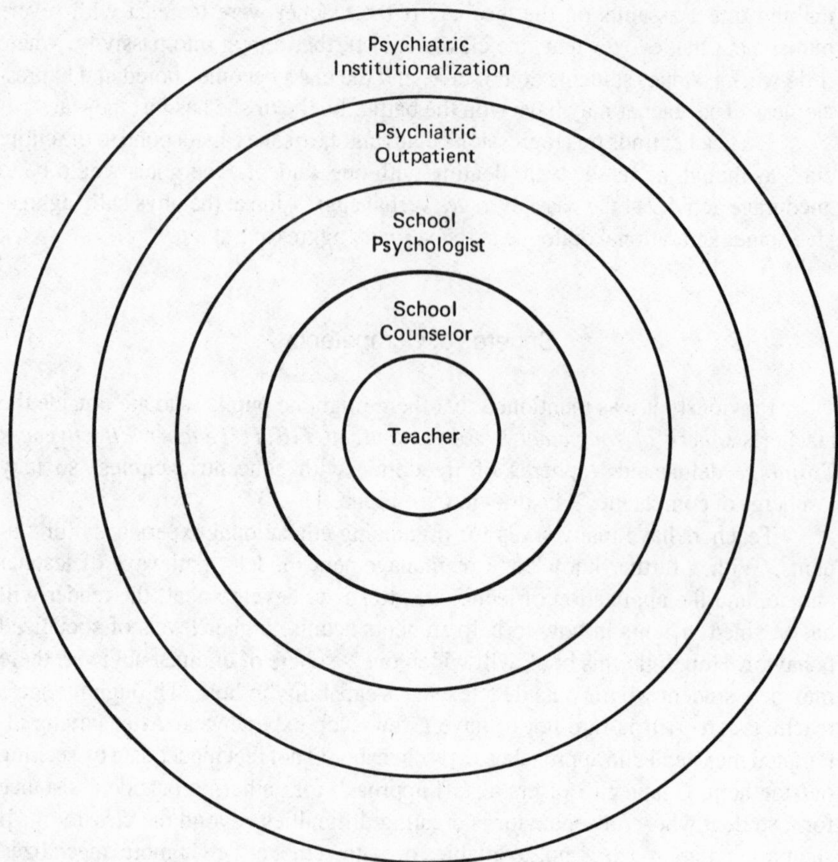

FIGURE 12–2. *Spheres of Teacher Competency*

trying to deal with an emotionally deviant child. A student's failure to respond could even trigger a teacher's regression into irrational stages of action, such as a retreat to verbal and physical aggressions that are directed at the deviant student as well as the entire class.

Summary

In review, it has been suggested that a teacher can decide upon using particular techniques from the various models that are applicable to the stage theory of social development. The teacher's goal is to facilitate the student's behavior from one stage to the next, although it will not be until the final stages are reached that "adult" social behavior will be seen. A mismatch of teacher techniques to stages could contribute to a student's regressing to more immature behavior. It was theorized that group behavior in an entire class could also move forward or backward along the same continuum. Lastly, "spheres of teacher competency" were described to allow for the assessment of those students who can be helped by a classroom teacher and those who need to be referred to more specialized help for their problems.

13

"Mainstreaming" the Difficult Student: The School Staff as a Team

Once the classroom door is closed, the teacher enters a private world of intimate interaction with students that can be rewarding, dynamic, and exciting. This is teaching at its best. However, this relationship and interaction can also produce a hostile, frightening environment for the teacher and students, where little learning takes place. Teachers generally have been given the charge by parents, school administrators, and fellow teachers to be the "lion tamer" or to be an exponent of the "don't smile until Christmas" syndrome. The message is that you are given *this* number of students for *this* period of time, and—for "heaven's sake"—it is your responsibility to keep them under control. Your "long arm of control" should somehow even extend to those times when you are not supervising your students, such as on the school playground, in the school cafeteria, on the school bus, and during school assemblies and sporting events. "It was *your* Robert, Mrs. (or Mr.) Jones, who was causing a problem in the (whatever). *You* need to do something about him!" Such a demand on teachers suggests that they have omnipotent powers and are able to wave "the magical wand of fear" to get students to behave. (Often, this same demand is also unfairly asked of school principals, counselors, or school psychologists *by* teachers.) If you cannot appease your school administrator, fellow teachers, or parents, you will eventually find your teacher performance evaluation carrying such criticisms as "has difficulty with disciplining," a phrase that seems to reflect the ultimate sin of being a teacher. This causes teachers to feel they have been branded with the scarlet letter *D* for *discipline* and that they have been shunned by their colleagues who, in subtle ways, suggest to them that they are ineffectual and unworthy to be part of their profession.

We suggest that the larger a school becomes, the more rules and structure that seem to be needed, and, in turn, the teacher's "area of freedom" becomes more limited. Once these limitations and structures are established, they seem to become "sacred cows" and are rarely re-evaluated to see whether they are truly needed or are serving the purpose for which they were originally intended. This erosion of "freedom of the teacher" continues until one feels dehumanized or one has become a jailer rather than a creative teacher.

Let us therefore suggest that teachers turn from the view of the teacher as a "classroom island" to that of becoming part of a cooperative team effort involving some or all of the school staff. This support group would have a number of advantages:

1. The group could be supportive of the teacher who is, for the first time, attempting the various techniques suggested in the models previously presented.
2. They could recognize and work on the problem of the "difficult" student who rarely is a problem *only* in the classroom, but who also disrupts the school activities that generally affect the entire school staff.
3. The group could engage in a team effort that includes school administrators and permits a forum for re-evaluating the institutional rules that limit the teacher's "area of freedom," and they could arrive at rules that are based on what is best for the *individual* student rather than on what is administratively expedient.
4. The school staff, working as a team, could concentrate on the "difficult" student and, using the overt and covert techniques in the various models, the teacher behavioral pathways, and a developmental understanding and perspective, could gradually blend all these methods to create a common schoolwide mode of operation that would improve the atmosphere for all students.
5. They could engage in a team effort, based on the techniques previously presented, that will meet the new legal demand for "mainstreaming" the special or exceptional child into the social activities of the school, with the "least restrictive environment" for such children.

Although it is generally true that teachers who are mainstreaming exceptional children will have ranges of students with whom they might not have worked before, we are not assuming, and we do not wish the teacher to assume, that a mainstreamed student automatically will be a discipline problem. As with all students, most mainstreamed youngsters will exhibit a great degree of self-control, but a few will not. We do not view mainstreaming in the narrow sense of having "special" students from "Educationally Mentally Retarded," "Learning and Behaviorally Disabled," "Perceptually Impaired," "Brain Damaged," and "Emotionally Disturbed" classes entering the regular classroom. This is one aspect of mainstreaming, but its wider concept is more identical to the notion of a fully integrated democratic school. This is a school where all children, regardless of race, religion, sex, economics, ethnic background, and social, mental, or physical capabilities, have the constitutional right to be part of both the classroom and the school community. Therefore, in this discussion of mainstreaming, we are really talking about problems resulting from having a full, dynamic, heterogeneous classroom of students.

In having a variety of students in the classroom, there is a greater probability that a teacher will encounter a student whose behavior disrupts the class or the school as a whole. It might be a student who has an extraordinary intellect, a student from a culture that is foreign to the teacher, a student with a physical handicap, or possibly a retarded child. Hopefully, based on the content of this book, the teacher will have a range of strategies and models of student management to use with such students, to be both applied individually or by a team effort called "staffing."

Staffing: A Team Process

For the well-seasoned classroom teacher, the mere mention of being part of a team process brings forth shouts of, "Oh, no, not another meeting!" Such a verbal aggression from teachers seems to be justified, as every teacher can remember meeting after meeting that has dragged on with little or no results. The frustration produced from these futile attempts to work with others seems to drive teachers back into their classroom "islands" to "do their own thing." It can be hypothesized that the reasons for nonproductive meetings are the lack of a clear orderly process for solving problems, and the group members' lack of understanding regarding the possible solutions available to them. Teachers have sat in meetings for hours feeling unclear as to what the problem being discussed was, and finally they would become frustrated into a state of "helpless passivity" by their colleagues whose "personal wisdom" seems to be repeated at every faculty meeting. In order to overcome these "roadblocks" to good collective problem solving, a clear orderly process will be proposed based on the six steps for problem solving described in the Thomas Gordon model of *Teacher Effectiveness Training* (T.E.T.). This material is based on John Dewey's scientific problem-solving steps of (1) defining the problem, (2) generating a possible solution, (3) evaluating, (4) deciding on a solution, (5) implementing, and (6) evaluating the solutions. In order to minimize the personal wisdom or biased form of solution, we propose that the team use the overt and covert teacher techniques, pathways, and developmental constructs as a data base for reasoned solutions. The function of the team then becomes one of creative integration or application of these techniques and methods to fit the needs of their particular school or a particular student who is "difficult."

Individualized Educational Plan (IEP)

As a result of federal legislation and some state laws, there are now demands for school personnel to create a specific plan, called the Individualized Educational Plan (IEP), to insure that the "exceptional" pupil who is now in school or is returning to the regular classroom from a special class will continue to have an individualized and focused program. In order to meet legal requirements, the IEP needs to include:

1. a statement of the student's present performance
2. yearly goals
3. immediate objectives
4. services to be used (or who will work with the child)
5. a time line for such services
6. the amount of time to be spent outside the regular classroom
7. objective criteria for evaluating achievement of objectives and goals.

Such a plan ordinarily needs to be developed by a team that includes, at the minimum, the classroom teacher, a second teacher (possibly the teacher of exceptional children), and the parents or guardian. (The student can also be a part of such a meeting and procedures.) The agreed upon plan must be written and signed by those involved. (See Form 13–1.)

The process of staffing can be an ideal aid to be used by the team to develop a plan for the "exceptional" child as well as for the "difficult" student. Although the central goal of IEP is to establish an educational plan, in many cases the child's social behavior is such that his or her cooperative behavior needs to be established so that the teacher will be able to carry out the plan. The tools presented previously are applicable to all children and can be valuable for the teacher working with the exceptional student.

"Staffing" is a structured process whereby school personnel meet and formulate an individualized plan for responding to and assisting a "misbehaving" or "difficult" child to become a socialized part of the school and classroom. The staff meeting can include any of the school personnel who have contact with this child, including such people as the school bus driver, cafeteria workers, play-

Student's Name ______________________ Summary of Present Behaviors ______________________

School ______________________

Data of Staffing ______________________

Long-Term Behavioral Changes (1) ______________________

______ (2) ______________________

(3) ______________________ (4) ______________________

______________________ (5) ______________________

short-term behavioral change	specific covert/overt teacher techniques	person responsible	% of time	approx. date of completion	re-evaluation date

Specific educational changes ______________________ Staffing Members ______________________

Evaluation criteria for changes ______________________

Date of meeting ______________________

Re-evaluation date ______________________

FORM 13–1. *Individualized Educational (Socialization) Plan (IEP)* ground supervisors, guidance counselors, the principal, as well as the child's parents and even the child as participants. Such participants may wish to meet on a formal or informal basis every two weeks at a regular school meeting or during preparation periods. The number of participants can vary, but the ideal size of the group would be four to nine people. Hopefully, most of the staffing participants would already have an understanding of the ideas previously provided in the summarized models (Chapters 2 through 9), as well as the directional pathways and the developmental socialization continuum that is to be used as a content foundation or knowledge base. One might find that, in his or her group, members who represent all three theoretical positions (Non-Interventionist, Interactionalist, and Interventionist) would be involved. It is within a group where these differences among teachers of varying beliefs and classroom practices exist that the greatest range of options will be explored to determine how to intervene with the "misbehaving" or problem student. The value-clarification model suggests that choosing from alternatives provides the best forum for decision making.

In order to facilitate group problem solving, the staffing process or meeting is governed by specific rules that might initially appear to be rigid and arbitrary. However, these strict procedures as to who may speak and for how long are needed when a team attempts to work together, and the rules restrict the "personal wisdom chatter" that lacks direction and focus. Such rules also decrease the possibility of the process deteriorating into aimless meetings where nothing is resolved and no actions are taken, as such meetings quickly deflate the teacher's enthusiasm.

It has been described previously that when individuals begin to feel frustrated and unsuccessful, they also begin to retreat along the developmental socialization continuum from rational problem solving to a prerational behavior of verbal aggression, physical aggression, or helpless passivity. The structure of the staff meeting will hold to a minimum the "verbal aggression" and "not OK" view of students or parents, while at the same time it will maintain the support needed by staff members to generate rational solutions.

Staffing Agenda: Steps and Procedures

It is helpful at the beginning of a staff meeting to appoint a "timekeeper" who will announce each step and goal and will identify those who contribute. The timekeeper will serve as a monitor to channel the discussion to conform to the stated goals. (See Figure 13–1, Staffing Agenda.)

Step 1.: Statement of the Problem—"Overview of the Student's Behavior"

Purpose: Step 1 will provide the members of the group with a general description of the student's behavior and will state clearly those behavioral changes that the teacher would like to see in the student.

STAFFING AGENDA

Step	*Topic*	*Speaker*	*Time*	*Purpose*
1.	Statement of the problem	Teacher	3 mins.	To give general description of student's behavior and state changes desired.
2.	Background information from the teacher	Teacher	10 mins.	To present background information using collected data.
3.	Background information from the group	All Members	15 mins.	To add information about student's behavior in various contacts with others throughout the school day.
4.	Clarifying background information	All Members	8 mins.	To clarify information already given and establish changes in student's behavior.
5.	Generating possible solutions in written form	All Members	3 mins.	To have each member give possible solutions in writing.
6.	Generating possible solutions in verbal form	All Members	15 mins.	To verbally share all possible solutions with the group.
7.	Generating and evaluating a plan of action	All Members	15 mins.	To explore all solutions and look for interrelated or common abilities.
8.	Deciding on a solution, "the final written plan"	All Members	10 mins.	To decide upon a group plan with each member assigned responsibility.
9.	Implementing a commitment	All Members	1 min.	To have members make a commitment to plan by signing the written form.
10.	Re-evaluation schedule	All Members	5 mins.	To agree upon appropriate period of time for implementation of plan before re-evaluation.

FIGURE 13–1. *Staffing Agenda*

Time: 3 minutes

Procedure: The classroom teacher of the misbehaving student (or the staff member having the greatest difficulty with the student) begins the reporting. The teacher (or other staff member) will discuss any typical behaviors or incidents that have occurred and will describe the teacher actions or approaches that have been attempted. This teacher will end the report with a list of behavioral changes that he or she would like to see in the student. For example, "I would like to see Carol (1) attend school on a regular basis, (2) work with peers without fighting or destroying their products, and (3) complete her homework."

Step 2: Background Information from the Teacher

Purpose: To have the classroom teacher (or the staff member having difficulty with the student's behavior) present a baseline or systematic collection of data on the different facets of the student's behavior.

Time: 10 minutes

Procedure: The classroom teacher or any other member who has collected systematic data with the use of baseline methods suggested by the Behaviorists or the observations of the student in relationship with peers, family, or school staff as suggested by Glasser and Dreikurs is given the opportunity to report. A student background information form (see Form 13–2) can be developed by the school staff to organize information gathering. It is advisable during Step 2 that only the member with the organized data be permitted to report, and that questions and discussion be held for a later period. This procedure will provide an avenue to get the information on the table, not to clarify it.

Step 3: Background Information from the Group

Purpose: This step permits other members of the group to add any information they might have from their various contacts with the misbehaving student.

Time: 15 minutes

Procedure: Any members of the group who have contact with the student present their background information. It is urged that they try to use the same reporting criteria as those found on the school's student background information form to determine whether the student's behavior is consistent from situation to situation or with staff member to staff member. Again, as in Step 2, the staff members simply report their information and withhold discussion of the information until later.

Step 4: Clarifying Background Information

Purpose: To permit all members to ask clarifying questions concerning the background information previously presented.

Time: 8 minutes

Procedure: All members of the staff meeting now have the right to question the teacher or staff member who presented information in Steps 1 through 3, in order to discuss the student and his or her problems in greater detail. This is also

Student __________________________
Date _____________________________
Name of Staff Member __________________

Part I Student's Misbehavior(s)

1. Describe misbehavior(s)
   a.
   b.
   c.
2. How frequent is each type of misbehavior?
   a.
   b.
   c.
3. What time of day does it occur?
   a.
   b.
   c.
4. In what physical surroundings?
   a.
   b.
   c.
5. With which peers or adults?
   a.
   b.
   c.
6. In what kinds of activities is student engaged before misbehavior occurs?
   a.
   b.
   c.

Part II Teacher (or other) Actions

1. What do you do when student misbehaves?
   a.
   b.
   c.
2. How does student respond?
   a.
   b.
   c.
3. When are your actions most successful?
4. When are these actions least successful?

FORM 13–2. *Student Background Information*

Part III Student Motivation

1. What responsibilities (assignments, tasks, or orders) does student fulfill?
2. What types of reinforcement (positive and negative) does student receive?
   a. positive (and/or encouragement)
   b. negative (and/or logical consequences)
3. How does student respond to reinforcement?
   a. positive (and/or encouragement)
   b. negative (and/or logical consequences)
4. How does student relate to the group (physical aggression, verbal aggression, passivity, or other behaviors)?

Part IV When Student is *not* Misbehaving

1. Describe positive behaviors.
   a.
   b.
   c.
2. How frequent is each type of positive behavior?
   a.
   b.
   c.
3. What time of day does each behavior occur?
   a.
   b.
   c.
4. In what physical surroundings?
   a.
   b.
   c.
5. With which peers or adults?
   a.
   b.
   c.
6. In what kinds of activities is student engaged before positive behavior occurs?
   a.
   b.
   c.

Part V Additional Questions

1. What does student enjoy doing (hobbies or subjects)?
2. What does student do well (hobbies or subjects)?
3. Are there any reasons to suspect health or physical disabilities?

FORM 13–2. *Student Background Information (cont'd)*

the time to identify and explore what overt techniques have previously been tried with this student by the teacher or others. These questions should be concerned with asking and not presenting solutions in disguise. Such questions as, "Have you tried 'active listening'? It might work." or, "Last year, I had the same type of problem and I found that the classroom meetings worked. Do you think you could do that?" are really disguised solutions and will find their place in Step 5. The group can add to, modify, or alter the behavioral changes first proposed in Step 1 by the teacher. Step 4 is complete when all members agree upon the desired changes for the student being discussed.

Step 5: Generating Possible Solutions in Writing

Purpose: To have all members write down their solutions to the student's overt and covert behaviors or suggestions as to the educational changes that could be implemented to help this student.

Time: 3 minutes

Procedure: All staff members will write down their solutions in terms of what actions they or anyone else could take to help the student. It is during this process that each member should review mentally the teacher-student interaction models of Gordon, Values Clarification, Transactional Analysis, Dreikurs, Glasser, Behavior Modification, and Behaviorism with Punishment, as well as the directional pathways and the Developmental Socialization Continuum. This review will help the member to decide what teacher methods and techniques would be the most helpful and how one can organize these behaviors systematically in relation to the power to be given the student or to be used by the teacher. Writing these possible solutions now actively involves each member in these overt actions, and it means, in Glasser's sense, that the members have committed themselves to the problem-solving process.

Step 6: Generating Possible Solutions Verbally

Purpose: To have each staff member present his or her written ideas verbally to the other members of the group without evaluation or feedback.

Time: 5 minutes

Procedures: Each member presents his or her ideas orally to the group. The discussion of the ideas is reserved for a later step, in order not to inhibit the free flow of each member's ideas.

Step 7: Generating and Evaluating a Plan of Action

Purpose: To have all members verbally explore, in a "brainstorming" format, how each of the ideas presented in Step 6 can be interrelated and developed into a comprehensive, collectively agreed upon plan of action, both for long-term and short-term behavioral changes or objectives.

Time: 15 minutes

Procedure: Interaction among staff members now becomes of primary importance, as the members can fully discuss how their ideas are interrelated or have some commonalities. The models in the various schools of thought (Non-Interventionist, Interactionalist, and Interventionist), the directional pathways, and the overt techniques as they relate to the Developmental Socialization Continuum should be used as a framework for evaluating the solutions presented. The group might ask: "Do our solutions cluster into one model or school of thought? Do they suggest that we wish to begin with the pathway of minimum teacher power, maximum power, or shared power? Can the student's behavior be placed on the Developmental Socialization Continuum, and, if so, do the suggested solutions agree with the techniques proposed in Chapter 10? Can educational changes or changes in time or space affect some or all of the problems?"

It is important in this step to understand that the teacher and staff members have progressed from the "personal wisdom" kind of speculative thinking where teachers try to solve problems by "stabbing in the dark." The constructs, methods, and procedures provided for teachers and school staffs have brought the professionals out of the "darkness" of functioning as limited technicians, and have provided a framework for scientific problem solving, which is characteristic of a true professional.

Step 8: Deciding on a Solution—The Final Written Plan

Purpose: To decide on an orderly plan of action and to put that plan into writing.

Time: 10 minutes

Procedure: Working within the time limit of this step, the staff member must decide upon an agreed plan of action in which members will be responsible for carrying out the various segments of this plan. The use of an Individualized Educational Plan form can organize the writing of such a plan of action and the designation of responsibilities. (All members should receive a copy.)

Step 9: Implementing—A Commitment

Purpose: To have the staff members commit themselves to implementing the plan's procedures.

Time: 1 minute

Procedure: Much like Glasser's view of commitment, each staff member is asked to sign or initial the written plan, and, by so doing, agrees to actively carry out the procedures agreed upon and to return for follow-up re-evaluation. (All members should receive a copy of the plan.)

Step 10: Re-evaluation Schedule

Purpose: To have the members agree to a time for a return meeting to evaluate the plan after a period of implementation, in order to determine its effectiveness based on the collected data.

Time: 5 minutes

Procedure: The last step is used to decide when to meet again, and what each member will do to record the behavioral changes of the student. These records can be made through observation, baseline data, or experimental data.

Summary of Staffing Procedures and Agenda

The structured agenda with arbitrary procedures is a systematic or scientific problem-solving process loosely based on the six steps of problem solving described by Gordon in *T.E.T. Teacher Effectiveness Training* and attributed to John Dewey. Such techniques, of course, can be modified by a staff to fit its working style, but what is most imperative is the agreed upon structure for the staff meetings. (Some schools will write these procedures for the staff on a large chart and place it on the wall in the meeting room.) The solution generated by the staffing procedures must rest on the foundation of understanding the various overt and covert techniques in each model, and how models cluster under various "schools of thought." There is also a need for understanding the use of power that these techniques imply, and how that power can be positioned on the three directional pathways. Additionally, an understanding of the Developmental Socialization Continuum with its implied developmental perspective on prerational and rational behaviors gives a solid knowledge base from which teachers and staff personnel can make informed decisions. Finally, many educational changes will be made within the classroom or throughout the school in order to create a school atmosphere in which problem students become nearly nonexistent.

14

Strengths and Limitations of Today's Teacher-Student Interaction Models

In the earlier descriptions of the teacher-student interaction models, the theoretical assumptions of student motivation and central overt and covert behaviors were described in the context of the Teacher Behavior Continuum. The models were objectively presented and followed by illustrations of how various elements of each could be used in the three pathways of teacher beliefs and then applied to student social development. Implicit in the selection of the various elements was the belief that the models or various techniques within models worked best as power pathways or responses to asocial students. As yet, however, the individual strengths and limitations of these models have not been compared. In order to make these comparisons, it would be helpful to first review these models by scanning the outlines (see Figures 14–1 through 14–7), where one will find a more concise summary of the basic assumptions on motivation, overt teacher behaviors, key vocabulary, and educational insights that have been developed in Chapters 3 through 9. With this content in mind, we can now focus on the strengths and limitations of each model.

The Non-Interventionists

Thomas Gordon, Louis Raths, Merrill Harmin, Sidney Simon, Thomas Harris, Eric Berne, and other Non-Interventionists share a belief in the inner rationality of the student. They believe student misbehavior is the result of obstacles that block the full expression of rational thought. The goal of each of these Non-Interventionists is to use methods to remove those obstacles.

In discussions of the Non-Interventionist models, there are questions common to all. Three such questions are:

1. Do all students, regardless of age or intellectual capacity, have an inherent rationality?
2. Are all students, regardless of language ability, able to verbalize their own personal thoughts and feelings?
3. Inasmuch as an approach predicated on language and reasoning is time consuming, does the teacher have such time to spend with one student?

The Supportive Model of Thomas Gordon

It is difficult to take issue with Teacher Effectiveness Training's emphasis on a warm, accepting relationship between teacher and students and the subsequent need to help students to acquire healthy, positive self-concepts. Gordon is concerned with the teacher being, foremost, a person who is sensitive, warm and noncritical. The strength of his model is that he goes beyond the vague descriptions of becoming a "good" person and instead prescribes specific teacher actions and methods to attain that end. He tells the teacher how to use critical listening, acknowledgment responses, door openers, active listening, and "I" messages as tools for helping a student to verbally reflect upon his or her emotions and behavior. He also provides the teacher with Method III "no lose" problem-solving

Basic Assumptions on Motivation

Child is motivated by internal desire to be good. He or she is helped by a warm, accepting relationship with another that enhances his or her self-concept. The child is rational—capable of solving his or her own problems.

Overt Teacher Behaviors
—Critical Listening
—Acknowledgment responses
—Door openers ("Do you want to talk more?")

FIGURE 14–1. *Outline of Gordon's Teacher Effectiveness Training*

—Active listening
—"I" messages
—Influencing ("Watch your step.")

Covert Teacher Behaviors

—Method III "no lose"
—Daily actions
—Reorganizing space
—Reorganizing time: diffused, individual, and optimal
—six steps to problem solving
—"areas of freedom"

Key Vocabulary

—Ownership of problems
—Active listening
—"I"/"you" messages
—Door openers
—Method III "no lose"
—Teaching-Learning area
—Six steps to problem solving
—Twelve roadblocks to communication
—Diffused time
—Individual time
—Optimal time
—"areas of freedom"

Educational Insights

—"areas of freedom"
—Organizing time as diffused, individual, and optimal
—Organizing space

Strengths

—Child solves his or her problem, thus developing responsibility.
—Democratic rule-setting practice
—No bad feelings while solving problems (no winners or losers)
—Helps teacher to decide problem ownership

Limitations

—At what age is a child rational?
—Is the mentally retarded child rational?
—What about the child without language?
—The time required for the teacher to administer T.E.T. is prohibitive.
—T.E.T. cannot be used in every conflict situation (i.e., violent child).

FIGURE 14–1. *Outline of Gordon's Teacher Effectiveness Training(cont.)*

techniques and the six problem-solving steps to resolve conflict in a democratic, equalitarian manner. These techniques free the teacher and student from the common outcome of disciplinary actions where one party loses and feels inferior while the other wins and feels superior. Other strengths of Teacher Effectiveness Training are embodied in the concepts of "areas of freedom" and the problems of ownership. Thus the teacher need not feel responsible for every student problem that occurs. The teacher can determine those behavioral problems that belong to administrators or legal officials and thus be able to narrow the focus of his or her attention.

The stress on a warm and supportive environment has been mentioned as a strength; yet, as is often the case, a strength can have dimensions of weakness. Gordon gives teachers concrete actions for allowing a student to verbalize his or her actions and feelings, but solutions for dealing with students who are violent are not readily apparent. Gordon's "I" or influencing messages may not be strong enough when a student explodes in rage and strikes another student. Gordon's techniques can be helpful before or after the act, but what can be done during the student's actual act of violence? Doesn't the teacher have to win and the student lose if physical harm is to be avoided?

Another limitation of Teacher Effectiveness Training is that Gordon's underlying assumption of rationality can be questioned. Do students of all ages possess the cognitive structures to make rational and positive social decisions? Cognitive psychologists suggest a student is not truly rational (i.e., considerate of others) until around the age of adolescence. It may be unfair to expect a young pupil or an intellectually limited (i.e., mentally retarded) student to make wise choices. Such students might need the teacher to *tell* them what is best. Furthermore, Gordon's approach of having students verbalize their emotions reflects an obvious problem for the nonverbal student. Some students will refuse to talk, and some may have such a limited vocabulary that they cannot communicate what they are feeling. It would appear that the teacher can use entreaties such as door openers for verbal discourses with only those students who already have a degree of language proficiency.

Finally, perhaps the most frequent criticism of Teacher Effectiveness Training by teachers is that it takes a lot of time to listen and solve problems when working with a misbehaving student. When a teacher has thirty students in a class, is it feasible to use nondirective statements and personal conferences with a misbehaving student? Would it be simpler to deal with a student in a direct manner and return to the rest of the class?

The Communication Model of Eric Berne and Thomas Harris's *Transactional Analysis*

Transactional Analysis has great value in helping teachers and students decode and analyze the messages they send to each other. Normally, people speak

Basic Assumptions on Motivation

—The brain functions as a high fidelity recorder. It records feelings that become fixed—recording, recalling, reliving.

—People will change if hurt, bored, or if they know they can.

—When people transact they send messages from one of the ego states (PAC).

—Because of man's childish feelings of "not OK" his actions with others are for the purpose of receiving strokes.

Overt Teacher Behavior

—Confronting the student with the game he or she is playing and speaking to his or her *Adult.*

—Asking "adult" questions

—Sending "adult" directive statements

—Responding at suitable times with parent to parent or child to child to give "strokes"

—Responding to potential crossed or ulterior transactions with his or her Adult

Covert Teacher Behaviors

—Visually looking on to determine the inner state of the student

—Determining game being played

—Recognizing his or her own state (PAC) being used

Key Vocabulary

Parent, Child, Adult

—Strokes

—Tapes

—Hooking

—Transaction

—Transactional Stimulus

—Transactional Response

—Crossed-transaction

—Ulterior-transaction

—Complementary-transaction

—Warm fuzzies

—Cold pricklies

—I'm OK, You're OK

Games

—Uproar

—Chip on the shoulder

—Stupid

—Schlemiel

—Make me

—Clown

Educational Insights

—Teacher use of language (PAC)

—Student use of language (PAC)

—Types of stroking

FIGURE 14–2. *Outline of Berne and Harris's Transactional Analysis*

Strengths

- —By helping children through the stages you help develop your own maturity.
- —Provides a construct that enables teacher to critically evaluate his or her verbal-nonverbal interchange with students.
- —Helps student to learn to communicate with their Adult.
- —Separates feelings into states of PAC.

Limitations

- —May be hard to distinguish which of the three constructs is speaking.
- —The adult as a rational state in the early years of life is weak and can be easily displaced by Child's or Parent's demands.
- —Needs training or constant reflecting in order to begin implementation.
- —No clear plan for changing students' misbehaviors.
- —Works only with children with language.

FIGURE 14–2. *Outline of Berne and Harris's Transactional Analysis(cont.)*

according to how they feel at the moment. Such talk is so much a part of one's everyday behavior that it is difficult to "stand back" and listen to oneself. It is Berne and Harris's contention that language emanates from various aspects of personality *(Parent, Adult,* and *Child)* and can facilitate or hinder reasonable decision-making. In other words, the use of language between the teacher and the misbehaving student can facilitate or impede realistic solutions. Therefore, the strength of Transactional Analysis is providing the teacher with the means of 1) decoding his or her messages, 2) teaching the student the code, and 3) having a common framework for further student and teacher communications.

The limitation of Transactional Analysis for teachers is that it is basically descriptive. It helps in analyzing and using prescriptive language, but it does not provide any clear plan for changing student misbehavior. Furthermore, the *Adult* as a rational state in the childhood years is weak and can be easily displaced by the *Child* and *Parent* states. Therefore, it may not be of much value to a student to know what those states are if he or she can exert little control over the *Child* or the *Parent*. It may make a student feel more inadequate when he or she knows how he or she is acting (i.e., the *Child*) but does not have the inner control to do otherwise. This criticism of Transactional Analysis is similar to one of Teacher Effectiveness Training in that students, developmentally, may not have the language or cognitive skills to use the reasoning necessary to employ such abstract and categorical knowledge of personality states. Another problem is that it is sometimes difficult for a teacher to make the fine distinctions between the *Parent, Adult,* and *Child*. For example, when a student says, "No one is going to stop me from going outside," is that the impulsive *Child* meaning, "I feel like running away!" the *Par-*

ent meaning, "Every student is supposed to go outside fifteen minutes every day," or the *Adult* meaning, "I feel lousy and need to clear my head"? A teacher cannot know unless the circumstances are readily apparent or there is time to discuss the message thoroughly. Teacher and student need training and continued retraining with Transactional Analysis in order to use it. In a busy class, the time is not so readily available to stop and assess the deeper meaning of what the teacher or student has just said before taking action.

Basic Assumptions on Motivation

—Values as well as emotions and I.Q. influence behavior problems.
—When values experiences are given to children with certain behavior problems, the problems often ease in intensity and/or frequency.
—Students can arrive at values through a rational process of choosing, prizing, and acting.
—The process will lessen apathetic, confused, and irrational behavior and increase more positive, purposeful, and enthusiastic behavior.

Overt Teacher Behaviors

—Modeling
—Questions
—Listening carefully and patiently
—Clarifying responses
—Formal exercises

Covert Teacher Behaviors

—Establishing a mood of acceptance
—Developing respect for student values
—Focusing attention on an issue in life
—Looking for value indicators

1. attitude statements
2. aspirations
3. purposes
4. interests
5. activities

Key Vocabulary

—Values clarifying discussions
—Role-playing, contrived incidents, zig-zag lessons, devil's advocate, values continuum, thought sheets, weekly reaction sheets, open-ended questions, overdissenters, role-players, values confusion
—Process of valuing, choosing freely, choosing from alternatives, choosing

FIGURE 14–3. *Outline of Raths and Simon's Values Clarification*

after considering consequences, prizing, affirming, acting, repeating
—Values indicators, clarifying responses, activities, worries, problems, apathetic, flighty, uncertain, inconsistent, drifters, overconformers, positive, purposeful, enthusiastic, proud, aspirations, attitudes, feelings

Educational Insights
—Values clarification should be infused in the curriculum.
—Misbehavior should be viewed as a lack of values.

Strengths
—Helps underachievers to improve:
1. attitudes toward learning.
2. active participation.
3. raising of questions and alternatives.
4. perseverance.
5. self-direction.

—Students become more purposeful.
—Can be used anytime and anywhere.
—Stimulates thinking.

Limitations
—No ideas are given for what to do when faced with disruptive behavior.
—May delve too much into students' personal lives.
—Does not add to knowledge base about problems.

FIGURE 14–3. *Outline of Raths and Simon's Values Clarification (cont.)*

The Valuing Model of Louis E. Raths, Sidney Simon, and Others

These writers claim that some student misbehavior can be viewed as a lack of personal codes or values of conduct. Students who are given the opportunity to clarify their values will be more consistent and rational in correcting their behaviors. The use of valuing questions, values indicators, modeling, clarifying responses, and formal exercises enables the student to explore his or her reasons for actions. It is the position of values clarification that a student will not internalize and act upon values unless he or she has freely chosen them. A supportive, nonjudgmental environment is needed for free choice. If a teacher imposes his or her thoughts and standards and thus coerces a student to act according to someone else's judgments, then the valuing process as a guide for consistent action is for naught.

The strengths of this model are based on the infusion of the valuing process into the everyday, ongoing curriculum. It provides every student, particularly the low achiever, the opportunity to actively participate, raise questions, explore alternatives, and make individual choices, without the usual fear of being corrected. The process stimulates thinking and can be used informally and formally anytime and anywhere during the school day.

The major limitation of the valuing model is its advocacy of nonjudgmental teacher support toward any student value. For example, in a discussion about physical violence, the teacher needs to be just as acceptive toward the student who says, "One should not use physical violence, as the ends never justify the means," as the student who says, "If someone's standing in the way of my getting a good job, I'm going to tear that person apart limb from limb." The teacher can explore the latter student's rationale and listen to other alternatives, but, according to the values-clarification process, he or she should not say or indicate in any way that "tearing a person apart limb from limb" is wrong. Even if a teacher were to completely agree with using such an approach, it still seems difficult to be acceptive of all values. For those teachers who have strong personal beliefs, it could be a terrible strain not to make one's beliefs known. Furthermore, some teachers might object philosophically to the position that all values are acceptable and instead point out that, in a classroom, the teacher has the responsibility for enforcing certain rules, standards, and values regardless of what a pupil thinks.

Another limitation of the valuing process is that it is basically an indirect method of dealing with misbehavior. It provides no immediate solutions for solving a disruptive student's problem; rather, its "payoff" is over a long period of time. Thus, it must be employed with other methods. The teacher has to use the valuing process on a continual basis for an extended amount of time before he or she can detect results. What happens if, after all this time, the student's behavior still does not change? Was such a time-consuming endeavor worthwhile, or, instead, could the teacher have used other models that would have been implemented and evaluated much sooner?

The Interactionalists

The Interactionalists believe that appropriate behavior is learned as a result of a student coming into contact with the needs of others. The student learns the reciprocal relationship of individuals who accommodate each other in order to live in a social group. The appropriate medium for such learning is interaction with others. The student does not propose solutions that are wholly in his or her own self-interest, but rather finds answers that are acceptable to the teacher and the classmates. The teacher is not the nonjudgmental facilitator as espoused by the Non-Interventionists, but instead delineates boundaries of behavior. Within those boundaries, choices can be made.

Questions of application that critics might raise include the following:

1. If the student and teacher make mutual plans, do not these in reality become merely teacher plans to which students agree?

2. If interaction is based on communication, what happens to the nonverbal student?
3. Do all students want to belong to a group? After all, if it is true that some individuals enjoy being alone, then is social motivation going to work?
4. Isn't using the group to confront and solve a student's problems "heavy handed," manipulative, and emotionally damaging to a student with an inferiority complex?

Basic Assumptions on Motivation

—Man is a social being and his desire is to belong.
—Man is a decision-making organism.
—All behavior is purposeful and directed towards social goals.
—Man does not see reality as it is, but only as he perceives it to be.
—Man is a whole being who cannot be understood by some particular characteristics.
—Man's misbehavior is the result of faulty reasoning on how to gain social recognition.

Overt Teacher Behaviors

—Confrontation
—Engaging child in friendly conversation
—Disclosing and confirming mistaken goals to the child
—Asking the following questions:

1. Could it be that you want special attention? (attention-getting)
2. Could it be that you want to be boss? (power)
3. Could it be that you want to hurt others as they've hurt you? (revenge)
4. Could it be that you want to be left alone? (inadequacy)

—Class group discussion about all types of behavior (scheduled weekly)
—Confrontation about goals and misbehavior
—Continued encouragement to increase child's confidence (belief in self)
—Avoiding criticism so true motives can be learned and behavior corrected
—Use encouragement techniques such as:

1. Work for improvement, not perfection.
2. Commend efforts.
3. Separate the *deed* from *doer.*
4. Build on strengths, not weaknesses.
5. Show your faith in the child.
6. Mistakes should not be viewed as failures.

—Developing logical and natural consequences, logically structured and arranged by the adult, that must be experienced by the student.

FIGURE 14–4. *Outline of Dreikurs's Social Discipline*

Covert Teacher Behaviors

—Four Goals of Child's Misbehavior:

1. Attention-getting
2. Power-seeking
3. Revenge
4. Display of inadequacy

—Preventing above behavior by following these steps:

1. Observe child's behavior in detail.
2. Be psychologically sensitive to your own reaction.
3. Confront child (4) questions.
4. Apply appropriate corrective procedures.

Key Vocabulary

—Attention-getting
—Power and control
—Revenge
—Helplessness
—Encouragement
—Hidden motivation
—Natural and logical consequences
—Recognition reflex
—Role-playing
—Classroom discussion
—Sociometric test
—Reading stories
—Informal plays

Educational Insights

—Classroom as collective group
—Sociometric tests for analyzing individual's relationship to group
—Classroom operated as a democracy

Strengths

—Develops system of mutual respect (rewards and punishment *not* needed).
—Allows children time to solve their own problems during class discussion.
—Involves whole class in decision making.
—Helps to aid in socialization of individual.
—Step-by-step procedure according to goals to follow.
—Self-worth developed by teacher and child.
—Has natural and logical consequences.

Limitations

—Teacher may not always be able to determine child's true goal.
—Some children refuse to talk about incident.
—Passive child is always very difficult to help using this method.
—At times, it can be hard to determine consequences.

FIGURE 14–4. *Outline of Dreikurs's Social Discipline (cont.)*

The Social Model of Rudolf Dreikurs

Dreikurs's social model is based on the underlying assumption that every student (or human) wishes to belong. Misbehavior is a student's misdirected goal of belonging. Therefore, if a teacher can ascertain the student's misdirected goal (attention-getting, power, revenge, or inadequacy) he or she can counter with a plan to enable the student to use appropriate behavior to belong successfully.

The strengths of Dreikurs's model are in the concreteness of application. He tells the teacher how to uncover the student's goal and how to plan according to that goal. Among the techniques a teacher can employ are role-playing, classroom discussions, sociometric testing, and story telling. He advocates a system of mutual respect where natural or logical consequences are used rather than arbitrary punishment or systematic reinforcements. The model is predicated on an optimistic outlook by the teacher who does not "give up" on a student. Rather, the teacher becomes sensitive and appreciative of a student's attempts to improve rather than the improvement itself.

The limitations of the social model are varied. Determining a student's social goal may not be as simple as it appears. What if a teacher has a mixture of feelings toward a student, which include feelings of hurt (revenge), being beaten (power) and helplessness (inadequacy)? What if the teacher asks the student the four verifying questions and receives no recognition reflex? Another problem with verifying the goal lies with a student who does not want to know why he or she behaves as he or she does.

The use of encouragement and personal attention also can be viewed as rewarding a student for misbehavior. There are those who believe, for example, that a passive student needs to be drawn out forcefully by physically showing him or her how to raise one's hand, by demanding that the student finish work in a certain length of time, and so forth. Dreikurs's techniques put little pressure on a student to achieve. Another concern is the question of dealing in a caring way with a student who is hurting others. Will not other students see the special attention such students receive for being "bad" and act accordingly?

A further limitation is that the choice of logical consequences is at times difficult to make. What should happen to a student who incessantly talks but still finishes all of the assigned work? What is a logical consequence for this student? Certainly it is *not* having his or her mouth taped shut, staying after school, or taking a note home. After all, the student is doing all that is expected except for talking too much. It is not readily apparent what the teacher should do.

The Reality Model of William Glasser

Glasser believes that every student has the capacity to be rational and responsible. However, the student does not acquire this capacity by himself or herself. The teacher provides a classroom of relevant activities so that a student will

Basic Assumptions on Motivation

Relevance, responsibility, and reality are necessary for schools without failure. The child is rational. The child has capability to be responsible, but needs to learn moral or acceptable boundaries of living successfully in society. Persons must live in a world of other human beings and must satisfy their own needs in a way that does not infringe upon others. Each person has two basic needs, the need for love and the need for self-worth, which must be fulfilled in order to have a successful identity. Behavior problems are a result of these needs not being met. A person must be helped to acknowledge his or her behavior and then take actions in making it more logical and productive. A person must make a commitment to responsible behavior.

Overt Teacher Behaviors

—Confronting transgressions ("Stop that," "The rule is . . .")
—Asking "what" questions ("What are you doing?" "What are the rules?" "In what way is your behavior helping you?")
—Pressing for a plan ("I'll help, you're responsible.")
—Agreeing on natural consequence of plan
—Failure of plan—isolating in class (repeat 1–4)
—Failure of step 5—isolating in school (repeat 1–5)
—Failure of step 6—isolating outside of school (repeat 1–6)
—Referring to outside agency

Covert Teacher Behaviors

—Observing the student and the situation
—Assessing what the teacher is currently doing and what success the student is having
—Starting fresh by reversing classroom organization and/or activities

Key Vocabulary

—Heterogeneous
—Reality therapy
—Identity
—Nonjudgmental
—Class meetings
—Intense counseling
—Open-ended
—Problem solving
—Responsibility
—Success
—Self-image
—Involvement
—Signed statement
—Behavior
—Consequences
—Value judgment
—Tight circles
—Failure
—Thinking vs. memorization
—Commitment
—Relevance
—Class meetings
—Love

FIGURE 14–5. *Outline of Glasser's Reality Therapy*

Educational Insights

—Class meetings for 1. Problem-Solving, 2. Open-Ended, 3. Educational-Diagnostic
—Superior system of grades; do away with standard A–F
—Upward Bound Program
—Strength teaching
—Seminars for small groups
—Enrichment programs
—Tutors and counseling
—Community contact
—Make curriculum relevant
—No ability grouping

Strengths

—Behavior is student's responsibility.
—It has no failures.
—Has a step-by-step procedure for all students.
—Child must take responsibility for own actions.
—Involves all those responsible.
—Is a specific use of isolation.

Limitations

—Doesn't work well with child who doesn't care.
—Class meetings are hard to fit into secondary school.
—School changes might be hard to accomplish within school structure.
—It is difficult to start fresh each day.

FIGURE 14–5. *Outline of Glasser's Reality Therapy (cont.)*

want to succeed. The teacher then confronts the student by asking him or her to look at the behavior that is keeping him or her from succeeding. The student is asked to make a commitment to a future plan that will be enforced by the teacher.

Reality therapy provides the teacher with an understanding of human motivation based on the concepts of love and self-worth. Glasser provides the educator with covert behaviors for assessing the relevance of one's classrooms. The strength of the model is in the clear delineation of what a teacher needs to do for every misbehaving student. The student must be confronted with "what" questions and must be pressed for a plan. The success or failure of the plan becomes the responsibility of the student, not the teacher. Yet, if the initial effort results in failure, the teacher can keep the responsibility on the student by isolating him or her until another plan is developed and agreed upon. Again, if the plan is unsuccessful, the student and teacher can start again. Behavior that is having a detrimental effect on all class members can be handled in a classroom meeting where all classmates can develop a mutually agreeable plan with the misbehaving student.

The criticisms of Glasser's model first revolve around the educational problem of having to create a relevant classroom environment where a student has successful experiences. There are teachers who teach subjects that they know are not perceived by misbehaving students as interesting or relevant. Yet the teacher can do little to either change the subject matter or reorganize the classroom environment due to external circumstances (i.e., in situations where the principal, superintendent, or school board dictate all policies affecting curriculum and environment). Therefore, these educators have difficulty with the first step of Glasser's approach. They want the students to behave properly in their classroom regardless of whether or not they enjoy what is going on. A second limitation is the use of classroom meetings for a misbehaving student. Again there are classrooms and class schedules, particularly on the secondary level, that make such meetings improbable. When a teacher meets with a group of thirty students for one forty-five minute period a day and has specific learning outcomes for each class, he or she will be hard pressed to find the time to have ongoing meetings that take twenty to thirty minutes to conduct. Another criticism applies to the student who does not care about school: making a plan and using isolation with this student are not likely to be successful. A student who would rather not be in school might welcome the chance to be isolated in a comfortable area. Glasser suggests that a student will eventually choose to come out, and the teacher should not allow the student to reenter until a plan is made. If the student does not choose to return, how long is a teacher to wait? Additionally, there is the concern about "making a plan." The strategy is based on the student having a certain degree of organized thought and language proficiency; therefore, it does not address the student who may desire to be in class but does not know how to verbalize or systematize that desire. A final weakness may be the unrealistic hope that a teacher can begin each new plan with an optimistic outlook. It might be unrealistic to expect a teacher to continue to be optimistic after a student repeatedly breaks a series of contracts.

The Interventionists

The Interventionists believe that humans are shaped by external stimuli. A teacher needs to be aware of the stimuli a misbehaving student is receiving and should then change the environmental conditions so that appropriate behavior is more rewarding than inappropriate behavior. The teacher is therefore very much in control and should express explicit standards of conduct for the student.

The basic argument against Interventionist approaches is not whether they work but whether the ultimate consequences for the student are beneficial. For example, reinforcement programs implemented as part of a piloted national experiment in 1972[1] showed that severely underachieving and delinquent junior high school students could make drastic changes in their behavior if the rewards were great enough. Students who were constantly late, who whistled, moved around, and talked incessantly during class suddenly became the picture of punctuality and docility. They would arrive on time, sit down with folded hands, and be attentive to the teacher when they knew they could earn "tokens" redeemable for record players, transistor radios, bicycles, tickets to concerts, and the like. The questions debated are whether students *should* learn to behave for such materialistic reasons, and if so, what happens to a student when the obvious rewards for appropriate behavior end?

Basic Assumptions on Motivation

—Children are not born with self-control—we must help them mold it.
—Deal only with outward (external) behavior.
—Use scientific techniques to demonstrate effectiveness.
—Be concerned with unacceptable behavior the child exhibits and what interventions can be applied to change it.
—The cause of the behavior exists outside the child, in the environment.
—Motivation-reinforcers:
Positive—something we like
Negative—something we dislike
Primary—relating to basic body needs
Secondary—abstracts, symbols
—The consequences, more than any other factor, determine the behavior the individual exhibits.

Overt Teacher Behaviors

—Teacher controlling the situation, imitation and shaping, fading, and directive statements for contingency contracting
—Explicit modeling for imitation, forward and backward chaining, saturation, time out, rewards for reinforcement of desired behaviors; commands as directive statements
—Using conditioners in form of material and verbal rewards; child definitely knows what he will receive by his behavior
—Using variable intervals and variable ratios

Covert Teacher Behaviors

—Reinforcing only the behavior to be increased
—Before beginning behavior modification:
1. Select the behavior to be changed.
2. Collect and record baseline data.

FIGURE 14–6. *Outline of Axelrod, Homme, and Others' Behavior Modification*

3. Identify appropriate reinforcers.
4. Collect intervention data.

—Graphing baseline and intervention data to evaluate effectiveness
—Changing reinforcers periodically
—Reinforcing the behavior on a variable reinforcement schedule

Key Vocabulary

—Baseline data reversals
—Contingency contracting
—Positive and negative reinforcement
—Shaping
—Fading
—Operant conditioning
—Behavior
—Extinction
—Intermittent reinforcement
—Tokens
—Time out
—Differential reinforcement of other behaviors (DRO)
—Discrimination stimulus generalization
—Chaining

Educational Insights

—School subjects can be taught in sequential, reinforcing manners.
—Stimulation of physical environment (positive and negative) should be considered.
—Positive stimuli are most effective in all dimensions of schooling.

Strengths

—It is positively oriented, and reinforces good feelings and self-concept.
—Encourages success.
—Gives a structured setting for learning.
—Eliminates constant/continual contact with a child.
—Capitalizes on nonverbal communication.
—It works (scientifically tested).
—It can work with all children.
—It is efficient.

Limitations

—Many people feel behavior modification practices are unacceptable and unethical.
—It can have harmful effects if not used correctly. Can be abused by insensitive and unethical practitioners.
—Does not accept emotions as important.
—Does not let the child use his or her own rational abilities.
—Needs precise record keeping to determine its success.

FIGURE 14–6. *Outline of Axelrod, Homme, and Others' Behavior Modification (cont.)*

The Behavior Modification Model

The behavior modification model is based on the use of positive reinforcement. General behavior is broken down into smaller parts so that students have insured success. A student can feel successful and competent as he or she learns appropriate behaviors and receives verbal, social, or material rewards. Standards of behavior are uniform, consistent, and clear to all students. The teacher does not need to spend any time in class discussions about rules or to conduct individual conferences dealing with problem solving. He or she can spend more time on instructional matters. Behavior modification can be used with all students, regardless of their age or cognitive and language abilities. A reinforcement schedule can be implemented with a nonverbal, passive student as well as with a highly articulate, aggressive student. Although, at first, reinforcements need to be used fre-

Basic Assumptions on Motivation

—Respectful, responsible children result from families where the proper combination of love and discipline is present.
—Developing respect for the adult is critical in student management.
—The best time to communicate often occurs after punishment.
—Control without nagging.
—Don't saturate with excessive materialism.
—Avoid extremes in control and love.
—The adult is in charge—he or she must win.

Overt Teacher Behaviors

—Identifying the rules well in advance; letting there be no doubt about what is and what is *not* acceptable behavior; when the child cold-bloodedly chooses to challenge those known boundaries, giving him reason to regret it; at all times demonstrating kindness, love, and understanding (Discipline is not an antonym of love and discipline is not a synonym of punishment)
—Controlling child behavior by reinforcement (Reinforcement *must* be immediate)
—Using directive statements (contingency contracting): If you do X then you do or get Y. Even though one gains points for following the contract, he or she is also penalized if he or she does not follow it.

Covert Teacher Behaviors

—Seeing Behavior Modification (Positivist)
—Reminding yourself to maintain your "power", to use discipline, and to use kindness, love, and so on
—Reminding yourself to be immediate and consistent with reinforcers
—Reminding yourself to never let the child have the "upper-hand"
—Reminding yourself to be patient!!!

FIGURE 14–7. *The Behaviorism/Punishment Model*

quently, the teacher can eventually use a random interval schedule. Positive use of behavior modification can be scientifically tested by the classroom teacher. This technique usually will work, and it is an efficient way of reversing a student's disruptive actions.

The limitations of the model are both philosophical and practical. Behavior modification is an approach that attempts to change a student's observable behavior. However, some misbehavior may be the result of "inner" problems. A student who is being physically abused at home may be taking his or her hostility out on classmates. A reinforcement program that conditions cooperative class behavior and extinguishes physical aggression may be beneficial to the teacher, but it does not help the student (or parents) resolve the underlying home problem. Therefore, in many cases, behavior modification approaches may change the symptoms but do little to alleviate the actual problem. There is also the argument that, in a democratic society, it is unethical and unacceptable for schools to control an individual's behavior. Limiting behavior so that destruction or harm can be avoided is necessary in any society, but the notion of conditioning specific behavior would be more applicable to a totalitarian society. Educational concerns with behavior modification are that learning "to behave" is an important cognitive task, just as important as learning such school subjects as reading and mathematics. Therefore, if a student is not allowed to bring his or her mental operations into use by learning to clarify emotions, to weigh alternatives, and to decide upon solutions, then a major area of intellectual or rational development would be neglected. Another concern is more immediate to teachers in that such a scientific approach is predicated on precise delineation and measurement of a student's pretreatment behavior. To do this, a teacher needs to write down misbehavior in clear terms and to keep an accurate tabulation of frequency. Some teachers might resist spending the time and effort that this ongoing recordkeeping and "paperwork" involves.

The Behaviorism/Punishment Model

Some of the same strengths and limitations of the behavior modification model exist with the behaviorism/punishment model. These writers propose all the positive behavior modification approaches, but they also include the use of negative measures such as stern commands, physical intervention, and, at times, physical punishment. They advocate concern and patience with students, but establish as a firm base that the student must accept a teacher's authority. Their premise is that students go to school to learn academics, and therefore a teacher needs to deal with disruption quickly and efficiently. Although positive reinforcement is encouraged, it must be immediately effective or the teacher should directly take steps to make the consequences of a student's misbehavior unpleasant and not worth doing again. In other words, misbehavior should be less positively rewarding than more appropriate behavior.

The most prevalent concern with this model is whether punishment really works. Scolding or paddling would indicate to a student what he or she should not be doing, but it does not tell him or her what should be done instead. Punishment therefore would need to be administered in conjunction with positive reinforcement. If this is so, then why not simply ignore the misbehavior rather than punish it? Also, punishment would have the opposite effect of its intent. To have a student stay after school for refusing to obey the teacher would make the student more resentful and more disobedient. Another concern is that the teacher would be providing a model of behavior to the student that he or she may not wish the student to emulate. For example, if a teacher believes it is inappropriate for students to use physical means to resolve a conflict, but that students should use calm language to make their needs known, then the use of "punishment" by the teacher would be incorrect. If a teacher grabs or paddles a student for fighting, then he or she would

Key Vocabulary

—Discipline	—Kindness
—Control	—Love
—Reinforcement	—Understanding
—Consistency	—Respect for authority
—Responsibility	—Miracle tools
—Self-discipline	—Family and God
—Self-control	—Defiance

Educational Insights

—Discipline needs to be quick with the late bloomer, slow learner, and underachiever.
—Grades need to be viewed as reinforcers.
—The purpose of schools is for students to learn; misbehavior keeps student from learning.
—It is better to be strict at the beginning; "don't smile till December."

Strengths

—Use of class time is more efficient. Problems are handled quickly; the teacher spends a lot of time teaching academic skills.
—Behavior Modification is a scientific method; results can be proven.
—It is effective for all age levels and kinds of students.

Limitations

—Such techniques need to start very early when the child is young.
—It is undemocratic and authoritarian.
—It may fail to recognize "circumstantial" evidence for misbehavior.
—Releases child from personal responsibility and rational decision.
—Limits on physical punishment are established by the school board.
—Punishment may not work.
—It models teacher behavior that is inappropriate for students to engage in.

FIGURE 14–7. *The Behaviorism/Punishment Model (cont.)*

be clearly showing the student that "might does make right." The student would feel justified in continuing to fight, because he or she has seen that the teacher has resolved his or her frustrations in the same manner. Aside from the issues of whether punishment works or whether punishment is a poor model, there is also the reality that the matter of punishment is often strictly regulated by school board policy. Many school systems do not allow, or they severely restrict, various forms of punishment (such as paddling or detention after school).

Summary

There are no teacher-student interaction models today that, to our knowledge, do not have their critics. There is not now, and there possibly never will be, research that provides indisputable documentation that one model is predominately superior to others. It has instead been the purpose here to refresh the reader's memory of the significant features of each model through the presentation of skeleton outlines (Figures 14–1 through 14–7) and then to present some of the debated issues concerning each model.

Notes

1. "Performance Contracting Experiment in Remedial Education," Conducted by the Office of Economic Opportunity, Carl D. Glickman, Education Analyst for the Portland, Maine Project.

15

Conclusion: A Better Tomorrow

Ms. Zunn is a quiet, composed woman who has been a fourth-grade teacher for six years. At twenty-nine years of age she has established herself in the eyes of parents, peers, and administrators as an above-average educator. She is especially well regarded as a strong classroom manager. Her students have traditionally responded to her firm, calm manner with appropriately restrained behavior. They have always had true affection and respect for her.

This year, however, has not been one of Ms. Zunn's best. The community has changed, during her tenure, from a basically middle-class to more of a lower-middle-class mix. The new trailer parks and housing projects have brought in populations of children who are new to Ms. Zunn's experience.

Although the great majority of her students are well behaved, there is one student in particular who constantly disrupts the entire class. His name is Joshua. Joshua is eleven years old; he is new to the community and has already been in three different schools. His father is a warehouse manager, his mother a waitress, and he is the oldest of four children He is an indifferent student, does not speak often, and is quick to physically lash out at others. He does not respond to Ms. Zunn's calm, stern manner the way the other students do. When she tells him to stop what he is doing (talking, dropping books, or bothering others), he ignores her and continues. When she finally has to resort to physical restraint, he loses all control and begins yelling, thrashing his arms, and flailing at her.

Ms. Zunn is near her rope's end. Yesterday Joshua was hitting the girl seated next to him, and when Ms. Zunn intervened, he swore at her. This morning, when he entered the classroom, he immediately grabbed Tony's comic books and tore them up. Ms. Zunn ran over to him and said, "Joshua, go sit over in the corner." Joshua refused. When she began to pull him out of his seat, Joshua exploded, throwing the chair down on the floor, striking out at her, and finally, in pure rage, spitting at her. He broke away from her, ran out of the classroom, and disappeared.

Ms. Zunn could no longer retain her composure. She tells the class that she needs to leave the room for a minute. Stepping into the hall, she leans back against the wall and begins softly crying to herself. She thinks of how helpless the situation with Joshua has become. She feels incapable of helping him. His excessive behavior is ruining the work she wishes to do with the other children. She simply cannot bear thinking about facing a whole school year like this.

As you remember, the first chapter began with this story of Ms. Zunn and Joshua. Ms. Zunn's behavior can now be interpreted according to the Developmental Socialization Continuum. When her "tried and true" method of stern commands failed to change Joshua, Ms. Zunn retreated from rational behavior to prerational forms of verbal aggression (yelling), to "physical aggression" (grabbing), to finally a defeated state of "passivity" (crying). It is not surprising that many teachers similar to Ms. Zunn behave in primitive stages. Dealing unsuccessfully with a disruptive student can become wearisome and frustrating. In time, a teacher can begin to resent the student, feel guilty about the class, and think of himself or herself as inadequate.

When we left Ms. Zunn, she had little hope. Previously, she had been an effective teacher with years of experience in using a singular approach of stern commands to her disruptive students. She now finds this approach ineffective with Joshua, yet she has little training or knowledge for changing her behavior. Therefore, she has continued an approach that has accelerated Joshua's misbehavior. What hope does she have for a better tomorrow?

How does the teacher break this cycle of despair? Many well-meaning supervisors or colleagues will advise "to be patient and everything will improve." Such advice is of little use to a teacher who needs help. He or she wants to know what actions to take. Hoping for a miraculous change without implementing a concrete plan of action would be an exercise in fantasy. It is our belief that Ms. Zunn and other teachers want the very best for their students. These educators are intelligent and capable persons who, if given the knowledge base and "tools," will make informed changes for the better. This book has attempted to provide the knowledge base and many of the tools to achieve these changes.

The Knowledge and Choices for Today's Teacher

The teacher who has read this book will be aware of the following three schools of psychological thought when disciplining students:

1. *The Non-Interventionists,* who believe a student must learn to discipline himself or herself through the facilitation of his or her inner rationality.

2. *The Interactionalists,* who believe a student learns discipline from the interaction of his or her desires with those of the outside world.
3. *The Interventionists,* who believe a student learns appropriate behavior as a result of the influences of the outer environment.

Within each school of thought there are specific authors of various teacher-student interaction models who suggest specific teacher practices. Each of those practices has been interpreted along the Teacher Behavior Continuum. (See Figure 15–1.) At one end of the continuum, strategies are used whereby the child has the most control of his or her behavior and the teacher has minimal control (capital *C*, lowercase *t*), and at the other end the teacher subsumes the child's power (lowercase *c*, capital *T*).

The Non-Interventionist models stress the minimally controlling behaviors at the left of the continuum, the Interactionalist models emphasize the teacher behaviors in the middle, and the Interventionists stress the behaviors at the right of the continuum.

The popular advocates of discipline models, corresponding to schools of thought are:

Non-Interventionists

Thomas Gordon	Supportive Model
Eric Berne	Communication Model
Thomas Harris	
Louis E. Raths	Valuing Model
Merrill Harmin	
Sidney B. Simon and others	

Interactionalists

Rudolf Dreikurs	Social Model
William Glasser	Reality Model

Interventionists

Saul Axelrod	Behavior Modification Model
Lloyd Homme and others	
James Dobson	Behaviorism/Punishment Model
Siegfried Engelmann	

Each of the models provides specific *overt* and *covert* teacher behaviors. The teacher can immediately choose from such behaviors as "active listening" (Gordon), to "social questioning" (Dreikurs), to "off to the castle" (Glasser), to "sat-

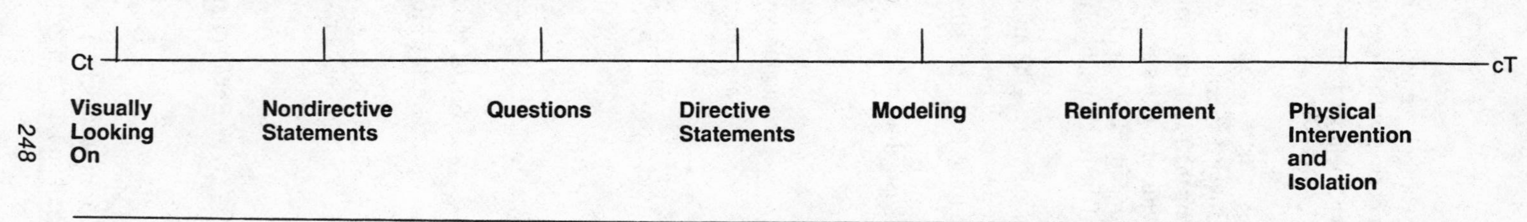

FIGURE 15–1. *Teacher Behavior Continuum (TBC)*

uration'' (Behavior Modification). However, for a more consistent, long-range plan, a teacher can choose a combination of the elements of various models to use through different eclectic pathways. The teacher can choose to work from student control to teach power *(Pathway I),* from teacher control to student power *(Pathway II),* or from shared power *(Pathway III).* The ultimate goal of all three pathways is to have the student be able to exercise control over his or her own behavior. Or, the teacher might prefer to base his or her decision of techniques on the student's stages of social development. Depending on the stage *(passivity, physical aggression, verbal aggression,* or *rational abilities*), he or she can choose those teacher practices that are most applicable.

The various choices a teacher can make are illustrated in Figure 15–2.

Another important element to consider is the school personnel who can be used to help the student. The misbehavior may be beyond the classroom teacher's *spheres of competency.* He or she might use a school *staffing* to develop an *individualized education plan* or to seek outside professional help.

The Professional Teacher

Many choices have been provided for the teacher. The authors have purposely refused to give a single "recipe" for action. Instead, the schools of thought, models, and pathways have been presented as information for the teacher to act on in his or her own way. Strengths and limitations of each model were presented, not to influence, but instead for the reader to consider the consequences of all the choices presented. The belief that has re-echoed throughout this book is that *there is no one approach to discipline or interaction that will be successful for all students.* In today's age of heterogeneity and pluralism, teachers will be most effective by diversifying and individualizing their approaches.

In the final analysis, we believe teachers will make wise choices. It is our contention that every teacher desires the best for his or her students. Within their own classrooms, only they truly know their students. If provided with the knowledge base for using the alternative "tools" of discipline, they then can make the appropriate applications.

A teacher is a professional. A professional can make decisions based on careful observation and analysis. A medical doctor, when confronted with an ill patient, will listen to the patient, monitor the body mechanisms, and observe the symptoms. The doctor will then not only use his or her past experience, intuition, or former training to determine a treatment, but he or she will add the knowledge acquired by having kept abreast of the latest research or theory. From this total picture, the physician will then decide what treatment is most suitable. If he or she is proven to be wrong, then the process begins again. Patients have confidence in a doctor who is knowledgeable, experienced, current, and intelligent. The patient's confidence in the doctor often helps in the cure; so it is with the student's

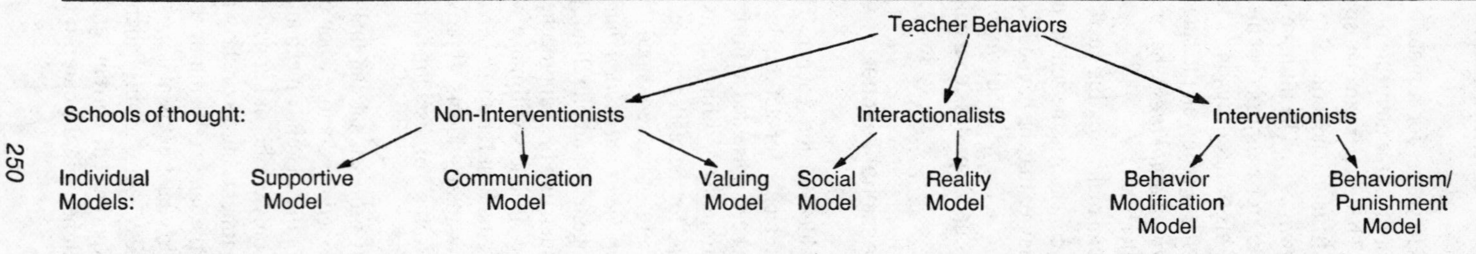

FIGURE 15–2. *Teacher Choices*

confidence in the teacher. Confidence comes from knowing of and being able to apply alternative remedies. Helplessness comes from not knowing what else to do.

A Better Tomorrow

The teacher who has read this book can be optimistic for good reasons. If current teacher behaviors with a disruptive student are unsuccessful, then there are many other actions that can be taken. Ms. Zunn, who was left weeping in the hall, can straighten up, "clear her head," reassess the situation, and decide on further action. She now has a range of strategies, models, and pathways to use. She and Joshua have every reason to expect a "better tomorrow."

Appendix A

Beliefs on Discipline Inventory*

This inventory is designed for teachers to assess their own beliefs on classroom discipline. It enables teachers to approximate to what extent they believe in the Interventionist, the Non-Interventionist, and the Interactionalist models of discipline. The inventory assumes teachers believe and act according to all three models of discipline, yet usually one predominates in their beliefs and actions.

The inventory is self-administered and self-scored. In the first part, teachers guess to what extent they believe in each of the three models. In the second part, teachers are given items in which they must choose one of two options given (a forced-choice format). A scoring key enables teachers to approximate the extent of their belief in each of the three models.

PART I. Prediction

Instructions: Rank the discipline models according to how you think you generally believe. Place *1* next to the model you think most dominates your beliefs, *2* next to the second, and *3* next to the third.

*Developed by Dr. Roy Tamashiro, The Ohio State University

Model	*Rank*
Interventionist	________
Non-Interventionist	________
Interactionalist	________

PART II. Forced Choices

Instructions: Select either A or B. You might not completely agree with either choice, but choose the one that is closer to how you feel.

1. A. Although children think, the decisions they make are not yet fully rational and moral.
   B. Students' inner emotions and decision-making processes must always be considered legitimate and valid.
2. A. Generally, I assign students to specific areas or seats in the classroom.
   B. Generally, my seating (or work area) assignments are open to negotiation.
3. A. No matter how limited the students' opportunities may be, students should still be given the responsibility to choose and make decisions.
   B. Teachers need to realize that, in addition to their effect on students during school hours, the students are greatly influenced by their families, the neighborhoods where they live, their peers, and television.
4. When the high noise level in the classroom bothers me, I will more likely:
   A. Discuss my discomfort with the students and attempt to come to a compromise about noise levels during activity periods.
   B. Allow the activity to continue as long as the noise is not disturbing or upsetting any student.
5. If a student breaks a classmate's portable tape player that she brought to school, I, as the teacher, will more likely:
   A. Scold both students, one for disrespecting other people's property, and the other for breaking a rule prohibiting her from bringing radios and tape players to school.
   B. Avoid interfering in something that the students (and possibly their parents) need to resolve themselves.
6. If students unanimously agree that a classroom rule is unjust and should be removed, but I (the teacher) disagree with them, then:
   A. The rule should probably be removed and replaced by a rule made by the students.
   B. The students and I should jointly decide on a fair rule.

7. When a student does not join in a group activity:
   A. The teacher should explain the value of the activity to the student and encourage the student to participate.
   B. The teacher should attempt to identify the student's reasons for not joining, and should create opportunities that respond to those reasons.
8. During the first week of class, I will more likely:
   A. Let the students interact freely and let the students initiate any rule making.
   B. Announce the classroom rules and inform students how the rules will be fairly enforced.
9. A. The students' creativity and self-expression should be encouraged and nurtured as much as possible.
   B. Limits on destructive behaviors need to be set without denying students their sense of choice and decision.
10. If a student interrupts my lesson by talking to a neighbor, I will more likely:
    A. Move the child away from other students and continue the lesson, because time should not be wasted on account of one student.
    B. Tell students how angry I feel and conduct a dialogue about how the students would feel about being interrupted.
11. A. A good educator is firm but fair in taking disciplinary actions on violators of school rules.
    B. A good educator discusses several alternative disciplinary actions with the student who violates a school rule.
12. When one of the more conscientious students does not complete an assignment on time:
    A. I will assume the student has a legitimate reason and that the student will turn in the assignment when she or he completes it.
    B. I will tell the student that she or he was expected to turn in the assignment when it was due, and then, with the student, we will decide on the next steps.

Scoring Key and Interpretation

Circle your responses on the following table and tally the totals in each table:

Table I		*Table II*		*Table II*	
2A	1A	4B	1B	2B	4A
3B	5A	6A	5B	3A	6B
7A	8B	9A	8A	7B	9B
11A	10A	12A	10B	11B	12B

Total number of responses in Table I __________
Total number of responses in Table II __________
Total number of responses in Table III __________

The responses in Table I represent the Interventionist model of discipline; the responses in Table II are Non-Interventionist; and Table III represents Interactionalist responses.

By examining which table contains the largest number of responses, you can identify the model of discipline that dominates your beliefs. The table with the second largest total of responses respresents your second most prominent belief model. Of course, the table with the fewest total responses represents the discipline model that you least believe in.

If you have an equal number of responses from each table (or close to equal), this *may* indicate that you are an eclectic rather than one who identifies clearly with any of the discipline models.

You may be interested in comparing your results on Part II of the Inventory with what you predicted in Part I of the Inventory.

This will give you an idea of how your predictions are to your beliefs, as measured by this inventory.

Naturally, this brief inventory is not definitive. However, it ought to give you a general picture of how much you believe in each of the three discipline models.

Appendix B

The following are three actual cases of how teachers of different beliefs made beginning choices and developed their own eclectic pathway of dealing with a "misbehaving student."* We asked the teachers to develop and report their cases using a standard format of gathering information about the student, interpreting the student's behavior according to their beliefs (i.e., Non-Interventionist, Interactionalist, and Interventionist), fixing the pathway, selecting beginning overt behaviors for two weeks, assessing the two-week progress, and considering future overt behaviors for the next two weeks. (The teacher's original words have in some cases been edited to read consistently with the writing style of this book.) Following each study are some of the authors' notes.

A Non-Interventionist Teacher–Pathway I Description of Student Behavior:

Georgette's misbehavior occurs most frequently during silent work periods in the classroom. She talks to her neighbors during such work times, her work is incomplete at the time the class period is finished, and she plays with items brought from home during this time.

This behavior occurs daily, most often in the morning reading periods. Georgette also gets out of her seat and walks to different people and talks to them during the work period. This occurs two or three times in the hour-and-a-half work period.

In interpreting Georgette's behavior, I feel I must first describe the work periods in which Georgette's problem is centered. The students are given their assignments to complete at their desk. After their work is finished, there are

*We would like to thank public school teachers Ms. Susan Dice, Ms. Donna Lawrence, and Ms. Tommy Jo Galbreath along with thirty other teachers for field-testing the ideas of this book and allowing us to use their reports.

various learning centers located around the room where the children can go. There has never been any strict rule about staying in their seats. However, Georgette is up talking to people five minutes after the work period has begun. She is not asking about directions for the work, as I have asked her if she needs help and she has said no.

She is an above-average student in all her work, and when she completes her seatwork, it is usually done correctly. She often does not complete it until she hears me call for the paper; then it's done hurriedly and turned in.

I realize that some of the problem is mine (Gordon's problem of ownership) as she is a good student. Yet she is also bothering other students and keeping them from their work. I interpret her behavior as the Non-Interventionists would. Georgette has simply not been aware of or thought about her behavior. If she could verbalize her actions, and if I could verbalize my problem with her actions, then she would change her behavior.

Fixing the Pathway

I will use Pathway I, "From Student Power to teacher Control"

Overt Behaviors

- Use Adult (T.A.) Language when talking to Georgette; don't be the *Parent*.
- Engage Georgette in discussions by using critical listening, acknowledgments, and door openers.
- Give "I" messages.

Assessment of Two-Week Implementation

The first step I took in trying to correct the behavior was to use "I" messages when Georgette walked over and distracted students and myself during work time. I would say, "Georgette, I have to stop listening to students in this reading group when you get up and talk to others. I can't hear what is being read to me." After such "I" messages, at a recess time I would have private talks with Georgette, asking her if she wanted to talk about her work being late or me getting annoyed. I remembered not to scold or lecture her, and if she didn't want to talk, not to pursue it. Well, after two weeks Georgette's behavior is the same: she has never responded to any of my door openers; she simply clams up and shrugs.

Future Overt Behaviors

I am going to continue private discussions with active listening, but I'm also going to ask the four questions of Dreikurs to see if she gives a recognition reflex. I suspect her goal might be attention, and if it is, I am going to make up a plan where she will have daily opportunities to receive special attention when her work is done.

Authors' Comments: We see that this teacher tried to use a combination of Non-Interventionist techniques to help the child to clarify her own behavior and to propose her own solution. Since the student did not respond, the teacher continues on Pathway I, by now also employing some of the Interactionalists' techniques of verifying the social goal and making a plan to help the student to acceptably achieve that goal. The strategy has obviously worked, for after two more weeks the teacher reports,

> After evaluating the progress shown by Georgette during the previous two weeks, I felt that Georgette was ready to re-evaluate and talk about her own progress. After talking to Georgette, we both felt the special attention wasn't needed any more. Georgette was very pleased with the good remarks she had been getting on her papers and thoroughly enjoyed my stopping at her desk once or twice a morning to encourage her. She felt she could now do her work without any trouble, but I could tell she really enjoyed the extra attention given during my stops. I then suggested that perhaps she might want to help around the classroom. She decided she would like to keep the arithmetic center straightened up and would like that to be her daily job. I agreed and told her we would talk again in a couple of weeks to see if she could handle getting her work finished and being in charge of the learning center.
>
> I feel Georgette has come a long way in dealing with her own problems and in understanding that we all must work together. I feel, in working with Georgette, she and I have turned a somewhat shaky relationship that could have made us both unhappy, into a positive, working relationship that is not only productive but satisfying to us both.

An Interventionist Teacher–Pathway II Description of Student Behavior:

> René reluctantly came to school in September. She was withdrawn, did not smile, and would not interact with other students. Her attendance was poor. The only time she talked to me was to ask when the school day would be over.
>
> During the next few months of school, René's behavior did not change. She would not communicate with me or other classmates. She would sit alone in the same location at each recess. If someone spoke to her, she would lower her head and not respond. She is not regarded as attractive and her clothes are old and shabby. Her schoolwork is poor; however, she will attempt any work that is given her. The school psychologist has tested René and reports that she is within the average IQ range. She has had medical checkups, and records indicate she is physically normal.

Interpretation of Behavior:

> We must look to her environment for the cause of misbehavior. All behavior can be explained as responses to environmental stimuli. I believe René acts the way she does because she's never been positively rewarded in the past when she has attempted to engage others. In fact, she probably has been shunned, teased, and scorned when she has tried to make friends with her new classmates.

Fixing the Pathway:

I am an Interventionist and believe in using Pathway II. I want to follow a pathway to put the teacher in control until wanted behavior is accomplished. I realize improvement will be slow, but I am confident some improvement will be seen by the end of this year.

The steps along the pathway are to observe, collect baseline data, classroom rearrangement, positive reinforcement, modeling and shaping.

Overt Behaviors:

There was one girl in our class who was attractive, outgoing and considerate. I suspected she might be able to get through to René. I decided to begin by rearranging the classroom and moving René beside Sue. I talked to Sue about befriending René, and she agreed. I arranged their seats so I could easily observe them.

My baseline experiment was very easy to do since René rarely ever talked.

For reinforcement, I smiled at her whenever I caught her quick glance. I touched her more often and talked to her just as I would the other students. However, I never put her on the spot for a reply that would take more than a nod of the head.

My long-range goal for René was for her to communicate and interact socially. To do this, she needed self-confidence. Every day for the first two weeks we had a class discussion about a story I read to the class for modeling. René has a weight problem that may make her feel different from the rest. The purpose of these stories was to show that everyone has a place and will be accepted as they are.

Assessment of Two-Week Implementation

Moving René beside Sue showed fast results. René would whisper occasionally but then look around to see if anyone was watching. When I caught René's eye, I would smile to show my approval.

Improvement was slight but successful, since she did say a few words occasionally. At the end of the two weeks I did a baseline experiment again. During the day she was speaking to me a minimum of four times and telling me about her former school.

Future Overt Behaviors

Now that René is beginning to interact with others, I plan to move towards greater student control. I plan to set up group projects so I can conduct classroom meetings (as Glasser suggests) with René and a small number of students. This way she might, after some time, feel free to talk in such a nonthreatening situation and eventually even propose ideas for the group.

Authors' Comments: Here we have a case of an Interventionist teacher beginning with positive reinforcement both in verbal and social form. This teacher has obviously eliminated the idea of using even more powerful techniques of satuation, physical punishment, or isolation, because of his sensitivity to the particular student. Since the reinforcement is successful, the teacher continues along Pathway II by next employing Glasser's classroom meetings.

An Interactionalist Teacher–Pathway III Description of Student Behavior:

The student is neat in appearance, well dressed, robust, and healthy looking. I have no reason to suspect that there is a health problem or other physical disability. However, the student does seem very tense, loud, and he handles materials, equipment, and games roughly.

He sometimes stays outside from five to ten minutes after lunch is over or remains in the restroom after the class has gone upstairs after the break. He then enters the room after the other students are quiet and settled into whatever activity they are doing. He always has a companion, though not always the same student. They come into the room making a lot of noise and disrupting whatever activity is taking place.

The student likes to take his time getting into lines in the room whenever the class is moving to another room. He usually then ends up, by his own design, at or near the end of the line. As soon as the teacher (who is at the front of the line) turns the other way to lead the class to its destination, the student in question knocks over displays in the room, takes things off the bulletin board by the door and drops them into the wastebasket, drops books from the box of books to be returned to the library into the wastebasket, kicks, pushes, fights, or otherwise causes a commotion at the end of the line, or leaves the line and takes another route to the place the class is going.

During class time, he talks without raising his hand and talks back to the teacher.

During class discussion periods or when the teacher is reading to the class or explaining something, he rocks back and forth in his seat.

Although the tardiness takes place mostly in the morning, the other misbehaviors take place about every fifteen to twenty minutes throughout the day.

This student always involves at least one other student when he comes in tardy or when he misbehaves outside the classroom. It isn't always the same student, but it is always one or several of the same five or six boys. Many of the students who frequently misbehave admire the student with whom I am working and will do just about anything he suggests, even though he always is the boss and frequently ends up screaming or physically fighting with them. He is both physically and verbally very aggressive.

Academically, the student has few problems. He seems to like most of the subject matter and his work is above average. He does, however, hurry through projects and assignments and, as a result, much of his work is below his best efforts. He does get right to work after assignments are made, works best under very structured circumstances, and loves to help with classroom housekeeping duties. He does, however, frequently undo some of the cleaning and straightening he has done so well in an effort to make these jobs last longer.

He responds well to positive reinforcement and encouragement.

My efforts to change his misbehavior up to the time this case study formally began included ignoring first offenses, conferences, directive statements, lost recesses, and isolation. None of these was effective for more than two days.

The student loves to draw, is interested in cars, trucks, motorcycles, science-fiction characters, and looks forward to his visits with his father, who lives in another state and takes him home with him every other Saturday.

Interpretation of Behavior

In attempting to interpret my student's goals in his behavior, I asked myself the four questions Dreikurs suggests that teachers covertly ask themselves concerning their own emotions when this child misbehaves. I do feel annoyed and I sometimes feel beaten and intimidated. I think most of Mark's misbehavior is directed toward the goal of attention-getting from his peers and from me, but I feel sometimes his goal is power.

In conference later, I asked my student the four sequential questions Dreikurs suggests:

Could it be that you want special attention?
Could it be that you want your own way and hope to be boss?
Could it be that you want to hurt others as you feel hurt by them?
Could it be that you want to be left alone?

From his reactions, I concluded that my first interpretations seemed correct, and I must try to find ways to give this student attention when he is not behaving appropriately and ways that he can have power that are useful to the class and rewarding to him, without engaging in a power struggle with the teacher.

Fixing the Pathway

I am a teacher who believes as the other Interactionalists do that boundaries must be established and that students must be made aware of what those boundaries are. I like to share responsibilities, decision-making, and power with my students, but I also reserve the right to clarify the rules and, once they are agreed upon, to enforce them.

I try to be actively involved with my students in warm, caring relationships, and I strive always to give them as much freedom as they can handle without hurting others or hampering the atmosphere for learning for others.

The pathway I chose to use after I used Dreikurs's model for interpreting the student's behavior was Pathway III beginning with the techniques of the Reality Therapy model by Dr. William Glasser. Having earlier in the year tried methods using less teacher control and finding them not successful with this student, I liked the idea of helping the student to acknowledge the reality of his own inappropriate behavior and of giving that student the responsibility for making an acceptable plan for his own future behavior that will not infringe on the rights of others.

Overt Behaviors:

After interpreting Mark's behavior and evaluating my past behavior with him and the approaches that did not work, I listed the changes I thought we could start with.

The changes desired first were:

Line up without fighting, kicking, or pushing.
Raise his hand when he wants to talk.
Come to class when the bell rings.
Take time to work carefully, and to do a good job.

Overtly, I will:

- Ask him the "what" questions; press for a plan; have him sign the agreement.
- Tell him that I will give him the attention he wants when he is not talking out of order. Then I will make it a point to talk to him before school starts and again when he returns to my class from English at 11:30. I will call on him at least once every half hour during the afternoon for at least two weeks. I will also give him time to share his drawings once each day for one month.
- Talk to him eight times each day when he is not talking out of order. Give him attention when he is behaving.
- Praise him for promptness when he comes to class on time and when he doesn't linger in the restroom after the rest of the class has returned to the room.
- Make sure this student lines up near the front of the lines when going to the restroom, to lunch, or to the library, since most of the misbehavior in lines occurs when this student is at the back of the line and I am at the front.
- When papers are very carelessly done, hand them back to be redone.
- When the student takes his time, works carefully, and turns in papers that are 90% accurate, post the papers on the bulletin board.
- Have class meetings the last fifteen to twenty minutes each day so that all the students can discuss anything that is bothering them at school or anything that pertains to them that they'd like to talk about.

Assessment of Two-Week Implementation:

I think giving Mark attention before he misbehaves has helped him to fulfill his need for recognition and attention. He has worked hard to keep his commitment to raise his hand when he wants to speak. My goal those first two weeks was for him to raise his hand at least half of the time when he wanted to talk. He has reached this goal.

He has not, during these two weeks, been late to class. I have made sure this student was at or near the front of the line whenever he must line up. So far, this has decreased the number of problems in lines by about half. However, he still gets involved in fights once he enters the restroom.

His papers have been done more carefully, and all except two math papers have been at least ninety percent accurate. I have returned only one writing paper to be redone.

This student chose to have fifteen minutes free art time every Thursday afternoon if he has kept his agreement all week. He also gets to help me do bulletin boards when they need to be changed.

The student has agreed to stay after school for fifteen minutes to re-evaluate his behavior when he doesn't keep his plan. So far, we haven't had to do this.

The class meetings held the last fifteen to twenty minutes each day have improved the whole class's overall behavior and concern for one another. During this time, students have been very frank about how this student's misbehavior has hurt them. This, as much as any single thing, I think, has helped the disruptive student to see that students he felt he was impressing did not like having their thinking interrupted and did not like to be pushed and bullied in line and on the playground.

While classroom behavior has improved, behavior on the playground is still quite aggressive from this student, both physically and verbally.

Future Overt Behaviors

I will continue to re-examine my classroom behavior and my use of classroom time, and I will continue to strive for activities that motivate the students, capitalize on students' interests, and that help each child to fulfill his or her needs to feel worthwhile and to be involved with a teacher who cares about him or her. Specifically, with Mark I will continue to help him to achieve his goals for attention and power in ways that are acceptable and not disruptive to the class. Our conversations before class will continue, with the emphasis being Mark telling me what he wishes to talk about and what he values.

For the next two weeks, I will press for Mark to raise his hand seventy percent of the time for when he wants to talk, while giving him attention when he is behaving without talking out and giving him time to share his interests and his art with the class, through demonstrations and displays. I'll continue to let him know I appreciate his coming to class on time so that we can all begin our work without the interruptions caused by late-arriving students.

I think it is now time for us to sit down together to work out a new plan to improve aggressive behavior that is still taking place in the restroom, in the art room, at the library, and on the playground. If need be, I will make a contingency contract for him Since Mark is seldom alone in these aggressive activities, I feel the conference now should involve him and the other five boys who are from time to time involved with him in the negative acts or who

> follow his misbehavior and disruptions by disruptive attention-getting behaviors of their own. They are all strongly influenced by his leadership.
>
> The class meetings will continue, but from now on we will meet just on Mondays and Thursdays from 2:40–3:00, except when there is a special need to meet more often.
>
> I will continue to believe that these students can and will improve their behavior when our relationships to each other are warm and trusting and when they are meeting their needs to feel worthwhile and successful.

Authors' Comments: This Interactionalist teacher pursuing Pathway II has given us a good example of the "fork in the road." She chose to begin with overt behaviors, Dreikurs's questions, Glasser's "what" questions, making a plan, and classroom meetings, as well as a liberal dose of Behavior Modification praise. After two weeks of having some techniques be successful, she proposes to have more individual conferences with Mark now that he feels free to vent his feelings and attitudes. Now she uses active listening and value questions to let Mark explore his inner feelings. Yet, in areas where Mark has not made satisfactory progress, the teacher increases her power by making his group come up with a plan or abide by her contingency contract.

Appendix C

Moral Reasoning: From Seven Years To Adulthood

Jean Piaget,[1] the noted child psychologist, was instrumental in providing the basis for Lawrence Kohlberg's[2] later work in the area of moral development. Piaget demonstrated that it was not until the child was eleven years old, or older, that he or she became intellectually able to evaluate abstract moral dilemmas. The values in such issues as future roles or occupations, sexual relationships, acceptance or rejection of religious principles, and relationships to figures of authority have little meaning to the young child. Piaget, and later Kohlberg, discovered that what a kindergartener or first-grade child thinks is "naughty" and what an adolescent thinks is right or wrong are dramatically different. An understanding of how reasoning varies among students can help the teacher who wants to communicate with a variety of students. The teacher is ordered by an understanding of moral growth in deciding what disciplinary techniques will best lead children to make more mature moral decisions about what is right or wrong and what, in turn, affects their actions towards others.

Let us provide an example of such divergences in student reasoning. Piaget interviewed many children across different age levels to gather their responses to common dilemmas. One of Piaget's typical dilemmas reads as follows:

> A. A little boy (or a little girl) goes for a walk in the street and meets a big dog who frightens him very much. So he then goes home and tells his mother he has seen a dog that was as big as a cow.
>
> B. A child comes home from school and tells his mother that the teacher has given him good marks, but it was not true; the teacher had given him no marks at all, either good or bad.[3]

Piaget then asked the various youngsters which child was the naughtiest. He found that children younger than first-grade age (prerational period) simply could not understand the problem and therefore could not give an intelligible response However, students in the early elementary grades did have a definite point of view Their reasoning was generally of this manner.

Fel (Age 6)

Which of these two children is naughtiest? —The little girl who said she saw a dog as big as a cow. —Why is she the naughtiest? —Because it could never happen. —Did her mother believe her? —No, because there never are (dogs as big as cows). —Why did she say that? —To exaggerate. —And why did the other one tell a lie? —Because she wanted to make people believe that she had a good report. —Did her mother believe her? —Yes. —Which would you punish most if you were the mother? —The one with the dog because she told the worst lies and was the naughtiest.

Bug (Age 6)

Which is the naughtiest? —The one with the cow. —Why is he the naughtiest? —Because it isn't true. —And the one with the good marks? —He is less naughty. —Why? —Because his mother would have believed, because she believed the lie.[4]

The replies are typical of boys and girls in *early* elementary school. "Naughtiness" or lying is measured by the degree of its credibility to adults. The lie about the good marks is "not so bad" because the mother will be easily taken in by it. Piaget demonstrated through these types of stories that the refinement of moral judgment and reasoning is a developmental process. Not until the ages of eleven or older does moral reasoning begin to change from being centered on "those more powerful adults" (believable to mother or father) to reasons of intent and justice when living cooperatively with others. The following are the responses of older children to the same vignettes.

Kei (Age 10)

Which is the naughtier? —The lie about the teacher. —Why? —Because he deceived his mother. —But so did the other. —But he (the one of the teacher) had said something the teacher hadn't said. —The other one too had said something that wasn't true. (Our counter-suggestions, no matter how insistent, are ineffectual.) —He had told a great big lie. The teacher hadn't said he was good. —Why is it naughtier than the lie about the dog? —Because you can see better that it (the lie about the dog) is not true. You can't tell with the lie about the teacher. —Why did he say he had seen a dog as big as a cow? —To make them believe he had seen something marvelous.[5]

What teachers should infer from the information just given is that, based on the child's experience and maturing intellectual abilities, what students understand as right or wrong will be dramatically different at different ages. If this develop-

mental growth process is disregarded, teachers will be making demands on students to evaluate behavior and problems that they do not yet have the intellectual abilities to fully understand. Also, teachers will be using techniques and methods that may inhibit or retard the moral growth of students.

Levels of Moral Reasoning

The work of Lawrence Kohlberg[2] has followed Piaget's findings with more exact stages of reasoning.

In the Developmental Socialization Continuum (DSC), one can see how moral levels I through VI are further substages of the two stages, social interaction through language and conceptualization through language. All moral reasoning levels begin at the rational age of seven years.

Moral Level I—Punishment and Obedience Orientation

Characteristic of early elementary grade students, this is a level where reasoning is based on the physical consequences of an act. The determination of goodness or badness is made regardless of the person's intention or motive. For example, let's look at two situations:

> Tommy is helping his mother to set the table, and accidentally the door closes on him as he is passing through it and it knocks the plates from his hands; all twelve plates break.
>
> Jimmy wants to get a cookie from the cupboard while his mother is away. He climbs onto a chair and attempts to get to the cookies that are on a high shelf. He bumps one cup, and it falls and breaks.

A child with Moral Level I reasoning would say that Tommy was the "naughtiest": he broke twelve items and Jimmy only broke one item. The Moral Level I child would judge and declare that Jimmy should receive harsh *physical* punishment.

Moral Level II—Instrumental-Relativist Orientation

It is not until around the ages of nine to eleven that students begin to understand motive. With the two stories just described, the Moral Level II child would suggest that Tommy was only helping and should not be punished for an accident. On the other hand, Jimmy was "bad"; he was doing something he knew was wrong. The Moral Level II child would further suggest that Jimmy should be punished by having to pay the logical consequence (Dreikurs). Jimmy might give up his allowance or do extra work at home to pay for a replacement. This logical consequence at Moral Level II is for the sole purpose of re-establishing the social order: "If things are broken, one must work to replace them."

Moral Level III—The Interpersonal Concordance or "Good Boy–Nice Girl" Orientation

Towards adolescence, moral reasoning reaches a stage of conforming to an image of what one should do based on what others will think. A good boy or girl of Level III would not knowingly take the cookies when told not to; therefore, Jimmy was wrong because he had disappointed his mother. This is the age of "peer review," when one reasons according to what classmates as well as adults might think, and it can be seen in conformity in dress and mannerisms among students of this age, in order to measure up and be "one of the gang," or a "good boy–nice girl."

Moral Level IV—Law and Order Orientation

Reasoning now shifts from what others might think to the unquestioned need for rules and regulations to sustain the social order. Jimmy attempted to "steal" the cookies, and stealing is against the law. What he did was wrong. It made no difference if he broke one cup or a hundred; his actions were illegal. Correct behavior in Level IV is obeying and upholding societal standards of conduct as rules for the common good. If everyone disobeyed the rules, there would be no society.

Moral Levels V and VI—Social-Contract Legalistic Orientation and Universal-Ethical Principles Orientation

According to Kohlberg, very few people ever reach Moral Levels V and VI. Right actions are defined in terms of general *individual* rights and standards based on a concept of democracy that overrides incompatible laws and orders. In Moral Level VI, reasoning is based on one's universal, self-chosen principles of what is good. Such a sense of justice transcends not only current law and order but also conventional concepts of government. In both Levels V and VI, the individual reasons to the rightness or wrongness of an act, not from selfish interests or standards upheld by authority, but rather on considerations of what is forever in the best interest of all people.

Notes

1. Jean Piaget, *Moral Judgment of the Child*, trans. Marjorie Gabain (New York: Free Press, 1965).
2. Lawrence Kohlberg, "The Cognitive-Developmental Approach to Moral Education," *Phi Delta Kappan*, ed. Stanley M. Elam, 56(1975); 10.
3. Piaget, *Moral Judgment of the Child*. p. 148.
4. Piaget, *Moral Judgment of the Child*, pp. 150–151.
5. Piaget, *Moral Judgment of the Child*, p. 158.

Index